铁路行业英语

Vocational English for Railway

主　编：刘　慧　林春香　应婷婷

副主编：肖映眉　李飞燕　邓　敏　李　瑶　续　莉

参　编：王　薇　全　敏　陈泓宇　冯琳佩　张　晶

　　　　肖　潇　尹珊波　李承翰　杨　冰　李建平

　　　　陈　燕　张晓艳　胡建平　司全龙　刘建军

主　审：周文革

北京理工大学出版社
BEIJING INSTITUTE OF TECHNOLOGY PRESS

版权专有 侵权必究

图书在版编目（CIP）数据

铁路行业英语 / 刘慧，林春香，应婷婷主编．

北京：北京理工大学出版社，2025.1．

ISBN 978-7-5763-4726-5

Ⅰ．U2

中国国家版本馆 CIP 数据核字第 2025SN7188 号

责任编辑：王晓莉　　**文案编辑**：王晓莉
责任校对：刘亚男　　**责任印制**：施胜娟

出版发行 /	北京理工大学出版社有限责任公司
社　　址 /	北京市丰台区四合庄路 6 号
邮　　编 /	100070
电　　话 /	（010）68914026（教材售后服务热线）
	（010）63726648（课件资源服务热线）
网　　址 /	http://www.bitpress.com.cn
版 印 次 /	2025 年 1 月第 1 版第 1 次印刷
印　　刷 /	保定市中画美凯印刷有限公司
开　　本 /	889 mm×1194 mm　1/16
印　　张 /	16.25
字　　数 /	388 千字
定　　价 /	98.00 元

图书出现印装质量问题，请拨打售后服务热线，负责调换

铁路作为国家重要基础设施和民生工程，在服务国家战略需求方面发挥着举足轻重的作用，尤其在服务"一带一路"沿线国家基础设施建设中，铁路建设是重要的组成部分。随着我国职业教育国际化进程的推进，职业教育与企业"同船出海"步伐不断加快，为铁路行业培养大量急需的技术技能人才，呈现出广阔的发展前景。因此，编写一本既涵盖铁路行业英语知识，发挥语言服务职教出海功能，又能够融入思政教育元素，提升学生综合素质的教材，显得尤为重要。

本教材立足新时代铁路行业"车、机、工、电、辆、信"方向的人才培养需求，以习近平新时代中国特色社会主义思想为指导，注重培养学生铁路行业英语基础知识和语言表达技能的同时，加强对学生的价值引导，提升其核心素养。教材选择职业岗位、职业安全等元素，引导学生学会交流、思考、表达，明确学生职业岗位发展方向，增强安全意识；搭配设置巧妙的语言输出训练，致力于培养学生英语环境下对铁路行业知识的理解和应用能力，引领学生实现全方位融合发展，助力培养满足建设社会主义现代化国家需要的铁路行业高素质技术技能人才。通过课文、对话和视频等多种素材，展现中国铁路情境，引导学生了解铁路，激发他们讲好中国铁路故事，为推动国家铁路高质量发展贡献自己的力量。

结合习近平新时代中国特色社会主义思想中关于爱岗敬业、勇于创新、担当作为等要求，我们在教材中融入了詹天佑精神、火车头精神、大国工匠精神、高铁精神、劳模精神等元素，旨在引导学生树立正确的世界观、人生观、价值观，激发学生的家国情怀和使命担当，增强安全意识，从而更好地适应未来的工作岗位，确保铁路行业工作的安全与高效。每个主题都设计了递进式的九大学习任务，即明学习目标、导主题内容、学行业词汇、习情景案例、演职场情景、练职业写作、讲中国铁路故事、测章节知识和评学习效果。

本教程具有以下特色：

1. 课程内容模块化

本教材将铁路行业知识与英语语言知识深度融合，创新性地整合为"铁道运输""铁道机电""铁道工程""铁道电信"四个英语语言知识模块。每个模块都围绕主题情境，设计了五个主题的听、说、读、写、演、讲等多样化的学习任务，全面涵盖了铁路行业"车、机、工、电、辆、信"等方向的主要就业岗位。

2. 学习内容情境化

在校内实训基地，教师深入讲解重点行业词汇，用英语真实地呈现岗位相关的行业知识，让学生在实际工作情境中理解并掌握基本的行业词汇。选择贴近铁路就业岗位与职业特色的的文体素材作为习情境案例的阅读文章，让学生初步了解工作场景、工作流程与岗位要求。演职场情景的听说任务基于未来的工作岗位以及中国铁路在国际合作中的经验和成果创设交际情境，让学生熟悉主要工作岗位的要求及作业标准，培养学生的国际化视野和跨文化交流能力。练职业写作环节，以图表形式梳理本节重要内容，营造职场英语交流情境，提升书面表达能力。

3. 思政教育融合化

在加强语言应用能力培养的同时，落实立德树人，德技并修！在"学行业词汇"和"习情境案例"任务中融入詹天佑精神、火车头精神、工匠精神，培养学生的岗位责任感、安全意识和担当意识，注重学生的职业素养与人生价值塑造。在"演职场情景"任务中，展示优秀学生示范视频，引导学生以模范为镜，向优秀看齐。在"讲中国铁路故事"环节，分享铁路榜样故事，传递榜样力量，塑造职业品质，树立职业理想。

4. 课程资源多样化

采用"英语教师＋专业教师"异质团队共建和师生共建的模式，英语教师与专业教师共同编写教材内容、教师团队与学生团队共同建设课程资源，在保证资源的专业性和原创性的同时，提供颗粒化的教学辅助资源和线上测试，实现课程"能学辅教"的功能定位。

5. 测评环节精准化

测章节知识环节，通过对学习目标达成效果的自我检测，培养学生自主学习，提高他们自我总结分析的能力。评学习效果环节，针对自主学习完善、语言思维提升、职场涉外沟通和多元文化交流等教学目标的达成，评估学习成果，不仅能有效提醒和帮助学生查漏补缺，还能帮助老师及时了解学生的学习状况，进行必要的教学反思。

本教材由湖南高速铁路职业技术学院刘慧、林春香、应婷婷主编。其中铁道运输模块主要由林春香、应婷婷、陈泓宇、刘慧共同编写，林春香统稿。铁道机电模块主要由刘慧、全敏、李瑶、李承翰共同编写，刘慧统稿。铁道工程模块主要由肖映眉、邓敏、张晶、冯琳佩、刘慧、林春香共同编写，刘慧统稿。铁道电信模块主要由王薇、李飞燕、续莉、肖潇共同编写，应婷婷统稿。

在教材编写过程中，我们得到了西南交通大学牵引动力国家重点实验室的研究员杨冰，湖南高速铁路职业技术学院的尹珊波、李建平、胡建平、司全龙、陈燕、张晓艳、詹冬桂、马占生、李培锁、刘孝凡、黄艺娜、李健、郑学贤、金林、郭丽丹等铁路专业老师，中铁大桥勘测设计院有限公司高级工程师龙潜江，衡阳铁路公安处法制交管支队法制大队大队长王超以及南京大学地理与海洋科学学院2023级李承翰同学的宝贵指导与帮助。

我们相信，通过学习本教材的内容，学生将能够深刻理解铁路行业的战略地位，激发出使命感和责任感，进而成长为铁路行业的高素质人才。此外，我们也希望本教材能够为职场英语教材编写领域注入新的活力，成为学生学习铁路行业英语的宝贵资源，使他们能在未来工作岗位上有效参与对外交流，积极宣传中国铁路，服务于国家"一带一路"建设与"职教出海"的长远目标。

目录

Module 1　Railway Transport　铁道运输 / 1

Topic 1	Introduction to Posts—Career Planning
	主题一　岗位介绍——职业规划 …………………………………………… 1
Topic 2	Passenger Service at Stations—Home from Home
	主题二　车站客运服务——宾至如归 …………………………………… 13
Topic 3	Passenger Service on Trains—Warmth Accompanies the Journey
	主题三　列车客运服务——温馨伴行 …………………………………… 25
Topic 4	Railway Freight Transport Organization—Unimpeded Transport
	主题四　铁路货物运输组织——物畅其流 ……………………………… 36
Topic 5	Railway Operation Organization—Precise Dispatch
	主题五　铁路行车组织——精准调度 …………………………………… 48

Module 2　Railway Electromechanics　铁道机电 / 62

Topic 1	Introduction to Posts—Career Planning
	主题一　岗位介绍——职业规划 ………………………………………… 62
Topic 2	Railway Vehicles—Be Steady and Safe
	主题二　铁路车辆——平稳安全 ………………………………………… 74
Topic 3	Railway Locomotives—Be the Main Player
	主题三　铁路机车——使命担当 ………………………………………… 87
Topic 4	EMU Train Overhaul—With Great Care
	主题四　动车组检修——精检细修 ……………………………………… 100
Topic 5	Electrified Railway—Be the Source of Power
	主题五　电气化铁路——动力之源 ……………………………………… 113

Module 3　Railway Engineering　铁道工程／126

Topic 1　Introduction to Posts—Career Planning
　　　　主题一　岗位介绍——职业规划 …………………………………………… 126

Topic 2　Railway Subgrade—Solid Foundation
　　　　主题二　铁路路基——坚如磐石 …………………………………………… 138

Topic 3　Railway Track 1—Seamless Connectivity
　　　　主题三　铁路轨道1——无缝连接 ………………………………………… 149

Topic 4　Railway Track 2—Precise Maintenance
　　　　主题四　铁路轨道2——严检慎修 ………………………………………… 162

Topic 5　Railway Bridge & Tunnel—Broad Thoroughfares
　　　　主题五　铁路桥隧——通衢广陌 …………………………………………… 175

Module 4　Railway Telecommunications　铁道电信／188

Topic 1　Introduction to Posts—Career Planning
　　　　主题一　岗位描述——职业规划 …………………………………………… 188

Topic 2　Railway Signaling—Be Safe and Reliable
　　　　主题二　铁路信号——安全可靠 …………………………………………… 201

Topic 3　Train Control System (TCS) —Be Precise and Stable
　　　　主题三　列车运行控制系统（TCS）——精准平稳 ……………………… 214

Topic 4　Railway Communication—Be Connected and Smooth
　　　　主题四　铁道通信——连通畅通 …………………………………………… 227

Topic 5　Train Dispatching Command System—Be Efficient and Intelligent
　　　　主题五　列车调度指挥系统——高效智能 ………………………………… 239

参考文献／251

Module 1
Railway Transport

铁道运输

Topic 1 Introduction to Posts—Career Planning
主题一 岗位介绍——职业规划

Task 1 Learning Objectives 明学习目标

Task Description: Get to know the learning content and clarify learning objectives.
任务描述: 了解学习内容,明确学习目标。

知识目标: 掌握与"岗位介绍"主题相关的行业英语词汇

技能目标:
1. 能读懂与本主题相关的文章
2. 能听懂与本主题相关的职场情景对话
3. 能模拟表演职场情景对话,能用英语讲述中国铁路榜样故事
4. 能用英语完成与主题相关的书面表达

素质目标: 了解"最美铁路人"客运值班员李军的榜样故事,学习她热心、真心、耐心、贴心、爱心、诚心服务旅客的精神,在未来岗位上以更加饱满的热情和更加专业的服务,为旅客提供安全、舒适、便捷的出行体验

Introduction to Posts 岗位介绍

学行业词汇: passenger duty officer, passenger clerk, ticket clerk, train conductor, freight duty officer, freight clerk, station dispatcher, shunting master, coupler, etc.

习情境案例: 《铁路运输角色百态,共筑安全畅通之旅》
1. 铁路运输专业学生的就业方向
2. 铁路运输组织与管理行业的岗位设置
3. 每个岗位的工作职责与素养要求

体验职场情景:
- 行业情景会话听说
- 行业情景会话展示
- 职业英语写作训练

讲中国铁路榜样故事

最美铁路人 李军
"旅客贴心人"

Task 2 Lead in 导主题内容

Task Description: Watch the video, complete the following exercises and learn about the post setting of railway transport organization and management.

任务描述：观看视频，完成练习，了解铁路运输组织与管理工作的岗位设置。

As an important transport mode in modern times, railway transport plays a major role in long-distance transport. It achieves the movement of passengers and freight by loading them onto trains and carrying them along railway tracks. The various work involved in organizing the movement of passengers and freight, as well as the movement of locomotives, **rolling stock**, and trains, is collectively referred to as railway transport organization and management. To be concrete, it covers passenger transport, freight transport, and train operation organization.

Generally speaking, passenger transport is to handle matters about passengers and luggage. It is mainly the responsibility of passenger service staff, such as **the passenger duty officer**, **the passenger clerk**, **the ticket clerk**, **the train conductor**, and the **train attendant**. Freight transport is to handle matters about freight and the relationship between railway and the **consignor or consignee**. It is mainly the responsibility of freight transport staff, such as **the freight duty officer** and **the freight clerk**. Train operation organization involves the operation and movement of locomotives, rolling stock, and trains. It is mainly undertaken by the train operation staff, such as **the station master on duty**, **the station duty officer**, **the assistant station duty officer**, **the station dispatcher**, **the shunting master**, and **the coupler**.

Task 2.1 Complete the following mind map.

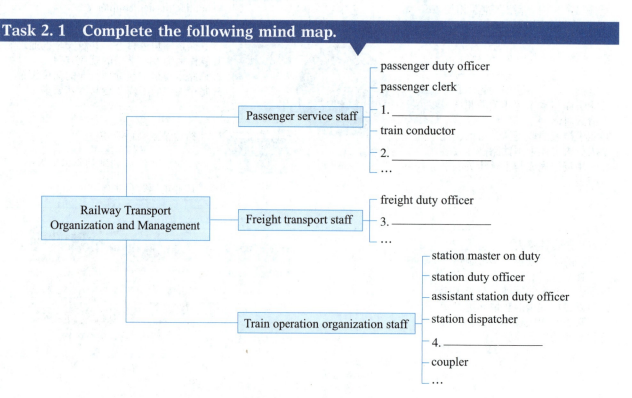

Task 3 Vocabulary Study 学行业词汇

Task Description: Learn the industry vocabulary, complete the following exercises, and master the English expression of titles and responsibilities of posts in railway transportation organization and management.

任务描述：学习行业词汇，完成练习，掌握铁路运输组织与管理各岗位名称及其职责的英文表达。

1. passenger duty officer

The **passenger duty officer** is the **shift leader** of the passenger service staff at a station. They are responsible for overall management and **supervision** of passenger service at the station.

2. passenger clerk

The **passenger clerk** is under the guidance of a passenger duty officer, and engages in specific passenger services at stations, such as assisting passengers with entering and exiting the station, waiting for trains, **boarding and alighting** from trains.

3. ticket clerk

The **ticket clerk** handles services like ticket sales, refunds, rebooking, and transfers. They should also ensure safety in **bills and fares**.

4. train conductor

The **train conductor** takes overall charge of passenger service on trains, and coordinates the work of the crew members, to ensure a safe and comfortable ride for passengers.

5. train attendant

The **train attendant** is under the guidance of the train conductor, and responsible for specific passenger services on trains, including dining service, assisting with boarding and alighting, keeping carriages clean and maintaining carriage order etc.

Module 1   Railway Transport   铁道运输   3

🎧 6. freight duty officer

The **freight duty officer** organizes and directs freight transport at railway stations, and also handles issues related to cargo losses and damages. They are regarded as the "chief commander" of the operation organization in the freight yard.

🎧 7. freight clerk

The **freight clerk** is responsible for specific tasks such as receiving goods, preparing for carriage, **tracking** goods, **monitoring** loading and unloading procedures, and handling abnormal situations during transportation etc.

🎧 8. station master on duty

The **station master on duty** leads the transport organization of the shift team, ensuring the transport organization is carried out safely and orderly.

🎧 9. station duty officer

The **station duty officer** organizes and directs **train reception**, **train departure, and shunting operations**, strictly according to the **train operation diagram**, relevant plans and operation standards. They direct the operations of all trains in a station.

🎧 10. assistant station duty officer

The **assistant station duty officer** assists the station duty officer in handling train reception, train departure, and shunting operations, etc.

🎧 11. station dispatcher

The **station dispatcher** is called the "designer" for shunting operations. and make **team work plans**, **phase work plans**, and **shunting operation plans**, etc. They should be familiar with the **station tracks** and train operation equipment.

🎧 12. shunting master

The **shunting master** serves as the "**commander**" of shunting operations, directing all activities of shunting locomotives and shunting workers. They direct shunting workers to complete shunting operations, based on the corresponding shunting operation plan.

🎧 13. coupler

The **coupler** is the **executor** of shunting commands. They carry out shunting operations under the direction of the shunting master.

🎧 14. passenger and freight station

A **passenger and freight station** refers to a station that handles both passenger and freight transport services.

Task 3.1 Match the words or phrases with the definitions.

1. _____ shunting master
2. _____ passenger clerk
3. _____ ticket clerk
4. _____ train attendant
5. _____ freight duty officer
6. _____ station dispatcher
7. _____ coupler
8. _____ station duty officer

A. the "designer" for shunting operations
B. directing the operation of all trains in a station
C. engaging in specific passenger services at stations
D. the executor of shunting commands
E. the "commander" of shunting operations
F. being responsible for specific passenger services on trains
G. handling ticket services
H. organizing and directing freight transport at railway stations

Word Bank

● New Words

consignor /kənˈsaɪnə/ n. 托运人,发货人
consignee /ˌkɒnsaɪˈniː/ n. 收货人
undertake /ˌʌndəˈteɪk/ v. 承担,从事
supervision /ˌsuːpəˈvɪʒn/ n. 监督
guidance /ˈɡaɪdns/ n. 指导
board /bɔːd/ v. 登上(火车、轮船或飞机)
alight /əˈlaɪt/ v. 从(汽车、火车等)下来
bill /bɪl/ n. 票据,账单

fare /feə/ n. 票款,车费
track /træk/ v. 跟踪; n. 轨道
monitor /ˈmɒnɪtə/ v. 监视,监控
commander /kəˈmɑːndə/ n. 指挥官
executor /ɪɡˈzekjətə/ n. 执行者
inspect /ɪnˈspekt/ v. 检查
escort /ˈeskɔːt/ v. 陪护,护送
recruitment /rɪˈkruːtmənt/ n. 招聘

Module 1 Railway Transport 铁道运输

coupler /ˈkʌplə/ n. 连结员

◎ Phrases & Expressions

rolling stock　车辆	shift leader　班组长
passenger duty officer　客运值班员	train reception　接车
passenger clerk　客运员	train departure　发车
ticket clerk　售票员	shunting operation　调车作业
train conductor　列车长	train operation diagram　列车运行图
train attendant　列车员	station track　站线
freight duty officer　货运值班员	team work plan　班组计划
freight clerk　货运员	phase work plan　阶段计划
station master on duty　值班站长	shunting operation plan　调车作业计划
station duty officer　车站值班员	security check lane　安检通道
assistant station duty officer　助理值班员	prohibited goods　违禁品
station dispatcher　车站调度员	come into play　发挥作用
shunting master　调车长	take charge of　负责……

Task 4　Passage Study 习情境案例

Task Description：Read the article, complete the following exercises, and learn about how the diverse roles in railway transport jointly build a safe journey.

任务描述：读懂文章，完成练习，了解铁路运输各岗位人员如何共筑安全畅通之旅。

The diverse roles in railway transport, jointly building a safe journey!

As soon as passengers enter the station, a journey filled with warm service begins. Ticket clerks are busy dealing with various ticket services in the ticket office. And passenger clerks can be seen everywhere at the entrance, the **security check lanes**, the waiting room, and the platform etc. They have frequent contact with passengers, **inspecting** for **prohibited goods** in detail, responding to all kinds of inquiries in patience, and organizing passengers to boarding and alighting in order. After passengers board the train, the train conductor leads train attendants to fulfill on-train service.

The freight duty officer and freight clerk are the "guardians" of freight transport. They are responsible for loading, transporting and unloading of goods. Under their guard, the goods can always be delivered safely and punctually.

At a passenger and freight station, many passenger trains and freight trains depart and arrive at the same time. How could that be possible? This is where the operation staff **come into play**. Station masters on duty are the "Great Steward" of the shift team. They **take charge of** any relevant issue of the team, and ensure that all work is carried out safely and orderly. The station duty officer issues the commands for the arrival and departure of all trains in a station. They should ensure punctual and safe operation of all trains. The station dispatcher, shunting master and coupler are responsible for shunting operation. They organize the locomotives and rolling stock to move purposefully on the station tracks and ensure the safety of locomotives, rolling stock and staff.

In summary, the diverse roles in railway transport fulfill their own duties and jointly build a safe journey for passenger travel and freight transport.

Task 4.1　Read the passage. Then, choose the correct answers.

1. Where are passenger clerks most likely to be found?
   A. Inside the train carriages.　　　　　B. In the ticket office.
   C. At the entrance, platform, and waiting hall.　　D. At the yard.
2. Who issues the commands for the arrival and departure of all trains in a station?
   A. The station dispatcher.　　　　　　B. The station attendant.
   C. The yardmaster.　　　　　　　　　D. The station master.
3. Which staff members are involved in organizing locomotives and rolling stock for safe movement?
   A. Train conductors and attendants.
   B. Freight agents and clerks.
   C. Station dispatcher, yardmaster, and coupler.
   D. Passenger clerks and security personnel.

Task 4.2　Read the sentence pairs. Fill in each blank with the best word or phrase.

1. station master on duty/passenger clerk
   A. A _____ organizes passengers to get on the train orderly.
   B. A _____ is the "Great Steward" of a shift team.
2. train conductor/yardmaster
   A. The _____ is responsible for shunting operation.
   B. The train attendant is under the leadership of _____ .

  Task ⑤　Vocational Situation Experience 演职场情景

Task Description: Experience the situational conversation and complete the following exercises, so as to enhance English application ability related to professional positions.
任务描述：体验岗位情景会话，完成练习，提升与职业岗位相关的英语应用能力。

Task 5.1 Listen to the conversation, and fill in the blanks.

Situation description: A trainee is about to finish his internship. And the recruitment for a railway bureau will begin next month. He is asking an experienced instructor for advice to apply for an appropriate post.

Trainee: Hi, Mr. Wang. May I have a few minutes of your time, please?

Instructor: Of course. What can I do for you?

Trainee: I heard a **recruitment** for a railway bureau will be here next month. I have no idea about which post to 1. _____ _____. Could you give me some advice?

Instructor: Sure. Students majoring in Railway Transportation mainly have three career paths, namely passenger service post, freight transport post, and train operation post.

Trainee: Each post has different responsibilities and requires different 2. _____. Right?

Instructor: Yes. Since you are good at communication and enjoy interacting with others, I think post of 3. _____ _____ or train attendant in passenger service would be a good fit for you.

Trainee: Is it because these two posts are in frequent 4. _____ with passengers?

Instructor: Exactly. When passengers run into difficulties, they may ask them for help in 5. _____ _____ _____.

Trainee: I do enjoy interacting with people and helping others. I think I will try applying for these two posts. Thank you very much!

Instructor: My pleasure. I hope it helps!

Task 5.2 Listen again and mark the statements as true (T) or false (F).

____ 1. The instructor believes that the trainee is suitable for freight transport posts.

____ 2. Students majoring in Railway Transportation have three possible career paths to choose from.

____ 3. The trainee decides to apply for the position of station dispatcher.

Task 5.3 Act out the roles with a partner.

Task 6 Vocational Writing Practice 练职业写作

Task Description: Refer to the information in the following table, describe the professional quality requirements for different posts and clarify your employment intention.

任务描述：参考下列表格信息，描述不同岗位的职业素养要求，明确就业意向。

Quality Requirements for Key Posts in Railway Transport Organization and Management

Post Category	Key Posts		Quality Requirements
	Initial Posts	Promoted Posts	
Passenger Service	Passenger clerk	Passenger duty officer	① Be willing to help ② Enjoy interacting with others
	Train attendant	Train conductor	① Be willing to help ② Enjoy interacting with others ③ Accept "Business Trip-like" shift duties for a ride
Freight Transport	Freight clerk	Freight duty officer	Be insightful and adaptable
Train Operation	Assistant station duty officer	Station duty officer	① Be meticulous ② Be good at communicating with others
	Coupler	Shunting master	① Be able to bear hardships ② Strictly observe relevant operating instructions and safety standards

Module 1 Railway Transport 铁道运输

Task 7 Telling Stories of China Railway 讲中国铁路故事

Task Description: Watch the story of railway role models and complete the following exercises to develop the awareness and ability to tell stories of China Railway in English.

任务描述：观看铁路榜样故事，完成练习，培养用英语讲述中国铁路故事的意识和能力。

7.1 What abilities do you think a passenger duty officer should master to provide better serving for passengers?

_____
_____
_____
_____
_____
_____
_____

7.2 Watch the video again and search online for more information about Li Jun, learn about her major achievements and how she became a "guardian of passengers". Then work in groups to tell Li Jun's story and share the inspiration and motivation you gain from her spirit.

_____
_____
_____
_____
_____
_____
_____

Task 8 Topic Test 测章节知识

> **Task Description**: Review this topic and complete the topic test to develop self-testing skills and summarizing analysis skills.
>
> **任务描述**：复习本章节内容，完成章节测试，培养自我检测和总结分析的能力。

◎ **Choose the correct answers.**

1. Which of the following is not specifically covered by railway transport organization and management?
    A. Freight transport. B. Passenger transport.
    C. Train operation organization. D. Air traffic control.

2. What is the primary responsibility of the ticket clerks?
    A. Loading and unloading freight. B. Conducting safety checks on passengers.
    C. Handling ticket-related services. D. Ensuring on-time departures.

3. Who are responsible for providing on-train service once passengers board?
    A. Station attendants. B. Train conductors and attendants.
    C. Freight agents. D. Passenger clerks.

4. What is the freight clerk primarily concerned with：
    A. The safety of passengers. B. The delivery of goods.
    C. Train shunting operations. D. Responding to passenger inquiries.

5. What is the role of the station master?
    A. Leading train attendants.
    B. Leading the transport organization of the shift team.
    C. Conducting security checks.
    D. Issuing commands for freight trains only.

◎ **Mark the following translations as true (T) or false (F).**

6. The train conductor leads train attendants to fulfill on-train service.
    译文：列车长带领列车员完成列车上的客运乘务工作。

7. Under their guard, the goods can always be delivered safely and punctually.
    译文：在他们的守护下，总是能安全、准确地发送货物。

8. They take charge of any relevant issue of the team.
    译文：他们负责解决团队纠纷。

9. They should ensure punctual and safe operation of all trains.
    译文：他们必须确保列车运行准点、安全。

10. The station dispatcher, shunting master and coupler are responsible for shunting operation.
    译文：车站调度员、调车长、连结员负责调车作业。

Module 1 Railway Transport 铁道运输 11

Task 9 Self-assessment 评学习效果

Task Description：Tick the items and self-assess learning outcomes.
任务描述：勾选选项，自我评估学习效果。

教学目标	评分项目
自主学习完善	□Have a good habit of independent learning 有良好的自主学习习惯 □Be clear about learning objectives 明确学习目标 □Know about learning content 了解学习内容 □Complete learning tasks effectively 有效完成学习任务 □Finish the section test consciously 自主进行知识检测
语言思维提升	Master the pronunciation, spelling, definition, and simple usage of the following vocabulary： 掌握下列词汇的发音、拼写、释义及简单应用： □board □alight □shunting □executor □coupler □passenger duty officer □security check lane □train conductor □station dispatcher □shift leader □train reception □train departure □train diagram □prohibited goods Be able to read and understand articles related to this topic and talk about them in English： 能读懂本主题相关文章并用英语简单介绍： □Possible career paths for students majoring in Railway Transport 　铁路运输专业学生的就业方向 □Diverse posts in railway transport 　铁路运输岗位设置 □Job responsibilities and quality requirements of each post 　每个岗位的工作职责与素养要求
职场涉外沟通	□Be able to understand workplace situational conversations related to this topic 　能听懂本主题相关的职场情景对话 □Be able to simulate workplace situational conversations related to this topic with a partner 　能与搭档一起模拟本主题相关的职场情景对话 □Be able to introduce the given theme in written form 　能用英语完成主题相关的书面表达
多元文化交流	□Be able to work in groups to tell the story of China railway role models in English 　能小组合作用英语讲述本主题相关的中国铁路榜样故事

Topic 2 Passenger Service at Stations
—Home from Home

主题二 车站客运服务——宾至如归

Task 1 Learning Objectives 明学习目标

Task Description: Get to know the learning content and clarify learning objectives.
任务描述: 了解学习内容，明确学习目标。

知识目标: 掌握与"车站客运服务"主题相关的行业英语词汇

技能目标:
1. 能读懂与本主题相关的文章
2. 能听懂与本主题相关的职场情景对话
3. 能模拟表演职场情景对话，能用英语讲述中国铁路榜样的故事
4. 能用英语完成与主题相关的书面表达

素质目标: 了解"新时代铁路榜样"客运员马成良的榜样故事，学习他用真诚和周到的服务为旅客搭建起温暖驿站的精神品质，在未来岗位上以更加饱满的热情和更加专业的服务，为旅客提供安全、舒适、便捷的出行体验

Passenger Service at Stations 车站客运服务

- **学行业词汇**: train ticket, boarding and alighting organization, ticket service, real-name verification, passenger flow, priority service for passenger in need, fast-check lane, traffic connection, etc.

- **习情境案例**: 《客流高峰来袭，客运站是这样应对的》
  1. 缓解客流压力的办法
  2. 车站内外的优质服务
  3. 重点旅客服务

- **体验职场情景**:
  - 行业情景会话听说
  - 行业情景会话展示
  - 职业英语写作训练

- **讲中国铁路榜样故事**:

新时代铁路榜样　马成良
"美丽驿站的温暖守护"

Module 1 Railway Transport 铁道运输 13

Task 2 Lead in 导主题内容

Task Description: Watch the video, complete the following exercises and learn about the work content of passenger service at stations.

任务描述：观看视频，完成练习，了解车站客运服务的工作内容。

Being crowded and **bustling**. This may be your first impression of train stations. But, once you enter the station, you will find everything is going on in perfect order. Passengers **queue up** for each process **consciously**. This can not do without service organization done by passenger service staff at the station.

Passenger stations play a **critical** role in the organization of railway passenger transport. They are the originating, transferring and **terminating** locations for passenger transport. They undertake many tasks, such as selling train tickets, printing **reimbursement vouchers**, providing passengers with a place to wait for the train. They serve as the link between the railway and passengers.

Passenger service at a station mainly covers ticket service, passenger boarding and alighting organization, and the other relevant services. Ticket service at stations includes ticket sales, ticket rebooking and ticket refund. Passenger boarding and alighting organization involves in services at the station entrance, security check lanes, waiting hall, platform and exit etc. The other relevant services are dining service, sanitation service, inquiry service etc.

Task 2.1 Complete the following mind map.

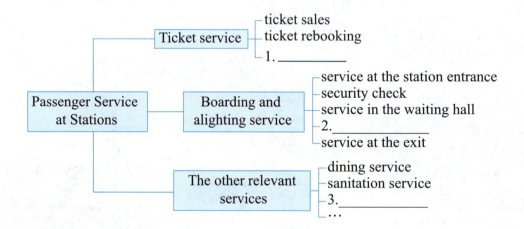

Task ③ Vocabulary Study 学行业词汇

Task Description: Learn the industry vocabulary, complete the following exercises, and master the English expressions related to passenger service at stations.

任务描述：学习行业词汇，完成练习，掌握与车站客运服务工作相关的英文表达。

🎧 1. train ticket

The **train ticket** is a physical **certificate** for passengers to board the train. It serves as a legally **binding** contract.

🎧 2. ticket service

Ticket service at stations refers to the process where tickets are sold, rebooked and refunded at the ticket window or through the ticketing vending machine.

🎧 3. boarding and alighting organization

Boarding and alighting organization is a comprehensive work. It involves in station entrance and security check, waiting for a train, ticket checking, platform service and arrival service etc. This is an important work of the passenger transport department in a station.

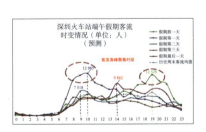

🎧 4. passenger flow

The **passenger flow** refers to passenger **volume** and **flows** over a certain direction in a certain period. It is an important basis for making passenger transport plans.

🎧 5. real-name verification

Real-name verification is a kind of information verification conducted at the entrance, the ticket gate, or on the train. It is to make sure that the identity information of a ticket holder **matches** his/her ticketing information.

6. fast-check lane

The **fast-check lane** is a special access allowed for passengers in a hurry, where they have **priority** in security check and ticket check if the time left for departure is less than a certain period. (The time period varies from 15 minutes to 30 minutes at different stations.)

7. priority service for passengers in need

Priority service for passengers in need is a series of priority and convenience given to passengers in need, e. g., the aged, children, patients, the disabled, and the pregnant. They have priority in purchasing tickets, entering the station, checking tickets, and boarding the train.

8. traffic connection

Traffic connection is a type of transport service which connects different kinds of vehicles to transfer passengers in a short time.

Task 3.1 Match the words or phrases with the definitions.

1. _____ train ticket
2. _____ ticket service
3. _____ passenger flow
4. _____ fast-check lane
5. _____ boarding and alighting organization
6. _____ real-name verification
7. _____ priority service for passengers in need
8. _____ traffic connection

A. a special access allowed for passengers who are in a hurry
B. a series of priority and convenience given to passengers in need
C. comprehensive and important work in a station
D. connecting different kinds of vehicles to transfer passengers
E. a kind of information verification
F. a physical certificate for passengers to board the train
G. the process where tickets are sold, rebooked and refunded
H. passenger volume and flows over a certain direction in a certain period

Word Bank

⊙ New Words

bustling/ˈbʌslɪŋ/*adj.* 热闹的
consciously/ˈkɒnʃəsli/*adv.* 自觉地
critical/ˈkrɪtɪkl/*adj.* 关键的，重要的
terminate/ˈtɜːmɪneɪt/*v.* 终止，结束
certificate/səˈtɪfɪkət/*v.* 证明，凭证
binding/ˈbaɪndɪŋ/*adj.* 有约束力的
volume/ˈvɒljuːm/*n.* 总数，总量
flow/fləʊ/*n.* 流量

match/mætʃ/*v.* 与……一致
priority/praɪˈɒrəti/*n.* 优先，优先权
surge/sɜːdʒ/*v.* 激增
tackle/ˈtækl/*v.* 应对
predict/prɪˈdɪkt/*v.* 预测
dizzy/ˈdɪzi/*adj.* 头晕的
conventional/kənˈvenʃənl/*adj.* 传统的，
老一套的

⊙ Phrases & Expressions

queue up　　排队等候
reimbursement voucher　　报销凭证
boarding and alighting organization
　　乘降组织
passenger flow　　客流
real-name verification　　实名制验证
fast-check lane　　急客通道
priority service for passengers in need
　　重点旅客服务
traffic connection　　交通接驳

peak passenger flow　　客流高峰
be confronted with　　面临
passenger-concentrated station
　　客流集中站
peak hours　　高峰时段
be endowed with　　被赋予
place stress on　　加强
manual ticket checking gate
　　人工检票通道

 Task Passage Study 习情境案例

Task Description：Read the article, complete the following exercises, and learn about how passenger stations tackle peak passenger flow.
任务描述：读懂文章，完成练习，了解铁路客运站如何应对客流高峰。

When peak passenger flow comes, passenger stations tackle it like this!

When the holiday comes, railway passenger stations **are confronted with** a **surge** in passenger flow. How do passenger stations **tackle** it?

Real-name verification is the first "gate" for passengers to enter the station. A **passenger-concentrated station predicts** passenger flows each day, and increases the verification gates and

 Module 1　RAILWAY TRANSPORT　铁道运输　17

security check lanes during **peak hours**. By this way, time for passengers to enter the station can be reduced. Besides, additional clerks are arranged at fast-check lanes, where passengers in a hurry **are endowed with** priority.

Inside the bustling waiting hall, passenger clerks are busy but not **dizzy**. They organize passengers to check tickets in sequence, and provide various inquiry services in patience.

Platform service is crucial. During peak hours, quantities of originating, terminating, and passing trains may surge. Passenger clerks at the platform would enhance guidance on in-station transfer and exit, so that arriving passengers can transfer or exit in a short time.

Arrival services at the exit are seen as "the Last Mile" of the journey. Passengers arrive late at night may have trouble in traffic connection. To solve this problem, passenger-concentrated stations communicate with local traffic departments to extend service hours of nearby buses and subways.

Furthermore, passenger-concentrated stations also **place great stress on** priority service for passengers in need. **Conventional** service ways are kept available, such as 24-hour ticket sales windows and **manual ticket checking gates**. So that the travel needs of the aged and the people incapable of getting on the Internet can be satisfied.

When peak passenger flow comes, staff at passenger stations and even all railway workers stick to their posts. It is their dedication and service that make every passenger feel warmly accompanied.

Task 4.1 Read the passage. Then, choose the correct answers.

1. Which way can be used to tackle passenger flows during peak times?
   A. By reducing the number of verification gates.
   B. By increasing verification and security check facilities.
   C. By allowing only ticket holders to enter the waiting hall.
   D. By limiting the number of passengers allowed inside the station.

2. What is the primary responsibility of passenger clerks inside the waiting hall?
   A. To sell tickets.
   B. To organize ticket checking in sequence.
   C. To keep passengers quiet.
   D. To provide food and beverages.

3. How do railway stations help passengers arriving late at night?
   A. By providing free hotel accommodations.
   B. By offering discounts on taxi rides.
   C. By arranging private shuttles.
   D. By working with local traffic departments to extend bus and subway services.

Task 4.2 Read the sentence pairs. Fill in each blank with the best word or phrase.

1. passenger flows/security check lanes
    A. They predict _____ every day.
    B. More _____ are opened during peak time.
2. fast-check lanes/priority service
    A. _____ is provided for passengers in need.
    B. _____ are provided for passengers in a hurry.

Task 5 Vocational Situation Experience 演职场情景

Task Description：Experience the situational conversation and complete the following exercises, so as to enhance English application ability related to professional positions.

任务描述：体验岗位情景会话，完成练习，提升与职业岗位相关的英语应用能力。

Task 5.1 Listen to the conversation and fill in the blanks.

Situation description：A trainee is assigned to work at a platform as a passenger clerk. He is consulting an experienced instructor about the job responsibilities, and try to qualify himself for this new job.

Trainee: Hello, Mr. Wang. I will work on the platform next week. Would you tell me some matters 1. _____ _____?

Instructor: Well. Before a train comes in, you need to be on site and 2. _____ _____ the track is clear.

Trainee: I see. What should I do as passengers arrive?

Instructor: You need to remind them to stand behind the white safety line and wait in line for the train.

Trainee: Is it to prevent them from getting into the tracks?

Instructor: Yes. After all, safety comes first.

Trainee: I notice there are 3. _____ in different colors on the platform. I'm afraid passengers will get confused.

Instructor: So, another important task is to help passengers find the correct landmarks.

Trainee: Does it mean our work is finished after passengers get on the train?

Instructor: No. After the 4. _____ _____ rings, you need to ask the people seeing off to leave in time.

Trainee: So passenger clerks at the platform do have quite a bit of work to do.

Instructor: Definitely. And don't forget the passengers getting off the train. You need to guide them to exit or transfer quickly.

Trainee: Get it. I will get well 5. _____ _____ this new job. Thank you very much!

Task 5.2 Listen again and mark the statements as true(T) or false(F).

____ 1. The trainee is assigned to work as a passenger clerk at a platform.

____ 2. The landmarks on the platform are in the same color.

____ 3. The work is finished after passengers get on the train.

Task 5.3 Act out the roles with a partner.

Task 6 Vocational Writing Practice 练职业写作

Task Description: Please describe job responsibilities and matters needing attention for passenger clerks at different workplaces, so that you can better understand and grasp relevant job requirements and skills.

任务描述：请描述客运员在不同岗位地点的工作职责与注意事项，以便更好地理解和掌握客运员的工作要求和技能。

Job Responsibilities and Matters Needing Attention for Passenger Clerks
车站客运员的岗位职责与注意事项

Workplace	Job Responsibilities and Matters Needing Attention
Entrance	① Guide passengers to line up for ticket verification ② Assist passengers in need ③ Be proficient in using verification facilities
Security check	① Inspect luggage for prohibited goods and excessively carried items ② Don't miss any prohibited goods or excessively carried items ③ Don't make any misidentification ④ Politely remind passengers of the way to handle prohibited goods and excessively carried items
Waiting hall	① Keep order ② Answer passengers' inquiries ③ Offer necessary help
Ticket gate	① Inform time for check-in in advance ② Guide passengers to line up for ticket check ③ Be proficient in using ticket check facilities and check tickets rapidly and accurately
Platform	① Be on site in advance and make sure the track is clear ② Guide passengers to find correct landmarks and wait in line for the train ③ Assist priority passengers in boarding ④ Assist passengers in exiting and transferring ⑤ Avoid passengers from falling into the station tracks
Exit	① Guide passengers to exit in order ② Answer to passengers' inquiries ③ Assist passengers in transferring to other vehicles ④ Ensure the route for exit is clear

Module 1 Railway Transport 铁道运输

Task 7　Telling Stories of China Railway 讲中国铁路故事

Task Description: Watch the story of railway role models and complete the following exercises to develop the awareness and ability to tell stories of China Railway in English.

任务描述：观看铁路榜样故事，完成练习，培养用英语讲述中国铁路故事的意识和能力。

7.1　As the role model of the railway industry in the new era, Ma Chengliang interpreted the true meaning of "serving the people" with his own actions. Please provide examples of how he has become a warm sunshine in the hearts of passengers through his meticulous and thoughtful service.

_____
_____
_____
_____
_____
_____

7.2　Watch the video again and search online for more information about Ma Chengliang to learn more about his exemplary deeds. Then work in groups to tell Ma Chengliang's story and share the inspiration and motivation you gained from his spirit.

_____
_____
_____
_____
_____
_____
_____
_____

Task 8　Topic Test 测章节知识

Task Description：Review this topic and complete the topic test to develop self-testing skills and summarizing analysis skills.

任务描述：复习本章节内容，完成章节测试，培养自我检测和总结分析能力。

◎ **Choose the correct answers.**

1. Where are passengers in a hurry given express and priority services?
   A. At the ticket counter.　　　　B. In the waiting hall.
   C. At fast-check lanes.　　　　D. On the platform.

2. What is referred to as the "Last Mile" of passengers' journey?
   A. The platform where passengers board the train.
   B. The walk from the train to the waiting hall.
   C. The services provided at the exit.
   D. The ticket checking process.

3. Which of the following is NOT a part of the boarding and alighting organization process?
   A. Ticket checking.　　　　B. Train dispatching.
   C. Waiting for a train.　　　　D. Boarding and alighting the train.

4. Who is responsible for the passenger organization at stations?
   A. Train conductors.　　　　B. Freight handlers.
   C. Passenger transport staff.　　　　D. Security guards.

5. What should a passenger clerk at the platform do before a train arrives?
   A. Check the train schedule.　　　　B. Assist passengers with luggage.
   C. Remind passengers to board.　　　　D. Confirm the track is clear.

◎ **Mark the following translations as true(T) or false(F).**

6. A passenger-concentrated station predicts passenger flows each day.
   译文：客流集中站每天预测客流情况。

7. Inside the bustling waiting hall, passenger clerks are busy but not dizzy.
   译文：候车大厅内客流如织，乘客们忙而不乱。

8. During peak hours, quantities of originating, terminating, and passing trains may surge.
   译文：在催促期间，始发、终到和途经列车数量激增。

9. Passengers arrive late at night may have trouble in traffic connection.
   译文：白天到达的旅客可能在交通接驳上遇到困难。

10. It is their dedication and service that make every passenger feel warmly accompanied.
    译文：正是他们的奉献与服务，使每位旅客感受到温暖陪伴。

Module 1　Railway Transport　铁道运输　23

Task 9　Self-assessment 评学习效果

Task Description：Tick the items and self-assess learning outcomes.
任务描述：勾选选项，自我评估学习效果。

教学目标	评分项目
自主学习完善	☐Have a good habit of independent learning 有良好的自主学习习惯 ☐Be clear about learning objectives 明确学习目标 ☐Know about learning content 了解学习内容 ☐Complete learning tasks effectively 有效完成学习任务 ☐Finish the section test consciously 自主进行知识检测
语言思维提升	Master the pronunciation, spelling, definition, and simple usage of the following vocabulary： 掌握下列词汇的发音、拼写、释义及简单应用： ☐certificate ☐flow ☐verification ☐priority ☐predict ☐passenger flow ☐real-name verification ☐fast-check lane ☐priority service ☐rush-hit station ☐place stress on ☐expense reimbursement voucher ☐boarding and alighting organization
	Be able to read and understand articles related to this topic and talk about them in English： 能读懂本主题相关文章并用英语简单介绍： ☐Ways to relieve passenger flow pressure 　缓解客流压力的办法 ☐The enhanced services inside and outside stations 　车站内外的优质服务 ☐Priority service for passengers in need 　重点旅客服务
职场涉外沟通	☐Be able to understand workplace situational conversations related to this topic 　能听懂本主题相关的职场情景对话 ☐Be able to simulate workplace situational conversations related to this topic with a partner 　能与搭档一起模拟本主题相关的职场情景对话 ☐Be able to introduce the given theme in written form 　能用英语完成主题相关的书面表达
多元文化交流	☐Be able to work in groups to tell the story of China railway role models in English 　能小组合作用英语讲述本主题相关的中国铁路榜样故事

Topic 3　Passenger Service on Trains
—Warmth Accompanies the Journey
主题三　列车客运服务——温馨伴行

Task ❶　Learning Objectives 明学习目标

Task Description: Get to know the learning content and clarify learning objectives.
任务描述：了解学习内容，明确学习目标。

掌握与"列车客运服务"主题相关的行业英语词汇　**知识目标**

1. 能读懂与本主题相关的文章
2. 能听懂与本主题相关的职场情景对话
3. 能模拟表演职场情景对话，能用英语讲述中国铁路榜样故事
4. 能用英语完成与主题相关的书面表达
技能目标

了解"最美铁路人"米尔班·艾依提的榜样故事，学习她工作中始终将旅客的需求放在首位、积极促进民族团结的精神品质，在未来岗位上以更加饱满的热情和更加专业的服务，为旅客提供安全、舒适、便捷的出行体验
素质目标

Passenger Service on Trains 列车客运服务

- 学行业词汇：bedding, earplug, passenger service crew, luggage handler, dining car attendant, railway policeman on board, D-series high-speed sleeper train, quiet carriage, etc.
- 习情境案例：《D907/908次列车：沪港动卧，优质服务伴您梦行！》
  1. 高铁动卧列车D907/908的运行信息
  2. 高铁动卧列车D907/908的温馨服务
  3. 高铁动卧列车D907/908开行的意义
- 体验职场情景：
  - 行业情景会话听说
  - 行业情景会话展示
  - 职业英语写作训练
- 讲中国铁路榜样故事

最美铁路人　米尔班·艾依提
"开放在列车上的最美石榴花"

Task ② Lead in 导主题内容

Task Description: Watch the video, complete the following exercises and learn about the membership structure of passenger train crew.

任务描述：观看视频，完成练习，了解客运列车乘务组的人员构成。

For passengers, most of their journey time is spent on a train. Therefore, providing good passenger service on trains has great significance for ensuring safety, convenience, and **comfort** of passengers. Passenger service on trains is offered by a train crew under the leadership of the train conductor. The train crew on **ordinary speed train** includes the **passenger service crew** (train conductor, train attendant, **broadcaster, luggage handler, dining car attendant**, etc.), railway policeman on board, and **vehicle inspection crew**. The train crew on high-speed train is composed of train conductor, train attendant, **on-board mechanist**, the railway policeman on board, and the driver.

Passenger transport differs from freight transport. Passengers on a trip have diverse material and cultural needs. So, passenger service on a train should put passengers' needs and experience in the first place, to ensure a comfortable and happy trip.

Task 2.1 Complete the following mind map.

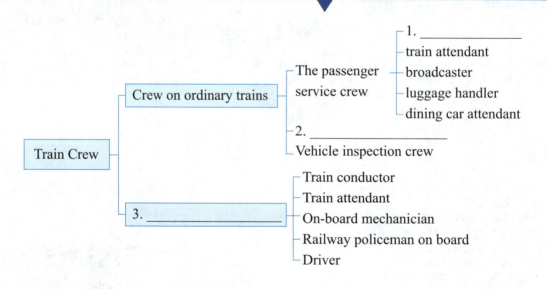

Task ③ Vocabulary Study 学行业词汇

Task Description: Learn the industry vocabulary, complete the following exercises, and master the English expressions related to passenger service on trains.

任务描述：学习行业词汇，完成练习，掌握与列车客运服务工作相关的英文表达。

🎧 **1. passenger service crew**

The **passenger service crew** is mainly responsible for tasks such as serving passengers, checking tickets, cleaning, taking care of passengers in need, and ensuring safe boarding and alighting etc. It consists of train conductor, train attendant, broadcaster, luggage handler, dining car attendant, etc.

🎧 **2. railway policeman on board**

The **railway policeman on board** assists the passenger service crew in keeping order on the train, settling **disputes** among passengers, and ensuring the safety of passengers.

🎧 **3. vehicle inspection crew**

The **vehicle inspection crew** is responsible for ensuring the operation safety of a passenger train from its **originating station** to the **terminating station**. During running, they need to inspect various devices and handle **failures** timely. After the train arrives at the destination, they need to check the **running gear** of the train.

🎧 **4. D-series high-speed sleeper train**

The **D-series high-speed sleeper train** refers to D-series high-speed trains with sleeping coaches. It is a more convenient and comfortable choice for passengers on a long journey.

🎧 **5. passenger transport depot**

The **passenger transportation depot** is responsible for the management of passenger train crew, the arrangement of crew work, and the on-board dining service, etc.

🎧 **6. quiet carriage**

The **quiet carriage** is a special carriage where there is lower noise and fewer interference. Hence, a more quiet and comfortable riding environment can be provided for passengers.

Module 1　Railway Transport　铁道运输　27

Task 3.1 Match the words or phrases with the definitions.

1. _____ passenger service crew
2. _____ vehicle inspection crew
3. _____ passenger transport depot
4. _____ railway policeman on board
5. _____ D-series high-speed sleeper train
6. _____ quiet carriage

A. inspecting various devices and handle failures timely
B. serving passengers directly
C. D-series high-speed trains with sleeping coaches
D. managing passenger train crew
E. assisting the passenger service crew in keeping order on the train
F. a carriage with lower noise and fewer interference

Word Bank

New Words

comfort /ˈkʌmfət/ n. 舒服, 舒适
broadcaster /ˈbrɔːdkɑːstə/ n. 广播员
dispute /dɪˈspjuːt/ n. 纠纷
failure /ˈfeɪljə/ n. 故障
undergo /ˌʌndəˈɡəʊ/ v. 经历, 经受
inbound /ˈɪnbaʊnd/ adj. 到达的
Cantonese /ˌkæntəˈniːz/ n. 广东话, 粤语
tag /tæɡ/ n. 标签
brand-new /ˌbrænd ˈnjuː/ adj. 崭新的

bedding /ˈbedɪŋ/ n. 床上用品
customized /ˈkʌstəmaɪzd/ adj. 定制的
exclusively /ɪkˈskluːsɪvli/ adj. 专用的
disposable /dɪˈspəʊzəbl/ adj. 一次性的
earplug /ˈɪəplʌɡ/ n. 耳塞
overnight /ˌəʊvəˈnaɪt/ adj. 夜间的
gallery /ˈɡæləri/ n. 展览馆
embroidery /ɪmˈbrɔɪdəri/ n. 刺绣

Phrases & Expressions

ordinary speed train   普速列车
passenger service crew   客运乘务组
luggage handler   行李员
dining car attendant   餐车乘务员
railway policeman on board   乘警
vehicle inspection crew   检车乘务组
on-board mechanician   随车机械师
originating station   始发站
terminating station   终点站
running gear   走行部

D-series high-speed sleeper train
　　高铁动卧列车
passenger transportation depot   客运段
quiet carriage   静音车厢
service supplies   服务备品
internationally universal socket
　　国际通用插座
eye mask   眼罩
disposable earplug   一次性耳塞

Task 4 Passage Study 习情境案例

Task Description: Read the article, complete the following exercises, and learn about the upgraded services on D-series high-speed sleeper train numbered D907/908.

任务描述：读懂文章，完成练习，了解沪港动卧 D907/908 次列车上的优质服务。

"D907/908: A Dreamy Journey from Shanghai to Hong Kong with Upgraded Comforts and Services!"

From June 15, 2024, a D-series high-speed sleeper train numbered D907/908 started to serve passengers. It departs in the evening and arrives in the morning, running between Shanghai Hongqiao Station and Hong Kong West Kowloon Station.

Shanghai Passenger Transport Depot takes on crew duties. The selected crew members have many years of work experience and can communicate in simple English. They have **undergone** theoretical training and on-board practice. Now they are good at ticketing services for passengers **inbound** to Hong Kong. They can also provide services in **Cantonese**.

Besides, carriage decorations and **service supplies** have been fully upgraded. In addition to luggage **tags, internationally universal sockets** are provided. **Brand-new bedding** is **customized** with special tags. The bedding is **exclusively** used. There is also a reading corner on the train to provide passengers with more cultural experience.

D907 departs from Shanghai Hongqiao Railway Station at 20:15. After about 11 hours, it terminates at Hong Kong West Kowloon Railway Station at 7:29 the next morning. For good passenger service, Shanghai Passenger Transport Depot creates a featured service of "A Sweet Sleep". Sleep aid devices are provided on the train, such as steam **eye masks, disposable earplugs**, and noise reduction stickers. With these devices, passengers can have a sweet sleep during the **overnight** journey. Crew members offer disturbance-free service at night. They answer passengers' inquiries in a soft voice to avoid disturbing other passengers.

From trains K99/100, T99/100, Z99/100, and G99/100 to D-series high-speed sleeper train D907/908, trains leaving for Hong Kong have always warmed passengers with sincere service. These trains have become a bridge of exchange between Shanghai and Hong Kong.

Task 4.1 Read the passage. Then, choose the correct answers.

1. What is the originating station for Train D907?
   A. Shanghai Pudong Airport.
   B. Shanghai Hongqiao Station.
   C. Beijing South Railway Station.
   D. Guangzhou South Railway Station.

Module 1　RAILWAY TRANSPORT　铁道运输

2. What type of sockets are provided in the carriages of Train D907/908?
   A. Locally specific sockets.
   B. Internationally universal sockets.
   C. USB charging ports only.
   D. Wireless charging pads.
3. How do crew members handle inquiries from passengers during the night?
   A. They ignore inquiries to avoid disturbance.
   B. They answer loudly and clearly.
   C. They answer in a soft voice.
   D. They refer passengers to automated machines.

Task 4.2 Read the sentence pairs. Fill in each blank with the best word or phrase.

1. luggage tags/disposable earplugs
   A. _____ are used to help passengers identify their own luggage.
   B. _____ protect the ears from harmful noise.
2. sleeper train/bedding
   A. The _____ is exclusively used on this train.
   B. D907/908 is a _____ .

Task 5 Vocational Situation Experience 演职场情景

Task Description: Experience the situational conversation and complete the following exercises, so as to enhance English application ability related to professional positions.

任务描述:体验岗位情景会话,完成练习,提升与职业岗位相关的英语应用能力。

Task 5.1 Listen to the conversation, and fill in the blanks.

Situation description: Li is a trainee from Changsha Passenger Transport Depot. He participates in a creativity competition to design folk-culture-themed carriages. Now, he is showing his project plan to his instructor, discussing how to meet the needs of different passengers and improve their ride experience.

Trainee: Hello, Mr. Wang. Would you like to help me with this plan of decorating a folk-culture-themed carriage?

Instructor: Of course. Let me see…Interior decorations of the carriage are designed according to Hunan 1. _____ . That is great.

Trainee: Thank you. Moreover, we plan to change Carriage 6 into a **gallery** for Hunan

Instructor: **embroidery**. This may help passengers gain more 2. _____ into Hunan embroidery.

Instructor: That sounds good. It would be much better if passengers have any chance to 3. _____ _____ Hunan embroidery by themselves.

Trainee: That's a great idea. I believe it will attract many passengers who are 4. _____ _____ Hunan embroidery. By that time, this carriage would be lively.

Instructor: But I'm afraid it may disturb some passengers who like quiet.

Trainee: Don't worry. This is a carriage special for exhibiting Hunan embroidery. It will not be used for 5. _____ _____ .

Instructor: Despite this, I still suggest adding a quiet carriage for those who prefer a quiet riding environment.

Trainee: That makes sense. Anyway, we should meet needs of different passengers.

Task 5.2 Listen again and mark the statements as true(T) or false(F).

_____ 1. The interior decorations of the carriage are designed based on Hunan local culture.

_____ 2. The trainee plans to change Carriage 6 into a gallery for Hunan pottery.

_____ 3. The quiet carriage is intended for passengers who prefer a peaceful ride.

Task 5.3 Act out the roles with a partner.

Task 6 Vocational Writing Practice 练职业写作

Task Description: Please select and describe one of the following services on a trains, and learn more about featured passenger service. So that, you can provide passengers with a more diversified ride experience at your future position.

任务描述: 请选择以下一种车厢服务进行描述,了解有特色的旅客列车服务内容,以便在未来岗位上更好地为旅客提供多元化的乘车体验。

Featured Passenger Services on Trains

Type of Service	Service Items
Quiet carriage	① Lower the broadcast volume ② Offer eye masks and earplugs ③ Offer "One-to-One" arrival reminder service
Intelligent catering reservation	① Reservations made online ② Offer food served on board or at stations along the way ③ Reservations made 1 hour earlier ④ Food is taken to the seat
Tourist trains with specific theme	① Carriage decorations with local culture features ② Enjoy attractions along the way ③ Provide featured services, such as themed catering, cultural lectures, and interactive games

_____

_____

_____

_____

_____

_____

_____

_____

Task 7 Telling Stories of China Railway 讲中国铁路故事

Task Description：Watch the story of railway role models and complete the following exercises to develop the awareness and ability to tell stories of China Railway in English.

任务描述：观看铁路榜样故事，完成练习，培养用英语讲述中国铁路故事的意识和能力。

7.1 Why is Mirban Eyiti called the "Most Beautiful Pomegranate Flower" on the train?

_____
_____
_____
_____
_____
_____
_____
_____

7.2 Watch the video again and search online for more information about Mirban Eyiti, introduce her major achievements. Then work in groups to tell Mirban Eyiti's story and share the inspiration and motivation you gained from her spirit.

_____
_____
_____
_____
_____
_____
_____
_____
_____

Task 8 Topic Test 测章节知识

Task Description: Review this topic and complete the topic test to develop self-testing skills and summarizing analysis skills.

任务描述:复习本章节内容,完成章节测试,培养自我检测和总结分析能力。

◎ **Choose the correct answers.**

1. What language skill is required for the crew members of Train D907/908?
   A. Mandarin only.　　　　　　　　B. Cantonese only.
   C. English only.　　　　　　　　　D. Mandarin, English and Cantonese.
2. Which of the following is NOT a sleep aid device provided on the train?
   A. Steam eye masks.　　　　　　　B. Disposable earplugs.
   C. Noise reduction stickers.　　　　D. Disposable toothbrush.
3. Which of the following is NOT a direct responsibility of a passenger transport depot?
   A. Arranging crew work schedules.　B. Managing the on-board dining service.
   C. Determining train ticket prices.　 D. Overseeing the train crew's duties.
4. Who leads the train crew in providing passenger service on trains?
   A. The train attendant.　　　　　　B. The vehicle inspection crew.
   C. The train conductor.　　　　　　D. The dining car attendant.
5. Which of the following is NOT a member of the train crew on an ordinary speed train?
   A. Train conductor.　　　　　　　 B. On-board mechanist.
   C. Railway policeman on board.　　D. Luggage handler.

◎ **Mark the following translations as true(T) or false(F).**

6. The train departs in the evening and arrives in the morning.
   译文:这列列车朝发夕至。
7. They have undergone theoretical training and on-board practice.
   译文:他们经过理论培训和跟车实习。
8. Brand-new bedding is customized with special tags.
   译文:全新的床单配有定制标签。
9. Sleep aid devices are provided on the train.
   译文:列车上提供了降噪设备。
10. These trains have become a bridge of exchange between Shanghai and Hong Kong.
    译文:这些列车成为沪港两地沟通交流的纽带。

Task 9　Self-assessment 评学习效果

Task Description：Tick the items and self-assess learning outcomes.
任务描述：勾选选项，自我评估学习效果。

教学目标	评分项目
自主学习完善	☐Have a good habit of independent learning 有良好的自主学习习惯 ☐Be clear about learning objectives 明确学习目标 ☐Know about learning content 了解学习内容 ☐Complete learning tasks effectively 有效完成学习任务 ☐Finish the section test consciously 自主进行知识检测
语言思维提升	Master the pronunciation, spelling, definition, and simple usage of the following vocabulary： 掌握下列词汇的发音、拼写、释义及简单应用： ☐comfort ☐failure ☐bedding ☐disposable ☐earplug ☐passenger service crew ☐luggage handler ☐dining car attendant ☐departure station ☐terminal station ☐running gear ☐railway policeman on board ☐D-series high-speed sleeper train
	Be able to read and understand articles related to this topic and talk about them in English： 能读懂本主题相关文章并用英语简单介绍： ☐The route of Train D907/908 　高铁动卧列车 D907/908 的线路 ☐The sweet services offered by Train D907/908 　高铁动卧列车 D907/908 的温馨服务 ☐The significance of Train D907/908 　高铁动卧列车 D907/908 开行的意义
职场涉外沟通	☐Be able to understand workplace situational conversations related to this topic 　能听懂本主题相关的职场情景对话 ☐Be able to simulate workplace situational conversations related to this topic with a partner 　能与搭档一起模拟本主题相关的职场情景对话 ☐Be able to introduce the given theme in written form 　能用英语完成主题相关的书面表达
多元文化交流	☐Be able to work in groups to tell the story of China railway role models in English 　能小组合作用英语讲述本主题相关的中国铁路榜样故事

Topic 4　Railway Freight Transport Organization —Unimpeded Transport

主题四　铁路货物运输组织——物畅其流

Task 1　Learning Objectives 明学习目标

Task Description：Get to know the learning content and clarify learning objectives.
任务描述：了解学习内容，明确学习目标。

知识目标
掌握与"铁路货物运输组织"主题相关的行业英语词汇

学行业词汇
truckload, fragile, dispatch, accommodate, allocate, utilize, container transport, full truckload transport, hazardous goods, dispatching operation, railway freight transport, etc.

技能目标
1. 能读懂与本主题相关的文章
2. 能听懂与本主题相关的职场情景对话
3. 能模拟表演职场情景对话，能英语讲述中国铁路榜样故事
4. 能用英语完成与主题相关的书面表达

习情境案例
《铁路货运：精准履约，安全护航》
1. 三种铁路货物运输方式
2. 铁路货物运输的基本作业
3. 货运员的工作职责和要求

Railway Freight Transport Organization 铁路货物运输组织

体验职场情境
行业情景会话听说
行业情景会话展示
职业英语写作训练

素质目标
了解"最美铁路人"货装安全护航人薛胜利的榜样故事，学习他的敬业精神、专注精神、创新精神以及奉献精神，在未来岗位上热爱工作，不断追求更高的目标

讲中国铁路榜样故事

最美铁路人　薛胜利
"货装安全护航人"

Task ❷ Lead in 导主题内容

Task Description: Watch the video, complete the following exercises and learn about the three types of railway freight transport.

任务描述: 观看视频, 完成练习, 了解三种铁路货物运输方式。

Railway freight transport occupies an important position in modern transportation industry. It has many advantages such as faster speed, larger transport capacity, less impact from weather, higher safety, and lower cost.

The types of railway freight transport are divided into three categories: full truckload transport, less-than-**truckload** transport and container transport.

Full truckload (FTL) transport is like a **giant appetite** designed specifically for large-scale cargo. When you have a large quantity of materials such as coal, oil, **mineral**, steel, grain and other goods that need to be transported, FTL transport is the best choice.

Different from full truckload transport, less-than-truckload (LTL) transport is an **exclusive** express service for small amounts of goods. It can easily handle goods with a weight of no more than 40 tons and a volume of less than 80 cubic meters.

Container transport is a standardized mode of transport in "boxes". As a "Transformer" of the freight industry, this standardized "box" can **accommodate** various goods. Whether it is food, daily necessities or industrial products, precise goods, valuable goods or **fragile** goods, all of them can be put into this "box", allowing for quick loading and unloading as well as convenient handover.

The above three modes of transport have their own characteristics, satisfying the diverse transportation needs of different customers.

Task 2.1 Complete the following mind map.

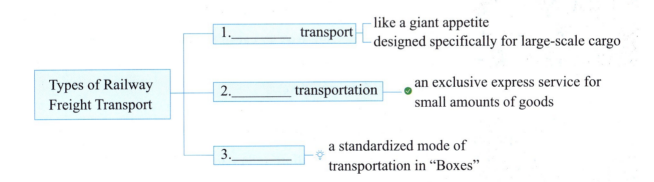

Task 3 Vocabulary Study 学行业词汇

Task Description：Learn the industry vocabulary, complete the following exercises, and master the English expressions related to railway freight transport organization.

任务描述：学习行业词汇，完成练习，掌握与铁路货物运输组织工作相关的英文表达。

🎧 1. full truckload transport (FTL)

The **full truckload transport** refers to the transportation mode utilized when a **batch** of goods needs to be loaded in one or more cars due to its weight, volume, shape or nature.

🎧 2. less-than-truckload transport (LTL)

The **less-than-truckload transport** refers to the transportation mode utilized when the weight, volume, shape and nature of a batch of goods do not require the exclusive use of a single truck for transportation.

🎧 3. container transport

The **container transport refers to** a "door-to-door" transportation mode that **utilize**s containers as carriers to **assemble** goods into containerized units. **It facilitates** loading and unloading by using large-scale handling machinery.

🎧 4. hazardous goods

The **hazardous goods** refer to all the goods that have the properties of explosion, **flammability**, poison, infection, **corrosion**, **radioactivity**. They are easy to cause personal injury, property damage or environmental pollution during the process of transportation, loading, unloading and storage.

🎧 5. dispatching operation

Dispatching operation refers to the various freight operations carried out at the dispatched station, including submitting the freight demand, acceptance, receiving inspection, charging and consignment, loading and so on.

🎧 6. on route operation

On route operation refers to the various freight operations on route, including handover and inspection, reloading and sorting, contract changing and **obstruction** disposal.

🎧 7. arrival operation

Arrival operation refers to the various freight operations carried out for the freight at the destination station. It mainly includes unloading, storage, delivery and the final settlement of **miscellaneous** fees.

🎧 8. open-top car

The **open-top car** is a kind of versatile railway car without a roof. It is primarily used for transporting goods such as coal, ores, building materials, machinery and equipment, steel, lumber and other cargoes.

🎧 9. boxcar

The **boxcar** refers to the freight car equipped with end walls, side walls, and a roof, as well as doors and windows on the side walls. It is primarily used for transporting boxed, bagged and bulk grains, as well as valuable goods that need to be protected from weather.

🎧 10. flatcar

The **flatcar** is a type of car that has no fixed ends and side walls. It utilizes its underframe to carry loads. It is mainly used for transporting goods such as steel, lumber, **gravel**, automobiles and containers.

🎧 11. refrigerated car

The **refrigerated car** has excellent **thermal insulation** properties and temperature control capabilities. It is mainly used for transporting fresh and live goods and **perishable** goods.

🎧 12. tank car

The **tank car** is a type of vehicle with a tank-shaped body, used for transporting various liquids, liquefied gases, powder articles and so on.

Module 1　Railway Transport　铁道运输　39

Task 3.1 Match the words or phrases with the definitions.

1. _____ full truckload transport
2. _____ less-than-truckload transport
3. _____ container transport
4. _____ dispatching operation
5. _____ open-top car
6. _____ boxcar
7. _____ flatcar
8. _____ tank car

A. a mode of freight transportation that doesn't need an entire truck

B. utilizing the underframe to carry loads

C. a versatile train car without a roof

D. a mode of freight transportation that needs one or more cars

E. all the freight tasks done at the dispatch station

F. a tank-shaped vehicle

G. a mode of transportation that uses containers to carry goods

H. a fully enclosed freight car

Word Bank

⊙ New Words

truckload/ˈtrʌkləʊd/ n. 一货车的容量；货车荷载
giant/ˈdʒaɪənt/ n. 巨人
appetite/ˈæpɪtaɪt/ n. 食欲；胃口
mineral/ˈmɪnərəl/ n. 矿物质；矿物
exclusive/ɪkˈskluːsɪv/ adj. 独有的；专用的
accommodate/əˈkɒmədeɪt/ v. 容纳
fragile/ˈfrædʒaɪl/ adj. 易碎的；易损的
batch/bætʃ/ n. 一批；一批生产量
utilize/ˈjuːtəlaɪz/ v. 利用，使用
assemble/əˈsembl/ v. （使）集合，（使）聚集
facilitate/fəˈsɪlɪteɪt/ v. 促进，推动
hazardous/ˈhæzədəs/ adj. 危险的；有害的
flammability/ˌflæməˈbɪləti/ n. 可燃性，易燃性
corrosion/kəˈrəʊʒn/ n. 腐蚀，侵蚀

radioactivity/ˌreɪdiəʊækˈtɪvəti/ n. 放射性
obstruction/əbˈstrʌkʃn/ n. 阻挠，妨碍
miscellaneous/ˌmɪsəˈleɪniəs/ adj. 混杂的，各种各样的
boxcar/ˈbɒkskɑː/ n. 货车车厢；有盖货车
flatcar/ˈflætkɑː/ n. 无盖货车；平台型铁路货车
gravel/ˈgrævəl/ n. 碎石，砂砾
refrigerated/rɪˈfrɪdʒəreɪtɪd/ adj. 冷冻的，冷却的
thermal/ˈθɜːməl/ adj. 热的，热量的
insulation/ˌɪnsjuˈleɪʃn/ n. 隔热；绝缘
perishable/ˈperɪʃəbl/ adj. （食物）易腐烂的，易变质的
consignment/kənˈsaɪnmənt/ n. 发送的货物，委托
consignor/kənˈsaɪnə/ n. 发货人；委托者
consignee/ˌkɒnsaɪˈniː/ n. 收件人；收货人

penalty/ˈpenəlti/n. （因违反法律、规定或合同而受到的）处罚；刑罚
diligent/ˈdɪlɪdʒənt/adj. 勤奋的；细致的
encounter/ɪnˈkaʊntə/v. 遭遇；偶遇

versatile/ˈvɜːsətaɪl/adj. 多功能的
sulfuric/sʌlˈfjʊərɪk/adj. 硫黄的；含多量硫黄的
edible/ˈedəbl/adj. 可食用的

⊙ Phrases & Expressions

railway freight transport　铁路货物运输
full truckload transport　整车运输
less-than-truckload transport　零担运输
container transport　集装箱运输
hazardous goods　危险货物
dispatching operation　发送作业

operation on route　途中作业
open-top car　敞车
refrigerated car　冷藏车
tank car　罐车
arrival operation　到达作业

 Task **Passage Study** 情境案例

Task Description：Read the article, complete the following exercises, and learn about the railway cargo transportation procedures and safety responsibilities.

任务描述：读懂文章，完成练习，了解铁路货物运输的流程与安全责任。

Railway Freight Transport: Precise Fulfillment, Safe Escort

Railway freight transport refers to the process in which the railway department serves as the carrier and accepts the **consignment** of the **consignor** to transport goods. The goods are transported from departure station to destination station via railway and delivered to the **consignee**. According to laws and regulations, the railway department is required to transport the goods to the destination safely, promptly and accurately as agreed upon in the contract. If the goods are damaged or delayed, the carrier must take responsibility and pay a **penalty**.

Goods with different nature varies in different transportation modes and storage measures. In order to ensure the safety of goods, goods that cannot be mixed due to their nature and different transportation conditions must not be consigned by one-batch freight, such as perishable and non-perishable goods, hazardous and non-hazardous goods.

The basic operations of railway freight transportation include dispatching operations, on route operations and arrival operations. The specific steps involve in the consignment, acceptance, preparing for carriage, loading, transportation, unloading, and delivery of the goods. Every operation procedure must follow strict codes and standards to ensure safe, timely, and accurate delivery of goods.

As freight clerks, we need to learn more about the characteristics, transportation requirements and safety standards of various types of goods. We are expected to be **diligent** and responsible in every cargo inspection to ensure that the quality and quantity of the goods meet transportation requirements. At the same time, we should monitor the transportation process, promptly identify and deal with problems, and ensure that the goods arrive at their destination safely and quickly.

Task 4.1　Read the passage. Then, choose the correct answers.

1. In railway freight transport, who is required to bear the liability for breach of contract and pay a liquidated damage if the goods are damaged or overdue, according to laws and regulations?
    A. The consignor.
    B. The consignee.
    C. The railway department (carrier).
    D. The insurance company.

2. Which of the following is NOT a specific step in the railway freight transportation process?
    A. Consignment of the goods.
    B. Acceptance of the goods.
    C. Transportation of the goods.
    D. Pricing of the shipment.

3. Which of the following is NOT included in the basic operations of railway freight transportation?
    A. Dispatching operations.
    B. Operations on route.
    C. Arrival operations.
    D. Packaging and labeling of goods.

Task 4.2　Read the sentence pairs. Fill in each blank with the best word or phrase.

1. follow/include
    A. The main steps _____ sending, receiving, moving, loading, transporting, unloading, and finally delivering the goods.
    B. All procedures must _____ strict rules to guarantee safe, on-time, and precise delivery of goods.

2. responsible/delayed
    A. We need to be thorough and _____ in checking cargo to make sure it meets shipping standards for quality and quantity.
    B. If goods are damaged or _____, the carrier takes responsibility and pays a penalty.

Task 5 Vocational Situation Experience 演职场情景

Task Description: Experience the situational conversation and complete the following exercises, so as to enhance English application ability related to professional positions.

任务描述：体验岗位情景会话，完成练习，提升与职业岗位相关的英语应用能力。

Task 5.1 Listen to the conversation, and fill in the blanks.

Situation description: A trainee is consulting an experienced instructor about the appropriate transportation modes for grain and seafood in order to master the knowledge and skills necessary for transporting these perishable goods efficiently and safely.

Trainee: Hello Mr. Fang, I've **encounter**ed a problem while studying 1. _____. Would you give me some suggestions on the transportation modes for grain?

Instructor: Of course. For the transportation of grain, we recommend using 2. _____.

Trainee: Why?

Instructor: Because boxcars 3. _____ _____ _____ transporting goods that need to be protected from moisture and sunshine. The top of the boxcar is 4. _____, which can prevent the grain from getting damp.

Trainee: I see, thank you very much. By the way, if I need to transport seafood, what kinds of car should I choose?

Instructor: A 5. _____ car. They are suitable for transporting frozen goods and food, as they have 6. _____ temperature control system. It can keep the seafood from going bad during transportation.

Trainee: Get it. Thanks for your answer!

Instructor: You're welcome. If you have any other questions, feel free to ask me.

Task 5.2 Listen again and mark the statements as true(T) or false(F).

_____ 1. For the transportation of grain, we recommend using flatcars.

_____ 2. The enclosed boxcar can prevent the grain from getting damp.

_____ 3. A refrigerated car is suitable for transporting frozen goods and food.

Task 5.3 Act out the roles with a partner.

Task 6 Vocational Writing Practice 练职业写作

Task Description: Refer to the following table, describe the types of railway freight cars and their characteristics, and learn about the main cargoes suitable for different types of cars in order to ensure the safety of freight transportation.

任务描述：参考表格内容，学会描述铁路货运车辆种类及其特点，掌握各种车型适合运输的主要货物，从而确保货物运输的安全。

Types of Railway Freight Cars

Vehicles	Main Goods for Transportation	Main Characteristics
Open-top car	Bulk cargoes: such as coal, mineral, lumbers and steel, etc.	① Large capacity ② High transportation efficiency ③ Strong adaptability ④ High cost-effectiveness
Box car	Goods that require protection against moisture and sunlight: such as grain, daily necessities, and instruments, etc.	① Good sealing ② Strong adaptability ③ Diverse types
Flat car	Bulk cargo: such as steel, lumber, machinery and equipment, automobiles, etc.	① **Versatile** ② Strong load-bearing capacity ③ Stable structure
Refrigerated car	Frozen goods and food: such as medicine, meat, seafood, fruit and vegetables, etc.	① Precise temperature control ② Good thermal insulation and heat insulation
Tank car	① Liquids: such as petroleum, gasoline, concentrated **sulfuric** acid and **edible** oil, etc. ② Liquefied gases: such as liquefied natural gas, etc. ③ Powdered goods: such as cement and flour, etc.	① Large capacity ② Low cost, high safety ③ Environmentally protected ④ Energy-saving

Task 7 Telling Stories of China Railway 讲中国铁路故事

Task Description: Watch the story of railway role models and complete the following exercises to develop the awareness and ability to tell stories of China Railway in English.

任务描述：观看铁路榜样故事，完成练习，培养用英语讲述中国铁路故事的意识和能力。

7.1 As the business supervisor of Songjiazhuang Station, what specific measures does Xue Shengli take to ensure cargo loading safety on the Datong-Qinhuangdao Railway?

7.2 Watch the video again and search online for more information about Xue Shengli, introduce his major achievements. Also, share the inspiration and motivation you gained from his spirit. Work in groups to tell the story of Xue Shengli.

Task 8　Topic Test 测章节知识

Task Description: Review this topic and complete the topic test to develop self-testing skills and summarizing analysis skills.

任务描述：复习本章节内容，完成章节测试，培养自我检测和总结分析能力。

◎ **Choose the correct answers.**

1. Which of the following is NOT a type of railway freight transport mentioned?
   A. Full truckload transport.　　　　B. Less-than-truckload transport.
   C. Container transport.　　　　　　D. Air freight transport.

2. Why might Full Truckload NOT be best for large quantities like coal, oil?
   A. More environmentally friendly.　　B. Fewer stops and transfers.
   C. Efficient use of truck capacity.　　D. Minimizes handling damage.

3. Which is the most accurate description of the railway's obligation in transporting goods?
   A. Saves shipper money.　　　　　　B. Provides compensation for damage.
   C. Ensures safe, prompt, accurate delivery.　D. Manages customs clearance only.

4. Which is NOT a reason for strict norms in transportation?
   A. Prevent accidents and damage.　　B. Ensure wrong delivery.
   C. Maintain customer satisfaction.　　D. Guarantee timely delivery.

5. Which of the following best summarizes the importance of monitoring the transportation process?
   A. Saves shipper money on costs.
   B. Enhances overall supply chain efficiency.
   C. Identifies and resolves issues for safe, timely delivery.
   D. Not necessary if contract clear.

◎ **Mark the following translations as true (T) or false (F).**

6. The basic operations of railway freight transportation include dispatching operations, operations on route and arrival operations.
   译文：铁路货物运输的基本作业包括发送作业、途中作业和到达作业。

7. Every operation procedure must follow strict codes and standards to ensure safe, timely, and accurate delivery of goods.
   译文：每一作业流程都必须遵循严格的规范和标准，以确保货物安全、及时、准确地送达。

8. As freight clerks, we need to learn more about the characteristics, transportation requirements and safety standards of various types of goods.
   译文：作为一名货检员，我们要了解各类货物的特性、运输要求和运输安全标准。

9. If the goods are damaged or delayed, the carrier must take responsibility and pay a penalty.
   译文：如果货物破损或逾期到达，承运人要承担违约责任，支付违约金。

10. Full truckload (FTL) transport is like a giant appetite designed specifically for large-scale cargo.
    译文：零担运输，如同一位巨人，专为大宗货物而生。

Task 9 Self-assessment 评学习效果

Task Description: Tick the items and self-assess learning outcomes.
任务描述: 勾选选项，自我评估学习效果。

教学目标	评分项目
自主学习完善	☐Have a good habit of independent learning 有良好的自主学习习惯 ☐Be clear about learning objectives 明确学习目标 ☐Know about learning content 了解学习内容 ☐Complete learning tasks effectively 有效完成学习任务 ☐Finish the section test consciously 自主进行知识检测
语言思维提升	Master the pronunciation, spelling, definition, and simple usage of the following vocabulary: 掌握下列词汇的发音、拼写、释义及简单应用: ☐truckload ☐fragile ☐dispatch ☐accommodate ☐allocate ☐utilize ☐container transport ☐full truckload transport ☐hazardous goods ☐dispatching operation ☐arrival operation ☐railway freight transport ☐less-than-truckload transport
	Be able to read and understand articles related to this topic and talk about them in English: 能读懂本主题相关文章并用英语简单介绍: ☐The three types of railway freight transport 　三种铁路货物运输方式 ☐The Basic operations of railway freight transportation 　铁路货物运输的基本作业 ☐The job responsibilities and requirements of freight clerks 　货运员的工作职责和要求
职场涉外沟通	☐Be able to understand workplace situational conversations related to this topic 　能听懂本主题相关的职场情景对话 ☐Be able to simulate workplace situational conversations related to this topic with a partner 　能与搭档一起模拟本主题相关的职场情景对话 ☐Be able to introduce the given theme in written form 　能用英语完成主题相关的书面表达
多元文化交流	☐Be able to work in groups to tell the story of China railway role models in English 　能小组合作用英语讲述本主题相关的中国铁路榜样故事

Topic 5　Railway Operation Organization
—Precise Dispatch

主题五　铁路行车组织——精准调度

Task 1　Learning Objectives 明学习目标

Task Description: Get to know the learning content and clarify learning objectives.
任务描述：了解学习内容，明确学习目标。

- 掌握与"铁路行车组织"主题相关的行业英语词汇 —— **知识目标**
- 学行业词汇：essential, exclude, dispatch, allocate, intermediate, marshaling yard, hump crest, disintegration shunting, marshaling shunting, railway operation organization, etc.

- 1. 能读懂与本主题相关的文章
  2. 能听懂与本主题相关的职场情景对话
  3. 能模拟表演职场情景对话，能用英语讲述中国铁路榜样故事
  4. 能用英语完成与主题相关的书面表达 —— **技能目标**
- 习情境案例：《车站行车组织如何编织安全高效运输网》
  1. 列车编组的工作内容
  2. 车站行车组织工作的主要内容
  3. 调车作业的种类和要求

- 体验职场情景：
  - 行业情景会话听说
  - 行业情景会话展示
  - 职业英语写作训练

- 了解"最美铁路人"车站值班员王军的榜样故事，学习他的敬业精神、专注精神、创新精神以及奉献精神，在未来岗位上热爱工作，不断追求更高的目标 —— **素质目标**

- 讲中国铁路榜样故事

Railway Operation Organnization 铁路行车组织

最美铁路人　王军
"车站值班员"

Task 2 Lead in 导主题内容

Task Description: Watch the video, complete the following exercises and lear about the work content of train marshaling.

任务描述: 观看视频，完成练习，了解列车编组的工作内容。

Passengers need to buy tickets when taking the train, and the railway freight also adopts the "one ticket for one vehicle" policy. The difference is that the direction of passenger trains is fixed, and passengers can board the train directly according to their tickets. However, the goods on the same freight train may be **destined** for different directions. In that case, we need to perform train **marshaling**.

Generally speaking, train marshaling involves regrouping trains bound for various directions based on their final destinations, and grouping freight cars for the same direction together. At the **marshaling yard**, the coupler performs break-up and make-up operations based on the type of cargo, transportation time limit, and transportation direction. The **shunting** locomotive pushes the carriages up to the "hump" as planned. Then the **coupler** separates the carriages as they pass the **hump crest**, allowing them to slide down smoothly onto the **designated** tracks. Once the number of carriages or the total weight on a particular track reaches the **criteria** for forming a complete train, the operational staff will inspect each carriage and **couple** them together. Thus the train marshaling for a freight train is completed. After the cargo inspector completes the pre-departure inspection, this freight train is ready to depart towards its destination!

Task 2.1 Complete the following mind map.

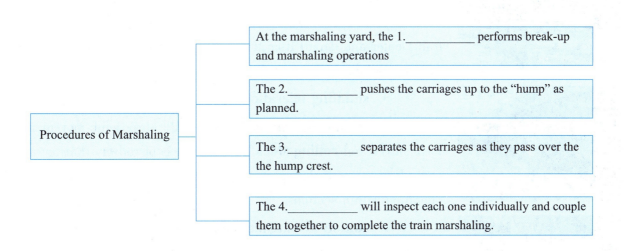

Task ❸ Vocabulary Study 学行业词汇

> **Task Description**: Learn the industry vocabulary, complete the following exercises, and master the English expressions related to railway operation organization.
>
> **任务描述**：学习行业词汇，完成练习，掌握与铁路行车组织工作相关的英文表达。

🎧 1. railway operation organization

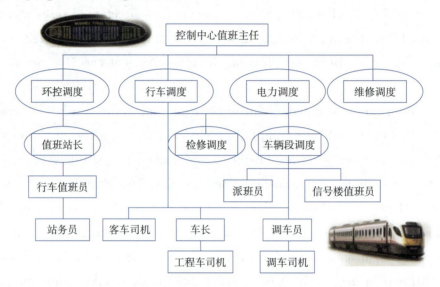

The **railway operation organization** is an **essential component** of railway transportation organization. It involves the comprehensive **utilization** of various technical equipment, the **rational** organization of train operation as well as the planning and organization of the transport process in railway.

🎧 2. train reception and departure operation

The **train reception and departure operation** refers to the necessary operations done according to established procedures when trains enter and depart from the station, in order to ensure the safety of train operation.

🎧 3. shunting operation

The **shunting operation** refers to all purposeful movements of locomotives and **rolling stock** in the process of railway transportation, **excluding** the arrival, departure, passing of trains at stations, and their operation within sections.

🎧 4. station dispatching command

The **station dispatching command** refers to the organization and command of the daily transportation activities at the station to ensure the smooth, efficient, and safe operation of trains.

🎧 5. section blocking

The **section blocking** refers to the operation method that allows only one train to operate within a section or block section at any given time. It guarantees the safe operation of the train.

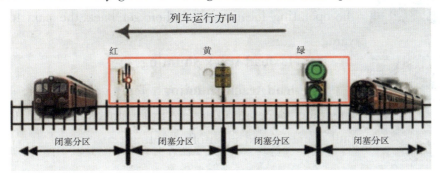

🎧 6. train operation diagram

The **train operation diagram** refers to a **graphical** representation of train operation schedules and **spatial** relationships, serving as the basis for organizing train operation across the entire railway network. It visually displays the **mutual** positions and corresponding relationships of each train in terms of time and space.

🎧 7. disintegration shunting

The **disintegration shunting** refers to the operations that **allocate** the inbound train sets or car groups to the fixed tracks of the shunting yard according to the destinations of cars or other needs.

🎧 8. marshaling shunting

The **marshaling shunting** refers to the operations that select and marshal cars to make up train sets or car groups according to the train formation plan, train operation diagram and other relevant regulations and requirements.

🎧 9. detaching and attaching shunting

The **detaching and attaching shunting** refers to the operations that add or remove cars, replace car groups for the transit trains, as well as detach or attach cars for pick-up and set-out trains at the **intermediate** station.

Module 1　Railway Transport　铁道运输

10. pickup and drop shunting

The **pickup and drop shunting** refers to the operations that send the cars to be loaded, unloaded or repaired from the marshaling yard to the operating locations and then get back the cars to the marshaling yard.

11. lead track shunting

The **lead track shunting** refers to a most basic mode of shunting operation. Generally there are two methods to be adopted such as push-pull shunting and push-off shunting.

12. push-pull shunting

The **push-pull shunting** refers to the operations that uses a locomotive to transfer a car from one track to a designated location on another track, and then detaching the car after it is parked properly.

13. push-off shunting

The **push-off shunting** refers to the operations that use a locomotive to push a train set to a certain speed, and then uncouple the hooks while the train is still in motion, allowing the detached car groups to coast towards a designated location by themselves.

14. hump Shunting

The **hump shunting** refers to the operations that rolls the detached cars from the hump crest into the designated lines in the shunting yard by their own **gravities** along with a certain **thrust** of the locomotive.

Task 3.1 Match the words or phrases with the definitions.

1. _____ railway operation organization
2. _____ reception and departure of train
3. _____ disintegration shunting
4. _____ push-pull shunting
5. _____ shunting operations
6. _____ couple-uncouple shunting
7. _____ marshaling shunting
8. _____ hump shunting

A. rolling detached cars down the hump crest into designated tracks in the yard, utilizing their own gravity assisted by locomotive thrust

B. transferring a car from one track to a designated spot on another using a locomotive, followed by decoupling upon proper parking

C. necessary procedures must be followed according to established procedures when trains enter and depart from the station

D. adding or removing cars, replacing car groups for the transit trains, and detaching or attaching cars for pick-up or set-out trains at intermediate stations

E. comprehensive utilization of technical equipment, rational train operation, efficient planning and organization of the transport process

F. forming train sets or groups based on train formation plan, train operation diagram and relevant regulations

G. allocating train sets or car groups to designated shunting yard based on destinations or other requirements.

H. **encompassing** all purposeful movements of locomotives and rolling stock in railway transportation, excluding station arrivals, departures, passings and section operations.

Word Bank

New Words

destine/ˈdestɪn/ v. 指定，选定
marshaling/ˈmɑːʃəlɪŋ/ v. （车辆）编组
shunting/ˈʃʌntɪŋ/ n. 调车；转线
hump/hʌmp/ n. 驼峰
crest/krest/ n. 峰顶
designated/ˈdezɪɡneɪtɪd/ adj. 指定的；标出的
criteria/kraɪˈtɪəriə/ n. （评判或做决定的）标准；准则
couple/ˈkʌpl/ v. （把设备等）连接
essential/ɪˈsenʃəl/ adj. 必不可少的；基本的
component/kəmˈpəʊnənt/ n. 组成部分
utilization/ˌjuːtəlaɪˈzeɪʃn/ n. 利用；使用
rational/ˈræʃənəl/ adj. 合理的
exclude/ɪkˈskluːd/ vt. 把……排除在外

dispatch/dɪˈspætʃ/ v. 派遣；发送
　　　　　　　　　n. 派遣；发送
graphical/ˈɡræfɪkl/ adj. 用图（或图表等）表示的
spatial/ˈspeɪʃəl/ adj. 空间的；与空间有关的
mutual/ˈmjuːtʃuəl/ adj. 相互的，彼此的
disintegration/dɪsˌɪntɪˈɡreɪʃən/ n. 分裂；解体
allocate/ˈæləkeɪt/ v. 分配；分派
intermediate/ˌɪntəˈmiːdiət/ adj. 居中的；中间的
gravity/ˈɡrævəti/ n. 重力
thrust/θrʌst/ n. 猛推，推力
encompass/ɪnˈkʌmpəs/ v. 包含；包括
comply/kəmˈplaɪ/ v. 遵从；服从

Phrases & Expressions

marshaling yard　编组场
hump crest　驼峰顶端
railway operation organization
　铁路行车组织
train reception and departure operation
　接发列车工作
shunting operation　调车工作
rolling stock　车辆
station dispatching and command work
　车站调度指挥工作
section blocking　区间闭塞

train operation diagram　列车运行图
disintegration shunting　解体调车
marshaling shunting　编组调车
detaching and attaching shunting
　摘挂调车
pickup and drop shunting　取送调车
lead track shunting　牵出线调车
push-pull shunting　推送调车
push-off shunting　溜放调车
hump shunting　驼峰调车

Task 4　Passage Study 习情境案例

Task Description: Read the article, complete the following exercises, and learn about the importance of train operation & shunting organization at the station.

任务描述：读懂文章，完成练习，了解车站行车与调车组织工作的关键性。

How Station Train Operations Weave a Safe and Efficient Transportation Network

During railway transportation, all movements related to locomotives, rolling stock, and trains belong to the scope of railway operation organization. Besides the movement along the railway track, a vast majority of train operation is carried out at railway stations. Therefore, organizing train operations properly at railway stations is of great significance for achieving safe, punctual, and efficient railway transportation.

The main content of train operation organization at railway stations includes reception and departure of trains, shunting operations, and station dispatching and command work. Train reception and departure operations encompass various procedures such as handling the section blocking, preparing receiving route and departure route, switching on/off home signal and starting signal, receiving and send-off trains, indicating train reception or dispatch, and putting the section into operation and reporting the positions of trains. Every station must have the ability to continuously receive and dispatch trains, and strictly follow the train diagram for operation. The work of reception and departure of train is uniformly commanded by station duty officer.

The formation of a train cannot be done without shunting. Shunting operations mainly include disintegration shunting, marshaling shunting, detaching and attaching shunting, pickup and drop shunting, other shunting and so on. Marshaling stations have a large amount of disintegration shunting and marshaling shunting, while intermediate stations generally only perform detaching and attaching shunting, pickup and drop shunting.

The shunting work at the station is under the unified leadership of the station dispatcher. Each shunting team is under the sole command of the shunting master. The shunting work must comply with relevant regulations to ensure shunting safety and efficiency.

Task 4.1　Read the passage. Then, choose the correct answers.

1. Which of the following is most critical for ensuring safe, punctual, and efficient railway transportation?
    A. The quality of locomotives and rolling stocks used.
    B. The maintenance of railway tracks and signaling systems.
    C. The proper organization of train operations at railway stations.
    D. The timely delivery of goods and passengers by trains.

2. Who is primarily responsible for commanding the work of receiving and departure of trains at railway stations?
    A. Train drivers.
    B. Station duty officer
    C. Rolling stock engineers.
    D. Track maintenance crews.

3. Which type of shunting operation is most common in marshaling yards?
    A. Detaching and attaching shunting.
    B. Pickup and drop shunting.
    C. Lead track shunting and push-pull shunting.
    D. Disintegration shunting and marshaling shunting.

Task 4.2　Read the sentence pairs. Fill in each blank with the best word or phrase.

1. station dispatcher/shunting master
    A. The _____ oversees the shunting work at the station in a unified manner.
    B. Each shunting team receives direction solely from its respective _____ .

2. ensure/command
    A. The process of receiving and dispatching trains is consistently _____ by the station duty officer.
    B. To _____ the safety and efficiency of shunting operations, it is imperative that all shunting work must comply with the relevant regulations.

Task 5 Vocational Situation Experience 演职场情景

Task Description: Experience the situational conversation and complete the following exercises, so as to enhance English application ability related to professional positions.

任务描述：体验岗位情景会话，完成练习，提升与职业岗位相关的英语应用能力。

Task 5.1 Listen to the conversation, and fill in the blanks.

Situation description: A trainee is consulting an experienced instructor about the types and requirements of shunting operations in order to better perform shunting tasks in future positions.

Trainee: Mr. Wang, is there a 1. _____ _____ going on over there?

Instructor: Yes, the locomotive is using the lead track to shunt the vehicles to a new track.

Trainee: I see, is this a type of 2. _____ _____ _____?

Instructor: That's right. Lead track shunting is one of the most basic types of shunting operations. It generally includes two forms: push-pull shunting and push-off shunting.

Trainee: Besides lead track shunting, are there any other shunting methods?

Instructor: Of course. There is another common shunting method called 3. _____ _____, which is the main approach for disintegrating trains at 4. _____ _____ .

Trainee: How does hump shunting take place?

Instructor: Hump shunting utilizes the gravity of the cars and a certain thrust of the locomotive to allow the detached cars to roll from the 5. _____ _____ into the designated lines.

Trainee: Get it. Anyone is allowed to perform shunting operation, isn't it?

Instructor: No. The movement of the shunting locomotives must be directed by the shunting master personally. The 6. _____ _____ must hold a valid certificate to ensure shunting safety and efficiency.

Trainee: I see. Thanks for your answer, Mr. Wang.

Instructor: You're welcome. If you have any questions, feel free to ask me.

Task 5.2 Listen again and mark the statements as true(T) or false(F).

____ 1. The locomotive is using the lead track to shunt the vehicles to a new track.

____ 2. Hump shunting is one of the most basic types of shunting operations, which generally includes two forms: push-pull shunting and push-off shunting.

____ 3. The movement of the shunting locomotives must be directed by the shunting operator personally.

Task 5.3 Act out the roles with a partner.

 Task Vocational Writing Practice 练职业写作

Task Description: Please summarize the types of shunting operations and the specific operation methods in order to grasp the characteristics of various shunting operations, the importance of shunting operations as well as the necessity for safe and efficient operations.

任务描述：请总结调车作业的类型和具体操作，以便掌握各种调车作业的特点、调车作业的重要性以及安全、高效操作的必要性。

Types of Shunting

Types	Description
Disintegration shunting	Allocate the inbound train sets or car groups to the fixed tracks of the shunting yard according to the destinations of cars or other needs
Marshaling shunting	Make up train sets or car groups according to the train formation plan, train operation diagram
Detaching and attaching shunting	Add or remove cars, replace car groups for the transit trains, as well as detach or attach cars for the pick-up and set-out trains at the intermediate station
Pickup and drop shunting	Send the cars to be loaded, unloaded or repaired from the marshaling yard to the operating locations and then get back the cars to the marshaling yard

Task 7　Telling Stories of China Railway 讲中国铁路故事

Task Description: Watch the story of railway role models and complete the following exercises to develop the awareness and ability to tell stories of China Railway in English.

任务描述：观看铁路榜样故事，完成练习，培养用英语讲述中国铁路故事的意识和能力。

7.1　As a station duty officer, how does Wang Jun embody the spirit of model workers with his practical actions?

7.2　Watch the video again and search online for more information about Wang Jun, introduce his major achievements. Also, share the inspiration and motivation you gained from his spirit. Work in groups to tell the story of Wang Jun.

Task 8　Topic Test 测章节知识

Task Description：Review this topic and complete the topic test to develop self-testing skills and summarizing analysis skills.

任务描述：复习本章节内容,完成章节测试,培养自我检测和总结分析能力。

◎ **Choose the correct answers.**

1. What is the primary purpose of train marshaling?
    A. To rearrange freight cars randomly without considering their final destinations.
    B. To assign specific locomotives to individual freight cars based on their weight.
    C. To group together freight cars destined for the same direction according to their final destinations.
    D. To increase the speed of trains by reducing the number of stops along the route.

2. Who is primarily responsible for separating the carriages as they pass over the the hump crest?
    A. The engineer driving the locomotive.　　B. The coupler.
    C. The railway dispatcher.　　D. The maintenance crew.

3. In the process of railway transportation where are a vast majority of train operations carried out?
    A. At railway stations.　　B. At marshaling yards.
    C. At platforms.　　D. On the train.

4. Which of the following is NOT included in the main contents of train operation organization work at railway stations?
    A. Receiving and departure of trains.
    B. Shunting operations.
    C. Station dispatching and command work.
    D. Track maintenance and repair.

5. Which person is responsible for commanding each shunting team during shunting work at the station?
    A. The station dispatcher.　　B. The shunting master.
    C. The train driver.　　D. The track inspector.

 Module 1　Railway Transport　铁道运输　59

◎ **Mark the following translations as true(T) or false(F).**

6. During railway transportation, all movements related to locomotives, rolling stock, and trains belong to the scope of railway operation organization.

    译文:铁路运输过程中,有关机车、车辆和列车的移动,都属于铁路行车组织范围。

7. The work of reception and departure of train is uniformly commanded by station duty officer.

    译文:车站内的接发列车工作由车站调度员统一指挥。

8. The formation of a train cannot be done without shunting.

    译文:列车的形成离不开调车。

9. The shunting work must comply with relevant regulations to ensure shunting safety and efficiency.

    译文:调车工作必须遵守相关规定,保证调车安全和调车效率。

10. Every station must have the ability to continuously receive and dispatch trains, and strictly follow the train diagram for operation.

    译文:每个车站都必须具备接发列车的能力,并严格按照列车图表行车。

Task 9 Self-assessment 评学习效果

Task Description：Tick the items and self-assess learning outcomes.
任务描述：勾选选项，自我评估学习效果。

教学目标	评分项目
自主学习完善	☐Have a good habit of independent learning 有良好的自主学习习惯 ☐Be clear about learning objectives 明确学习目标 ☐Learn about learning content 了解学习内容 ☐Complete learning tasks effectively 有效完成学习任务 ☐Finish the section test consciously 自主进行知识检测
语言思维提升	Master the pronunciation, spelling, definition, and simple usage of the following vocabulary： 掌握下列词汇的发音、拼写、释义及简单应用： ☐essential ☐exclude ☐dispatch ☐allocate ☐intermediate ☐marshaling yard ☐hump crest ☐disintegration shunting ☐marshaling shunting ☐hump shunting ☐lead track shunting ☐railway operation organization ☐receiving and departure of train
	Be able to read and understand articles related to this topic and talk about them in English： 能读懂本主题相关文章并用英语简单介绍： ☐Work content of train marshaling 　列车编组的工作内容 ☐The main contents of train operation organization work at railway stations 　车站行车组织工作的主要内容 ☐Types and requirements of shunting operations 　调车作业的种类和要求
职场涉外沟通	☐Be able to understand workplace situational conversations related to this topic 　能听懂本主题相关的职场情景对话 ☐Be able to simulate workplace situational conversations related to this topic with a partner 　能与搭档一起模拟本主题相关的职场情景对话 ☐Be able to introduce the given theme in written form 　能用英语完成主题相关的书面表达
多元文化交流	☐Be able to work in groups to tell the story of China railway role models in English 　能小组合作用英语讲述本主题相关的中国铁路榜样故事

Module 2
Railway Electromechanics

铁道机电

Topic 1　Introduction to Posts—Career Planning
主题一　岗位介绍——职业规划

 **Task 1　Learning Objectives** 明学习目标

Task Description: Get to know the content and clarify learning objectives.
任务描述: 了解学习内容，明确学习目标。

知识目标：掌握与"岗位介绍"主题相关的行业英语词汇

技能目标：
1. 能读懂与本主题相关的文章
2. 能听懂与本主题相关的职场情景对话
3. 能模拟表演职场情景对话，能用英语讲述中国铁路榜样故事
4. 能用英语完成与主题相关的书面表达

素质目标：了解"新时代·铁路榜样"机车检修工黄忆的榜样故事，学习他勤学精技、匠心修车、执着追求、勇于创新的精神，在未来岗位上热爱工作，不断追求更高的目标

Introduction to Posts 岗位介绍

学行业词汇：main driver, assistant driver, mechanist of EMU trains, catenary worker, locomotive depot, vehicle depot, vehicle inspector, etc.

习情境案例：《各司其职，共筑列车安全与正点运行》
1. 司机、检车员、动车组机械师、接触网工工作岗位的职责
2. 司机、检车员、动车组机械师、接触网工工作岗位的重要性

体验职场情景：行业情景会话听说　行业情景会话展示　职业英语写作训练

讲中国铁路榜样故事

最美铁路人　黄忆
"机车医生"

Task ② Lead in 导主题内容

Task Description: Watch the video, complete the following exercises and learn about the English names for major positions.

任务描述：观看视频，完成练习，了解主要岗位名称的英文表达。

Railway transportation is like a **sophisticated** and complex **interlocking** machine. Various railway departments can be viewed as parts and components of this machine. They all have their functions and responsibilities. To ensure the efficient and orderly operation of the machine, all parts and components must keep running around the clock. This may provide a continuous driving force for railway transportation.

A **locomotive depot** is mainly in charge of the use, comprehensive preparations, and overall **overhaul** of railway locomotives. A **vehicle depot** takes **principal** responsibility for the operation, preparations, and overhaul of railway vehicles. An **EMU depot** takes charge of the operation, overhaul, and **senior overhaul** of EMU trains. Besides, a **power supply section** is mainly responsible for the traction power supply for electrified railways, power supply for railway signaling, electric power supply for railway districts and overhaul and **maintenance** of electrical equipment.

After graduation, which post will you be engaged in? Do you know about it?

People working at a locomotive depot are mostly drivers. At a vehicle depot, you may serve as a vehicle inspector. At an EMU depot, you are probably a **mechanist** of EMU trains. As for the power supply section, you are mainly expected to be a **catenary worker**.

Task 2.1 Complete the following sentences with the correct word.

1. After graduation, if you work at a _____ _____, you are mostly likely to be a driver.
2. At a vehicle depot, you may serve as a _____ _____ .
3. If you work at an EMU depot, you are probably a _____ of EMU trains.
4. As for the power supply section, you are mainly expected to be a _____ _____ .

Task ③ Vocabulary Study 学行业词汇

Task Description: Learn the industry vocabulary, complete the following exercises, and master the English expressions for major positions and their basic responsibilities.

任务描述：学习行业词汇，完成练习，掌握主要岗位及其基本职责的英文表达。

1. vehicle inspector

The **vehicle inspector refers to** personnel who inspect and test the technical status of railway vehicles in operation, and perform maintenance and **troubleshooting** on them.

2. main driver

The **main driver** refers to the railway transportation professional who drives a train and ensure the safe and on-time running of it.

3. assistant driver (apprentice driver)

The **assistant driver** is an assistant and backup force of the main driver. He needs to assist the main driver in safe driving and routine maintenance of trains.

4. mechanist of EMU trains

The **mechanist of EMU trains** are specialized technical personnel responsible for the operation maintenance, on-board service, and fault handling of EMU trains.

5. catenary worker

The **catenary worker** is a technical job engaged in the repair, maintenance and management of electrified railways. They are mainly responsible for the **debugging**, regular maintenance, repair of catenary and overhead lines to ensure the stability and safety of power **transmission**.

6. overhaul

Overhaul is a process of inspecting, maintaining and repairing equipment and machine.

Task 3.1 Match the words or phrases with the definitions.

1. _____ vehicle inspector
2. _____ main driver
3. _____ assistant driver
4. _____ mechanist of EMU trains
5. _____ catenary worker
6. _____ overhaul

A. professionals who drive a train and ensure the safe and on-time running of a train
B. a process of inspecting, maintaining and repairing equipment and machine
C. technician responsible for operation maintenance, on-board service and fault handling of EMU trains
D. technical personnel engaged in repair, maintenance and management of electrified railways
E. an assistant and backup force of the main driver
F. personnel who inspect and test the technical status of railway vehicles in operation

Word Bank

New Words

sophisticated /səˈfɪstɪkeɪtɪd/ adj. 精密的,复杂巧妙的
interlocking /ˌɪntəˈlɒkɪŋ/ adj. 联锁的
overhaul /ˌəʊvəˈhɔːl/ n. 检修
principal /ˈprɪnsəpəl/ adj. 最重要的,首要的
maintenance /ˈmeɪntənəns/ n. 维护,保养,维持
mechanist /ˈmekənɪst/ n. 机械工;机械师
troubleshoot /ˈtrʌblʃuː/ v. 解决重大问题;排除……的故障
apprentice /əˈprentɪs/ n. 学徒,徒弟
debug /ˌdiːˈbʌg/ vt. 调试;除错
transmission /trænzˈmɪʃn/ n. 传递,传播
core /kɔː/ n. 核心,要点
lubricate /ˈluːbrɪkeɪt/ v. 润滑,给……加润滑油

tedious /ˈtiːdiəs/ adj. 冗长的,单调乏味的
restore /rɪˈstɔː/ v. 恢复,修复
bodyguard /ˈbɒdigɑːd/ n. 保镖
meticulously /məˈtɪkjələsli/ adv. 细致地;一丝不苟地
diagnosis /ˌdaɪəgˈnəʊsɪs/ n. 诊断,判断
routine /ruːˈtiːn/ adj. 常规的,例行的
eliminate /ɪˈlɪmɪneɪt/ v. 排除,根除
hazard /ˈhæzəd/ n. 危险,危害;(不可避免的)风险
dedication /ˌdedɪˈkeɪʃn/ n. 奉献,尽心尽力
internship /ˈɪntɜːnʃɪp/ n. 实习生;实习期
assessment /əˈsesmənt/ n. 评估,评价
cumulatively /ˈkjuːmjələtɪvli/ adv. 累积地

Phrases & Expressions

railway transportation 铁路运输
locomotive depot 机务段
vehicle depot 车辆段
EMU depot 动车段
senior overhaul 高级修理
power supply section 供电段

vehicle inspector 检车员,车辆检修员
refer to… 指的是……
main driver 正司机
assistant driver 副司机
mechanist of EMU trains 动车组机械师

catenary worker　接触网工	qualification examination　定职考试
be skilled at...　擅长……；熟练掌握……	Intermediate vehicle inspector　中级检车员
on-board mechanist　随车机械师	senior vehicle inspector　高级检车员
ground mechanist　地勤机械师	senior worker　高级工

 Task 4　Passage Study 习情境案例

Task Description: Read the article, complete the following exercises, and learn about the responsibilities and the importance of job positions of drivers, car inspectors, EMU train mechanists, and catenary workers.

任务描述：读懂文章，完成练习，了解司机、检车员、动车组机械师、接触网工这些工作岗位的职责和重要性。

Each Fulfilling Its Responsibilities, Jointly Ensuring Train Safety and Punctual Operation

Drivers are believed to be the **core** strength of a locomotive depot. They drive a locomotive on the railway lines to provide passengers with a high-quality travel experience. In addition to excellent driving skills, they need to be capable of handling sudden failures. They follow various operating procedures strictly to ensure the safe, smooth, and on-time running of each train.

Vehicle inspectors need to give a thorough and regular examination of vehicles. They need to **be skilled at** vehicle maintenance, such as running-in, **lubricating** and cleaning. They perform an inspection of the electric appliances and electronic devices of a vehicle. Although vehicle overhaul is **tedious**, their excellent maintenance quality enables them to restore all parts and components of the vehicle to their best conditions, ensuring its safe operation.

There are two categories of EMU train mechanists. One is the **on-board mechanist**; and the other is the ground mechanist. Like the "**bodyguard**" of an EMU train, the on-board mechanist monitors its operating state all the time. The **ground mechanist** is more like a "full-time doctor". They may provide meticulous overhaul and maintenance services for EMU trains in an **EMU depot**, including fault **diagnosis** and troubleshooting, repair and replacement of parts.

A catenary worker is considered to be the guardian of the railway power supply and the "Spiderman" above the railway lines. Walking through the night and high in the sky, they conduct catenary installation, maintenance, repair, and troubleshooting. Through 24-hour monitoring and **routine** overhaul, they are capable of **eliminating** potential **hazard**s of catenary and maintaining safety in railway power supply equipment and train operation.

Although there are differences in the above posts, all staff have a high sense of responsibility and professional **dedication**, jointly safeguarding the safe and on-time operation of trains.

Task 4.1 Read the passage. Then, choose the correct answers.

1. What are the purpose of the article?
   A. To give tips on applying for railroad jobs.
   B. To list qualifications for various open positions.
   C. To describe changes to the companies hiring policies.
   D. To understand the responsibilities of the main job positions in the rail industry.
2. Which of the following requires the "Spiderman" along a railway line?
   A. Catenary worker.   B. Vehicle inspector.
   C. Driver.   D. Brakeman.
3. Who need to give a thorough and regular examination of vehicles?
   A. Porter.   B. Catenary worker.
   C. Vehicle inspector. D. Driver.

Task 4.2 Read the sentence pairs. Fill in each blank with the best word or phrase.

1. driver/vehicle inspector
   A. A _____ need to be skilled at vehicle maintenance.
   B. A _____ run a locomotive at the railway track.
2. on-board mechanist/ground mechanist
   A. The _____ monitors an EMU train's operating state all the time.
   B. The _____ provides meticulous overhaul and maintenance services for EMU trains in a EMU depot.

 ## Task 5 Vocational Situation Experience 演职场情景

Task Description: Experience the situational conversation and complete the following exercises, so as to enhance English application ability related to professional positions.
任务描述:体验岗位情景会话,完成练习,提升与职业岗位相关的英语应用能力。

Task 5.1 Listen to the conversation, and fill in the blanks.

Situation description: A trainee who is a would-be driver in the locomotive depot, is consulting the experienced instructor about the promotion requirements for becoming a driver of EMU train, so as to improve himself in terms of skills, experience, safety regulations, professional qualities and other aspects.

Trainee: Nice to meet you, Mr. Wang. I'm going to work in the locomotive depot next week. May I ask you something about the driver for EMU trains?

 Module 2 Railway Electromechanics 铁道机电   67

Instructor: Nice to meet you, too. Xiao Zhang. To become a qualified driver of EMU trains, you will go through fire and water.

Trainee: Can you tell me more about it?

Instructor: First, you may start as an 1. _____, learn from an experienced driver, and practice basic skills.

Trainee: Do I have any chance to be promoted to an assistant driver if I pass the **internship assessment**?

Instructor: Sure. When your mileage exceeds 30,000 km, you are allowed to participate in an assistant driver **qualification examination**. If you can pass this exam, you will be an 2. _____ _____.

Trainee: Can an assistant driver drive the EMU train?

Instructor: No. After you study locomotive-relating affairs and on-vehicle services continuously for at least one year, or your driving mileage reaches 60,000km **cumulatively**, you can join the Railway Locomotive Driving Qualification Test. Once you pass the test, you become a 3. _____ of EMU trains in a real sense.

Trainee: That is not as easy as it sounds. But I am willing to spare no effort and meet the 4. _____.

Instructor: Good for you! The driver of EMU trains needs not only the solid professional skills but also a strong sense of responsibility.

Trainee: Thank you. I will keep it in mind and 5. _____ to become an outstanding driver of EMU trains.

Task 5.2 Listen again and mark the statements as true(T) or false(F).

____ 1. When your mileage exceeds 30,000 km, you will be an assistant driver.

____ 2. After an assistant driver's driving mileage reaches 60,000km cumulatively and pass the Railway Locomotive Driving Qualification Test, he will become a driver of EMU trains.

____ 3. An assistant driver can drive EMU train.

Task 5.3 Act out the roles with a partner.

Task 6 Vocational Writing Practice 练职业写作

Task Description: Refer to the table, learn to describe the basic promotion conditions for the main positions matched with your major, so as to better plan your personal career path.

任务描述：参考表格内容，学会描述与专业匹配的主要岗位的基本晋升条件，以便做好个人职业发展规划。

Career Development and Promotion Requirements for Key Posts of Different Majors

Majors	Key Initial Posts	Basic Requirements for Promotion	Key Promoted Posts
Locomotive operation and maintenance	Locomotive apprentice driver	① Mileage reaches 30,000 km ② Pass the assistant driver qualification examination	Assistant driver
	Assistant driver	① Study locomotive-relating affairs and on-vehicle services continuously for at least one year, or mileage reaches 60,000km cumulatively for assistant drivers ② Pass theory and actual practice examinations for drivers	Locomotive driver or driver of EMU trains
Railway vehicle techniques	**Intermediate vehicle inspector**	Pass exam or appraisal, and obtain a Certificate of Senior Vehicle Inspector	**Senior vehicle inspector**
EMU train overhaul techniques	Ground mechanist of EMU trains	① Improve relevant skills ② Pass assessment and obtain the Job Qualification Certificate for On-vehicle Mechanists of EMU Trains	On-board mechanist of EMU trains
Railway power supply techniques	Catenary worker	① Obtain the Job Qualification Certificate for Catenary Workers ② 3–5 years of working experience ③ Pass skill examinations and obtain the Job Qualification Certificate for Senior Workers.	**Senior worker**

Task 7　Telling Stories of China Railway 讲中国铁路故事

Task Description: Watch the story of railway role models and complete the following exercises to develop the awareness and ability to tell stories of China Railway in English.

任务描述：观看铁路榜样故事，完成练习，培养用英语讲述中国铁路故事的意识和能力。

7.1　What are Huang Yi's contributions in the field of locomotive brake system and wiper maintenance?

_____
_____
_____
_____
_____
_____
_____
_____

7.2　Watch the video again and search online for more information about Huang Yi, introduce his growth experience and get to know how he became a "Locomotive Doctor" in locomotive maintenance depot. Also, share the inspiration and motivation you gained from his spirit. Work in small groups to tell the story of Huang Yi.

_____
_____
_____
_____
_____
_____
_____
_____

Task 8 Topic Test 测章节知识

Task Description: Review this topic and complete the topic test to develop self-testing skills and summarizing analysis skills.

任务描述：复习本章节内容，完成章节测试，培养自我检测和总结分析的能力。

◎ **Choose the correct answers.**

1. What's position responsible for operating trains on railway lines?
    A. Vehicle inspector.   B. Catenary worker.
    C. Driver.   D. Mechanist of EMU trains.

2. Who assists the main driver in safe driving and routine maintenance of trains?
    A. Porter.   B. Assistant driver.   C. Conductor.   D. Brakeman.

3. What is involved in the overhaul?
    A. To inspect and repair the equipment and machines.
    B. To provide braking power.
    C. To ensure passenger comfort.
    D. To support the weight of the train.

4. What are the job responsibilities of the on-board mechanist?
    A. To increase the speed of the train.
    B. To provide comfort to passengers.
    C. To achieve coupling, hauling, and buffering of vehicles.
    D. To monitors EMU trains operating state all the time.

5. What qualities should catenary worker possess?
    A. Familiarity with basic catenary installation, maintenance and a rigorous attitude towards their work.
    B. Familiarity with basic and excellent driving skills.
    C. Familiarity with strong marketing abilities.
    D. Familiarity with vehicle advanced engineering degrees.

◎ **Mark the following translations as true(T) or false(F).**

6. Drivers run a locomotive at the railway track and provide passengers with a good ride experience.
    译文：司机驾驶机车在铁路线上运行，为乘客提供优质的乘车体验。

7. Vehicle inspectors need to give a thorough and regular examination of vehicles.
    译文：检车员定期对车辆进行深度"体检"。

8. They need to be skilled at vehicle maintenance, such as running-in, lubricating and cleaning.

译文：他们擅长对车辆进行运行、润滑、清洁等保养工作。

9. Like the "bodyguard" of an EMU train, on-board mechanist monitors its operating state all the time.

译文：地勤机械师如同动车组的"贴身保镖"，时刻监控着列车的运行状态。

10. Walking through the night and high in the sky, they conduct catenary installation, maintenance, repair, and troubleshooting.

译文：他们夜以继日对接触网进行安装、维护、检修与故障排除。

Task 9 Self-assessment 评学习效果

Task Description: Tick the items and self-assess learning outcomes.
任务描述：勾选选项，自我评估学习效果。

教学目标	评分项目
自主学习完善	☐Have a good habit of independent learning 有良好的自主学习习惯 ☐Be clear about learning objectives 明确学习目标 ☐Know about learning content 了解主题内容 ☐Complete learning tasks effectively 有效完成学习任务 ☐Finish the section test consciously 自主进行知识检测
语言思维提升	Master the pronunciation, spelling, definition, and simple usage of the following vocabulary: 掌握下列词汇的发音、拼写、释义及简单应用： ☐main driver ☐assistant driver ☐mechanic of EMU trains ☐catenary worker ☐locomotive depot ☐vehicle depot ☐vehicle inspector ☐apprentice ☐overhaul ☐lubricating ☐tedious ☐vehicle ☐troubleshooting
	Be Able to read and understand articles related to this topic and talk about them in English: 能读懂本主题相关文章并用英语简单介绍： ☐The job responsibilities of drivers, car inspectors, EMU train mechanists and catenary workers 　司机、检车员、动车组机械师、接触网工的工作职责 ☐The importance of job positions of drivers, car inspectors, EMU train mechanists and catenary workers 　司机、检车员、动车组机械师、接触网工工作岗位的重要性
职场涉外沟通	☐Be Able to understand workplace situational conversations related to this topic 　能听懂本主题相关的职场情景对话 ☐Be Able to simulate workplace situational conversations related to this topic with a partner 　能与搭档一起模拟本主题相关的职场情景对话 ☐Be able to introduce the given theme in written form 　能用英语完成主题相关的书面表达
多元文化交流	☐Be Able to work in groups to tell the story of railway role models 　能小组合作用英语讲述本主题相关的铁路榜样故事

Topic 2　Railway Vehicles—Be Steady and Safe
主题二　铁路车辆——平稳安全

Task ❶　Learning Objectives 明学习目标

Task Description：Get to know the content and clarify learning objectives.
任务描述：了解学习内容，明确学习目标。

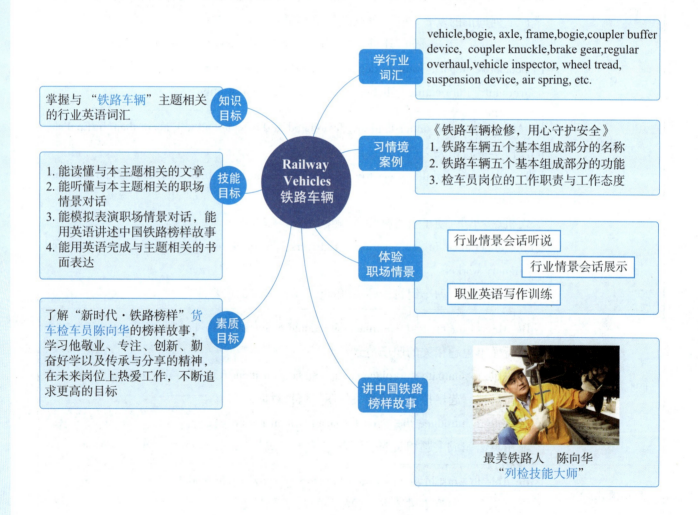

 **Task 2　Lead in 导主题内容**

Task Description: Watch the video, complete the following exercises and learn about the English names for the main components of a high-speed railway bogie.

任务描述：观看视频，完成练习，了解高铁转向架主要部件的英文表达。

High-speed trains run very fast, but their carriage can still remain steady, and even a **vertically** placed coin can **stand still**. What is the secret to the steady operation of high-speed trains?

In addition to smooth high-**precision** rails, steady operation of high-speed trains cannot be realized without bogies, which is a **critical component** of **vehicle**s. One of the key components that enable the coins to stand still is the **air spring** on the **bogie**. It is a suspension device **mount**ed between the car body and the bogie.

Bogies, like the legs of human beings, are considered to be the **running gear** of the **rolling stock**. A bogie is composed of wheels, **axle**s, **frame**s, and **suspension device**s. As the car body is mounted on the bogie, the bogie needs to be capable of bearing the weight of the car body. With the help of bogies, trains can move on **curve**d tracks smoothly and steadily. Besides, spring devices and **shock absorbers** installed on the bogie have the function of shock **absorption**. They can absorb and reduce **vibration**s from tracks, thus ensuring the steady running of rolling stock and the comfort and safety of passengers.

Task 2.1　Write down the English names of a high-speed railway's bogie components in the picture.

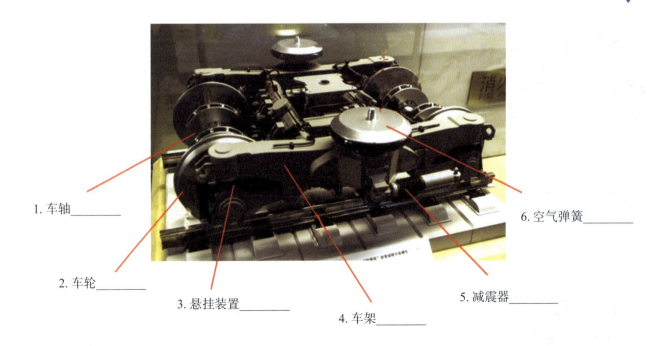

1. 车轴_____
2. 车轮_____
3. 悬挂装置_____
4. 车架_____
5. 减震器_____
6. 空气弹簧_____

Module 2　Railway Electromechanics　铁道机电　75

Task 3 Vocabulary Study 学行业词汇

Task Description: Learn the industry vocabulary, complete the following exercises, and master the English names and functions of main components of railway vehicles.

任务描述：学习行业词汇，完成练习，掌握铁路车辆主要部件名称及其功能的英文表达。

1. bogie

The **bogie**, also known as the running gear, is one of the key components of vehicles. As a frame, it supports the vehicle body. Through this frame, the wheelset can be connected to the carriage.

2. air spring

The **air spring** is a suspension device for shock absorption on railway vehicles. It is mounted between the vehicle body and the bogie. Each bogie is equipped with two air springs.

3. axle

The **axle** is a metal bar. It connects two wheels and thus forms a wheelset.

4. suspension device

The **suspension device** is a spring that bears the weight of bogie frames.

5. shock absorber

The **shock absorber** is a device used to reduce vibration and impact generated in the process of car running.

🎧 6. underframe

The **underframe** is the foundation of the car body. It is connected with wallboards and the roof into a whole to bear loads and impact forces.

🎧 7. coupler buffer device

The **coupler buffer device** is composed of a coupler, a buffer, and a coupler knuckle. It can be used to achieve coupling, hauling, and buffering of vehicles.

🎧 8. coupler

The **coupler** is a connecting device. It can be used to connect the locomotive with the vehicle, or realize the connection between vehicles.

🎧 9. buffer

The **buffer** is a device, which can be used to cushion the impact forces of a train, absorb the impact energy, and transfer the load.

coupler knuckle →

🎧 10. coupler knuckle

The **coupler knuckle** is the joint of coupler. Through a coupler knuckle, coupling and uncoupling of cars can be realized.

🎧 11. brake gear

The **brake gear** is a device. It can be used to implement braking, thus slowing down or stopping the vehicle rapidly.

🎧 12. regular overhaul

The **regular overhaul** means that all or partial components of the car need to be checked and repaired to some extent when the car is operated for a certain period of time or **mileage**.

🎧 13. routine maintenance

The **routine maintenance**, also known as daily repair, can timely find out and handle all car

Module 2　Railway Electromechanics　铁道机电　77

faults to ensure vehicles in service are in good technical condition. It plays a role of ensuring traffic safety.

🎧 **14. brake pipe**

The **brake pipe** is located under the underframe. It is a steel pipe running through the whole vehicle.

🎧 **15. wheel tread**

The **wheel tread**, also known as wheel rail **interface**, refers to the contact part that a wheel touches the rail surface.

Task 3.1 Match the words or phrases with the definitions.

1. _____ coupler buffer device   5. _____ coupler knuckle
2. _____ air spring   6. _____ bogie
3. _____ brake pipe   7. _____ axle
4. _____ brake gear   8. _____ suspension device

A. a metal bar connecting two wheels and thus forms a wheelset
B. being used to implement braking, thus slowing down or rapidly stopping the vehicle
C. the joint of coupler
D. being composed of a coupler, a buffer, and a coupler knuckle
E. a steel tubing running through the whole vehicle
F. being mounted between the vehicle body and the bogie for shock absorption
G. a spring that bears the weight of bogie frames
H. supporting the vehicle body and the wheelset can be connected to the carriage through it

Word Bank

⊙ New Words

vehicle/ˈviːəkl/ n. 车辆,机动车
vertically/ˈvɜːtɪkli/ adv. 垂直地
precision/prɪˈsɪʒn/ n. 精确,准确
bogie/ˈbəʊgi/ n. 转向架
critical/ˈkrɪtɪkl/ adj. 极其重要的, 关键的

component/kəmˈpəʊnənt/ n. 组成部分, 部件
mount/maʊnt/ v. 安装
axle/ˈæksl/ n. 车轴
frame/freɪm/ n. 车架,构架
curve/kɜːv/ adj. 弯曲的 n. 曲线

absorption/əbˈzɔːpʃn/n. 吸收;吸纳
vibration/vaɪˈbreɪʃn/n. 振动
mileage/ˈmaɪlɪdʒ/n. 行驶里程
interface/ˈɪntəfeɪs/n. 边缘区域,接合部位
skeleton/ˈskelɪtn/n. 框架,骨架
underframe/ˈʌndəfreɪm/n. 底架,车底架
cargo/ˈkɑːɡəʊ/n. 货物
joint/dʒɔɪnt/n. 关节,接合处
coupler/ˈkʌplə/n. 车钩
buffer/ˈbʌfə)/n. 缓冲器
knuckle/ˈnʌkl/n. 关节;钩舌
haul/hɔːl/v. 牵引,拉

implement/ˈɪmplɪment/v. 执行,贯彻
wear/əˈbreɪʒn/n. 磨损;磨耗
crack/kræk/n. 裂缝,裂纹;v. 破裂
deformation/ˌdiːfɔːˈmeɪʃn/n. 变形
primarily/praɪˈmerəli/adv. 首要地
constructure/kənˈstrʌktʃə/n. 结构,构造
maintain/meɪnˈteɪn/v. 保持,维持;维修
rigorous/ˈrɪɡərəs/adj. 严谨的,一丝不苟的
accordingly/əˈkɔːdɪŋli/adv. 相应地,因此
defect/ˈdiːfekt/n. 缺点,缺陷

☉ Phrases & Expressions

stand still　　静止,站着不动
air spring　　空气弹簧
running gear　　走行部
rolling stock　　车辆
suspension device　　悬挂装置
spring device　　弹簧装置
shock absorber　　减震器
consists of…　　包含,由……组成
in-vehicle facilities　　车内设备
coupler buffer device　　车钩缓冲装置
brake gear　　制动系统

be composed of…　　由……组成
side wall　　侧墙
end wall　　端墙
coupler knuckle　　车钩
regular overhaul　　定期检修
routine maintenance　　日常维修
due to…　　由于,因为……
workshop wagon　　车辆修理厂
vehicle depot　　车辆段
wheel tread　　车轮踏面

 Task **Passage Study** 习情境案例

Task Description: Read the article, complete the following exercises, and learn about the basic structure and functions of railway vehicles, as well as the job responsibilities and work attitude of vehicle inspectors.

任务描述:读懂文章,完成练习,了解铁路车辆的基本构造及其功能和检车员岗位的工作职责与工作态度。

Railway Vehicle Inspection, Carefully Guarding Safety

There are many kinds of railway vehicles, but their structures are basically the same. Generally, a railway vehicle **consist**s **of** five basic parts, that is the body, **in-vehicle facilities**, the bogie, the **coupler buffer device**, and the **brake gear**.

A vehicle body is the basic **skeleton** of a train. It **is** generally **composed of** the **underframe**, the **side wall**, the **end wall**, the floor, and the roof. It is the component in which passengers can sit or **cargo** can be loaded.

In-vehicle facilities are devices installed to meet the needs of passenger's comfort, convenient loading or unloading of goods and safe transportation.

A bogie serves as the "feet" of a train. A carriage is equipped with two bogies. The bogie supports the car body and can be used to realize the running of the train and ensure that the train passes curved tracks smoothly.

A coupler buffer device seems like the "**joint**" of a train. It is composed of a **coupler**, a **buffer**, and a **coupler knuckle** and can be used for coupling, **haul**ing, and buffering of vehicles.

As the "brake system" of a train, a brake gear is a device that can be used to **implement** braking, thus slowing down or stopping the vehicle rapidly.

Regular overhaul and **routine maintenance** of railway vehicles are necessary **due to wear**, **crack**ing and **deformation**s during operation. Moreover, the regular overhaul of a vehicle is **primarily** completed in a **workshop wagon** and a **vehicle depot**.

As vehicle inspectors, they need to be familiar with the basic vehicle **constructure**. They shall **maintain** a serious and **rigorous** attitude towards their work, check all parts and components of the vehicle meticulously, find out specific faults rapidly and **accurately** and take maintenance measures accordingly. In this way, all parts and components of the vehicle are ensured to be in the best state, which prevents accidents caused by faults.

Task 4.1　Read the passage. Then, choose the correct answers.

1. What are the five basic parts that generally constitute a railway vehicle?
    A. Engine, wheels, body, seats, and doors.
    B. Body, in-vehicle facilities, bogie, coupler buffer device, and brake gear.
    C. Car body, bogie, coupler, and brake system.
    D. Frame, roof, windows, doors, and bogies.

2. What is the primary function of a bogie in a railway vehicle?
    A. To provide comfort to passengers.
    B. To support the car body and ensure smooth running on curved tracks.
    C. To couple and uncouple railway vehicles.
    D. To implement braking and stopping of the train.

3. Why is regular overhaul and routine maintenance necessary for railway vehicles?
    A. To enhance the aesthetic appeal of the vehicles.
    B. To prevent wear and tear, cracking, and deformations during operation.
    C. To increase the speed and efficiency of the trains.
    D. To change the color and design of the vehicles regularly.

Task 4.2 Read the sentence pairs. Fill in each blank with the best word or phrase.

1. coupler buffer device/bogie
   A. A _____ serves as the "feet" of a train.
   B. A _____ seems like the "joint" of a train.
2. in-vehicle facilities/a brake gear
   A. _____ is a device that can be used to implement braking, thus slowing down or rapidly stopping the vehicle.
   B. _____ are devices mounted to make passengers comfortable during their trips, loading or unloading of goods convenient.

Task 5 Vocational Situation Experience 演职场情景

Task Description: Experience the situational conversation and complete the following exercises, so as to enhance English application ability related to professional positions.

任务描述：体验岗位情景会话，完成练习，提升与职业岗位相关的英语应用能力。

Task 5.1 Listen to the conversation, and fill in the blanks.

Situation description: A trainee is consulting the experienced instructor about the process and precautions for freight car inspection, ensuring that all parts are fixed before running the train again, in order to guarantee traffic safety.

Instructor: How is the 1. _____ _____ for this freight car?

Trainee: I have examined the brake gear and found something wrong. But I can't 2. _____ _____ why. Perhaps, there's something wrong with the brake pipe.

Instructor: I have inspected the 3. _____ _____. It is secure and nothing goes wrong.

Trainee: Then I wonder where the problem is. I need to check again more carefully.

Instructor: Is the bogie going well?

Trainee: The axle, the frame, and the suspension gear all 4. _____ normally, except for the wheels.

Instructor: What's wrong with the wheels?

Module 2 RAILWAY Electromechanics 铁道机电

Trainee: Some severe 5. _____ are found on the **wheel tread**.

Instructor: Get it. I will arrange for a repairman to fix it. We need to put it right before running again.

Task 5.2 Listen again and mark the statements as true(T) or false(F).

____ 1. The trainee found something wrong with the brake gear and the brake pipe.

____ 2. The trainee mentioned that the axle, the frame, and the suspension gear of the bogie were functioning normally.

____ 3. The instructor decided to arrange for a repairman to fix the wheel tread immediately.

Task 5.3 Act out the roles with a partner.

 Task **Vocational Writing Practice** 练职业写作

Task Description: Refer to the table, learn to describe the five basic parts of railway vehicles and get familiar with their structural and functional characteristics in order to better perform inspection tasks and ensure the safe operation of railway vehicles in your future position.

任务描述:参考表格内容,描述铁路车辆的五个基本组成部分,熟悉这些部分的结构和功能特点,以便在未来岗位上更好地执行检车任务,确保铁路车辆的安全运行。

Five Basic Parts and Functions of the Railway Vehicle

Items	Description	Functions
Vehicle body	Composed of the underframe, the sidewall, the end wall, the floor, the roof and so on	① To provide the space where passengers can sit ② To provide the space where goods are loaded
In-vehicle facilities	① Water supply devices ② Air conditioning and heating devices ③ Sitting and sleeping equipment	① To make passengers comfortable during their trips ② To make loading or unloading of goods convenient ③ To make transportation safe
Bogie	① Located at the lower part of a car ② Two bogies for one carriage	① To support the car body ② To act as running gear ③ To ensure the train passes the curved tracks smoothly

Items	Description	Functions
Coupler buffer device	Composed of a coupler, a buffer, and a coupler knuckle and so on	① To couple vehicles ② To haul vehicles ③ To buffer vehicles
Brake gear	Be used to implement braking	① To slow down ② To stop a vehicle rapidly

  Task 7　Telling Stories of China Railway 讲中国铁路故事

Task Description: Watch the story of railway role models and complete the following exercises to develop the awareness and ability to tell stories of China Railway in English.

任务描述：观看铁路榜样故事，完成练习，培养用英语讲述中国铁路故事的意识和能力。

7.1　How can a vehicle inspector conduct precise and error-free inspections of hundreds of checkpoints within five minutes of technical inspection time?

7.2　Watch the video again and search online for more information about Chen Xianghua, introduce his major achievements and get to know how he became a "skilled and benevolent doctor" in vehicle maintenance. Also, share the inspiration and motivation you gained from his spirit. Work in small groups to tell the story of Chen Xianghua.

Module 2　Railway Electromechanics　铁道机电　83

Task 8 Topic Test 测章节知识

Task Description: Review this topic and complete the topic test to develop self-testing skills and summarizing analysis skills.

任务描述：复习本章节内容，完成章节测试，培养自我检测和总结分析能力。

◎ **Choose the correct answers.**

1. What is the main function of the vehicle body in a train?
   A. To provide comfort to passengers.
   B. To support the weight of the train.
   C. To serve as the basic skeleton where passengers sit or cargo is loaded.
   D. To ensure smooth movement on curved tracks.

2. For which purpose are the in-vehicle facilities primarily installed?
   A. To enhance the appearance of the train.
   B. To make passengers comfortable and ensure safety during transportation.
   C. To reduce the weight of the train.
   D. To increase the speed of the train.

3. How many bogies are typically equipped on a carriage?
   A. One. B. Two. C. Three. D. Four.

4. What is the function of a coupler buffer device in a train?
   A. To provide braking power.
   B. To support the weight of the train.
   C. To achieve coupling, hauling, and buffering of vehicles.
   D. To ensure passenger comfort.

5. What qualities should vehicle inspectors possess?
   A. Familiarity with basic vehicle constructure and a rigorous attitude towards their work.
   B. Familiarity with basic vehicle constructure and excellent driving skills.
   C. Familiarity with basic vehicle constructure and strong marketing abilities.
   D. Familiarity with basic vehicle constructure and advanced engineering degrees.

◎ **Mark the following translations as true (T) or false (F).**

6. The brake gear is the brake system of a train.
   译文：制动装置是列车的刹车系统。

7. A vehicle body is the basic skeleton of a train, consisting of the underframe, side walls, end walls, floor, and roof.
   译文：车体是列车的基本骨架，由车架、侧墙、端墙、地板和车顶等部分组成。

8. Regular overhaul and routine maintenance of railway vehicles are necessary due to wear, cracking, and deformations during operation.

   译文：由于铁路车辆在运行过程中会发生磨损、裂纹和变形等，因此需要进行定期检修和日常维护。

9. The regular overhaul of a vehicle is primarily completed in a workshop wagon and a vehicle depot.

   译文：车辆定期检修场所主要是维修车间和车辆段。

10. An air spring is a suspension device for shock absorption mounted between the car body and the bogie.

    译文：空气弹簧是一种减震的悬挂装置，安装在车体与转向架之间。

Task 9 Self-assessment 评学习效果

Task Description: Tick the items and self-assess learning outcomes.
任务描述：勾选选项，自我评估学习效果。

教学目标	评分项目
自主学习完善	☐Have a good habit of independent learning 有良好的自主学习习惯 ☐Be clear about learning objectives 明确学习目标 ☐Know about learning content 了解学习内容 ☐Complete learning tasks effectively 有效完成学习任务 ☐Finish the section test consciously 自主进行知识检测
语言思维提升	Master the pronunciation, spelling, definition, and simple usage of the following vocabulary： 掌握下列词汇的发音、拼写、释义及简单应用： ☐vehicle ☐bogie ☐axle ☐frame ☐bogie ☐coupler ☐coupler buffer device ☐coupler knuckle ☐brake gear ☐regular overhaul ☐routine maintenance ☐vehicle inspector ☐shock absorber ☐wheel tread ☐suspension device ☐air spring
	Be Able to read and understand articles related to this topic and talk about them in English： 能读懂本主题相关文章并用英语简单介绍： ☐Names of five basic parts of a railway vehicle 　铁路车辆五个基本组成部分的名称 ☐Functions of five basic parts of a railway vehicle 　铁路车辆五个基本组成部分的功能 ☐The job responsibilities and work attitude of vehicle inspectors 　检车员岗位的工作职责与工作态度
职场涉外沟通	☐Be Able to understand workplace situational conversations related to this topic 　能听懂本主题相关的职场情景对话 ☐Be Able to simulate workplace situational conversations related to this topic with a partner 　能与搭档一起模拟本主题相关的职场情景对话 ☐Be able to introduce the given theme in written form 　能用英语完成主题相关的书面表达
多元文化交流	☐Be Able to work in groups to tell the story of railway role models 　能小组合作用英语讲述本主题相关的铁路榜样故事

Topic 3　Railway Locomotives—Be the Main Player
主题三　铁路机车——使命担当

Task ❶　Learning Objectives 明学习目标

Task Description: Get to know the content and clarify learning objectives.
任务描述：了解学习内容，明确学习目标。

知识目标
掌握与"铁路机车"主题相关的行业英语词汇

学行业词汇
locomotive, brake valve, console, traction motor, pointing and calling, key lever, reversing lever, steam locomotive, diesel locomotive, electric locomotive, etc.

技能目标
1. 能读懂与本主题相关的文章
2. 能听懂与本主题相关的职场情景对话
3. 能模拟表演职场情景对话，能用英语讲述中国铁路榜样故事
4. 能用英语完成与主题相关的书面表达

习情境案例
《机车：引领列车安全前行》
1. 铁路机车的三种类型及特点
2. 开火车前的五个主要步骤
3. 机车乘务员岗位的工作职责与工作态度

体验职场情景
行业情景会话听说
行业情景会话展示
职业英语写作训练

素质目标
了解"最美铁路人"动车组司机杨勇的榜样故事，学习他严于律己、忠诚担当、无私奉献的精神，在未来岗位上热爱工作，不断追求更高的目标

讲中国铁路榜样故事

最美铁路人　杨勇
"英雄司机"

Module 2　Railway Electromechanics　铁道机电

Task 2　Lead in 导主题内容

Task Description: Watch the video, complete the following exercises and learn about the English names for the main components on the driver's console in cab.

任务描述：观看视频，完成练习，了解司机室的驾驶操纵台主要部件的英文表达。

Is the **acceleration** and **deceleration** of trains also achieved by **stepping on** the **accelerator** and **brake pedals** like cars?

Actually, the acceleration and deceleration of trains is primarily controlled by the **speed control handle** on the driver's **console** in **cab**, just like **accelerator** pedal. Through this handle, a driver can control the train to accelerate, decelerate or **maintain** a **constant** speed.

The train's braking is controlled by the **driver's brake valve** on driver's console, like the braking pedal. The driver can **manually** push and pull it to stop the train.

The pedals that a train driver steps on are not the accelerators or brakes of the train. The rightmost pedal is called the **air whistle** pedal, just like a **horn**. When the train **encounters bends**, enters or exits stations, the driver steps on the air whistle pedal to sound as a warning. The middle pedal is a **safety alert device**, also known as an **anti-fatigue driving device**. When the train is running, the driver needs to step on it every 30 seconds. If the controls are not operated for a long time, an alarm will sound.

Task 2.1　Write down the English names of main components on the driver's console in the picture.

1. _____ 2. _____

3. _____ 4. _____

5. _____ 6. _____

7. _____ 8. _____

9. _____ 10. _____

Task 3　Vocabulary Study 学行业词汇

Task Description: Learn the industry vocabulary, complete the following exercises, and master the English expressions of locomotives.

任务描述：学习行业词汇，完成练习，掌握铁路机车的相关英文表达。

🎧 1. traction motor

The **traction motor** is the key component of the locomotive. It is connected to the wheelset and turns electric energy into mechanical energy in a traction state to make the locomotive run.

🎧 2. pointing-and-calling

At the earliest, the **pointing-and-calling** is derived from "pointing and confirming", a safety procedure specially used in the field of railway. In detail, it refers to pointing the finger at an object while confirming it orally, utilizing both their hands and mind together.

🎧 3. automatic brake valve

The **automatic brake valve**, commonly known as the main brake, is used to control the braking and relieving of the whole train.

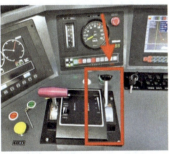

🎧 4. independent brake valve

The **independent brake valve**, commonly known as the minor brake, is used along with the automatic brake valve to control the braking and relieving of a locomotive independently.

🎧 5. key lever

As a part of the driver's controller, the **key lever** is used to change the running speed of the train by adjusting its position.

6. reversing lever

As a part of the driver's controller, the **reversing lever** is used to change the operating conditions of a locomotive, such as moving forward or backward.

7. main circuit breaker

The **main circuit breaker** is used to turn on or off the main switch of power supplies to an electric locomotive or electric multiple unit.

8. calling response

The **calling response** is a standardized mode of calling and responding, among staff on a train during railway transportation.

9. relieving

The **relieving** is the process of releasing or reducing the braking effect on a train that has already been applied with brakes.

Task 3.1 Match the words or phrases with the definitions.

1. _____ key lever
2. _____ reversing lever
3. _____ traction motor
4. _____ main circuit breaker
5. _____ automatic brake valve
6. _____ independent brake valve
7. _____ pointing-and-calling
8. _____ calling response

A. being used to turn on or off the main switch of power supplies to an electric locomotive
B. being used to control braking and relieving of the whole train
C. being used to change the running speed of the train with the change of position
D. pointing the finger at an object and confirming the object orally
E. being used to independently control braking and relieving of a locomotive
F. being used to control a locomotive to move forward or backward
G. a standardized calling and responding mode in railway transportation
H. turning electric energy into mechanical energy in a traction state

Word Bank

◉ New Words

locomotive /ˌləʊkəˈməʊtɪv/ n. 机车,火车头
acceleration /əkˌseləˈreɪʃn/ n. 加速,加快
deceleration /ˌdiːseləˈreɪʃn/ n. 减速
pedal /ˈpedl/ n. 踏板
handle /ˈhændl/ n. 把手,手柄; v. 处理
console /kənˈsəʊl/ n. 控制台,操纵台
cab /kæb/ n. 驾驶室
accelerator /əkˈseləreɪtə/ n. 油门;催化剂
maintain /meɪnˈteɪn/ v. 保持,维持
constant /ˈkɒnstənt/ adj. 恒定的,不变的;持续不断的
valve /vælv/ n. 阀,阀门
manually /ˈmænjuəli/ adv. 手动地
horn /hɔːn/ n. 喇叭;角
encounter /ɪnˈkaʊntə/ v. 遭遇,遇到

bend /bend/ n. 拐弯,弯道
traction /ˈtrækʃn/ n. 牵引,拖,拉
lever /ˈliːvə/ n. 操纵杆,控制杆
circuit /ˈsɜːkɪt/ n. 电路,回路
relieve /rɪˈliːv/ v. 缓解;减轻
diesel /ˈdiːzl/ n. 柴油;内燃机
electric /ɪˈlektrɪk/ adj. 电的,用电的,电动的
combustion /kəmˈbʌstʃən/ n. 燃烧
eliminate /ɪˈlɪmɪneɪt/ v. 淘汰,消除
gradeability /ˌɡreɪdəˈbɪləti/ n. 爬坡能力
investment /ɪnˈvestmənt/ n. 投资,投入
infrastructure /ˈɪnfrəstrʌktʃə/ n. 基础建设,基础设施
pantograph /ˈpæntəɡrɑːf/ n. 受电弓
sidetrack /ˈsaɪdtræk/ n. 侧线,侧道

◉ Phrases & Expressions

brake pedal　制动踏板
step on　踩上,踏上
speed control handle　调速手柄
accelerator pedal　油门踏板,加速踏板
driver's brake valve　司机制动阀
air whistle　风笛
safety alert device　安全警惕装置
anti-fatigue driving device　防疲劳驾驶装置
signal indicator　信号机
traction motor　牵引电动机
pointing-and-calling　手指口呼
automatic brake valve　自动制动阀
independent brake valve　单独制动阀
key lever　主控手柄
reversing lever　换向手柄

main circuit breaker　主断路器
calling response　呼唤应答
transport capacity　运输能力
steam locomotives　蒸汽机车
diesel locomotive　内燃机车
electric locomotive　电力机车
be driven by　由……驱动
be equipped with　配备有……
motive power　动力
power supply system　供电系统
thermal efficiency　热效率
locomotive inspection　机车检查
parameter setting　参数设定
departure confirmation　发车确认
assistant driver　副司机
a high sense of responsibility

高度的责任感
be familiar with 熟悉
driving simulation system
模拟驾驶系统

stopping command 停车指令
arrival signal indicator 进站信号机
double yellow lights 双黄灯

 Task ❹ Passage Study 习情境案例

Task Description:Read the article, complete the following exercises, and learn about the basic types and features of railway locomotives, as well as the job responsibilities and work attitude of locomotive drivers.
任务描述:读懂文章,完成练习,了解铁路机车的基本类型及特点和机车乘务员岗位的工作职责与工作态度。

Locomotive:Leading the train safely forward

A train cannot run very fast without its powerful locomotive. Locomotives are the power source for the trains. With no **transport capacity** itself, the locomotive pulls cars along the track to transport passengers or goods.

Based on different power sources, there are **steam locomotives, diesel locomotives**, and **electric locomotives**. Among them, a steam locomotive burns coal and **is driven by** steam; a diesel locomotive burns diesel and **is equipped with** an internal **combustion** engine that provides **motive power**; and an electric locomotive is driven by its **traction motor**. The power of the electric locomotive is supplied by an external **power supply system**.

The steam locomotive has been **eliminated** because of its extremely low **thermal efficiency**. Now, we can see some steam locomotives exhibited in railway museums.

The diesel locomotive has certain shortcomings, including heavy pollution and poor **gradeability**. However, it is hardly affected by weather and can smoothly run even in extreme weather conditions of rain and snow.

The electric locomotive needs a high **investment** in **infrastructure** and strict maintenance requirements, and tends to be easily affected by terrible weather. But, it has certain advantages, such as no air pollutants, less noise and higher speeds. Therefore, the working conditions of drivers and the comfort levels of passengers are all improved.

Locomotive drivers are technicians who control or drive a locomotive. They are commonly known as train drivers. To drive a train smoothly and steadily, a train driver needs to fulfill standardized procedures accurately, including departure preparations, receiving, **locomotive inspection**, **parameter setting**, door closing, and **departure confirmation**. In the process of driving, the main driver and **assistant driver** in the locomotive supervise and remind each other by repeating "pointing-and-calling" actions hundreds of times. With precise driving skills and **a high sense of responsibility**, they carry forward the spirit of the locomotive and lead the train to its destination safely and punctually.

Task 4.1 Read the passage. Then, choose the correct answers.

1. What are the three basic types of locomotives according to the passage?
   A. Steam locomotives, electric locomotives, and maglev locomotives.
   B. Steam locomotives, diesel locomotives, and electric locomotives.
   C. Diesel locomotives, high-speed trains, and electric locomotives.
   D. Hybrid locomotives, autonomous locomotives and specialty locomotives.

2. What are the advantages of electric locomotives?
   A. With heavy pollution and poor grade ability.
   B. With extremely low thermal efficiency and been eliminated.
   C. Producing no air pollutants, low noise and high speed.
   D. Being able to smoothly run even in extreme conditions of rain and snow.

3. What does a train driver need to do in order to drive a train smoothly and steadily?
   A. To fulfill standardized procedures accurately.
   B. To only focus on the scenic views along the route.
   C. To constantly check social media updates and respond to messages.
   D. To talk on the phone with the train dispatcher for the entire journey.

Task 4.2 Read the sentence pairs. Fill in each blank with the best word or phrase.

1. diesel locomotive/steam locomotive
   A. A _____ burns coal and is driven by steam.
   B. A _____ burns diesel and is equipped with an internal combustion engine.

2. train drivers/"pointing-and-calling"
   A. Both main and assistant drivers in the locomotive supervise and remind each other by repeating hundreds of _____ actions.
   B. Locomotive drivers are technicians who control or drive a locomotive. They are commonly known as _____ .

  Task 5 Vocational Situation Experience 演职场情景

Task Description: Experience the situational conversation and complete the following exercises, so as to enhance English application ability related to professional positions.
任务描述：体验岗位情景会话，完成练习，提升与职业岗位相关的英语应用能力。

Task 5.1 Listen to the conversation, and fill in the blanks.

Situation description: A trainee is consulting an experienced instructor about the process and precautions of a driving simulation system of electric locomotive, to get

familiar with the operational procedures of driving a locomotive, and guarantee traffic safety.

Trainee: Mr. Wang, I am not very familiar with this **driving simulation system**. Would you like to help me with it?

Instructor: My pleasure. Before operation, you need to be familiar with how to start and stop the train.

Trainee: OK. Before starting the train, I need to lift the **pantograph** first, close the main circuit breaker, then relieve the automatic and the independent 1. _____ _____, move the reversing lever one gear position forward, and finally slowly push the 2. _____ _____. The train will thus move forward. Is that right?

Instructor: Yes. How can we learn about the current speed and speed limits during train operation?

Trainee: From the LKJ 3. _____.

Instructor: You're right. If you receive a **stopping command**, how to do the operation properly?

Trainee: I should input the parking 4. _____ _____ after calling and responding. Now, the **arrival signal indicator** shows **double yellow lights**. This means that I need to stop the train at the **sidetrack**. Right?

Instructor: Correct. You may have a try. 5. _____ makes perfect. With more practice, you'll be good at it.

Trainee: Thanks for your guidance. Let me have a try!

Task 5.2 Listen again and mark the statements as true(T) or false(F).

____ 1. Before starting the train, the trainee needs to lift the pantograph first.

____ 2. The trainee mentioned that he could learn about the current speed and speed limits from the main circuit breaker.

____ 3. The double yellow lights shown in the arrival signal indicator means that the trainee needs to stop the train at the sidetrack.

Task 5.3 Act out the roles with a partner.

94　铁路行业英语

Task 6 Vocational Writing Practice 练职业写作

Task Description: Refer to the following table, describe the five main procedures before driving a train and get familiar with the key operations. So that you can better perform driving tasks and ensure the safe operation of trains in your future position.

任务描述：参考表格内容，描述开动火车前的五个主要步骤，熟悉操作要点，以便在未来岗位上更好地执行驾驶任务，确保火车的安全运行。

Five Main Procedures before Driving a Train Away

Main procedures	Key operations
Receiving	① Confirm the right train according to the fixed train number, the fixed platform, and the fixed station track ② Get ready to receive it
Locomotive inspection	① Enter the cab and begin to comprehensively check the running status of the locomotive ② Confirm all parts of the locomotive are in normal service
Parameter setting	① Input correct parameters according to the operating segment and the operation mode of a train ② Make sure that the train runs within the monitoring range of a onboard train control device all along
Door closing	① After passengers boarding or alighting ② Close the door according to the notification of the conductor
Departure confirmation	① Confirm relevant signals, speed, door state, and departure time ② Relieve braking and start the train

Task 7 Telling Stories of China Railway 讲中国铁路故事

Task Description: Watch the story of railway role models and complete the following exercises to develop the awareness and ability to tell stories of China Railway in English.

任务描述：观看铁路榜样故事，完成练习，培养用英语讲述中国铁路故事的意识和能力。

7.1 What spiritual qualities can we learn from Yang Yong?

7.2 Watch the video again and search online for more information about Yang Yong, introduce his major achievements and get to know how he became a "role model for modern railway". Also, share the inspiration and motivation you gained from his spirit. Work in small groups to tell the story of Yang Yong.

Task 8　Topic Test 测章节知识

Task Description：Review this topic and complete the topic test to develop self-testing skills and summarizing analysis skills.

任务描述：复习本章节内容，完成章节测试，培养自我检测和总结分析的能力。

◎ **Choose the correct answers.**

1. What is the acceleration and deceleration of trains achieved by?
    A. By main circuit breaker.　　　　　B. By speed control handle in cab.
    C. By accelerator and brake pedals.　　D. By driver's control of engine.

2. Why are steam locomotives eliminated?
    A. They run very quietly.
    B. They produce many pollutants.
    C. They are easy to maintain and repair.
    D. They have extremely low thermal efficiency.

3. Which of the following accurately describes the function of the automatic brake valve?
    A. It controls the braking and relieving of the entire train.
    B. It controls the braking and relieving of locomotives.
    C. It regulates the temperature of the train's brakes.
    D. It adjusts the power output of the train's engine.

4. Before starting the train, drivers need to _____ the main circuit breaker, then _____ the automatic and the independent brake valve.
    A. connect; relieve.　　　　B. connect; apply.
    C. close; relieve.　　　　　D. close; apply.

5. Which of the following is NOT essential for a train driver to ensure smooth and steady train operation?
    A. departure preparation.　　B. door closing.
    C. locomotive inspection.　　D. personal preference and intuition.

◎ **Mark the following translations as true(T) or false(F).**

6. With no transport capacity, the locomotive drives the vehicle to move on its track.
    译文：机车自身有运输能力，它牵引车辆沿轨道运行。

7. Based on different power sources, there are steam locomotives, diesel locomotives, and electric locomotives..
    译文：机车根据动力来源不同，分为蒸汽机车、内燃机车和电力机车。

8. An electric locomotive is driven by its traction motor.
    译文：电力机车通过机车上的牵引电动机驱动列车运行。

9. The diesel locomotive is hardly affected by weather and can smoothly run even in extreme conditions of rain and snow.

   译文：内燃机车受天气影响较大，在极端雨雪天气不能顺畅行驶。

10. In the process of driving, both a main and assistant driver in the locomotive supervise and remind each other by repeating hundreds of "pointing-and-calling" actions.

    译文：在驾驶过程中，机车上的主、副司机通过重复成百上千次的"手指口呼"动作，互相监督提醒。

Task 9　Self-assessment 评学习效果

Task Description: Tick the items and self-assess learning outcomes.
任务描述：勾选选项，自我评估学习效果。

教学目标	评分项目
自主学习完善	☐Have a good habit of independent learning 有良好的自主学习习惯 ☐Be clear about learning objectives 明确学习目标 ☐Know about learning content 了解学习内容 ☐Complete learning tasks effectively 有效完成学习任务 ☐Finish the section test consciously 自主进行知识检测
语言思维提升	Master the pronunciation, spelling, definition, and simple usage of the following vocabulary： 掌握下列词汇的发音、拼写、释义及简单应用： ☐locomotive ☐brake ☐console ☐screen ☐responsibility ☐whistle ☐traction motor ☐pointing and calling ☐key lever ☐reversing lever ☐automatic brake valve ☐independent brake valve ☐diesel locomotive ☐electric locomotive ☐steam locomotive ☐air whistle Be able to read and understand articles related to this topic and talk about them in English： 能读懂本主题相关文章并用英语简单介绍： ☐Three basic types and features of railway locomotives 　铁路机车的三种类型及特点 ☐Five main procedures before driving a train away 　开走火车前的五个主要步骤 ☐The job responsibilities and work attitude of locomotive drivers 　机车乘务员岗位的工作职责与工作态度
职场涉外沟通	☐Be able to understand workplace situational conversations related to this topic 　能听懂本主题相关的职场情景对话 ☐Be able to simulate workplace situational conversations related to this topic with a partner 　能与搭档一起模拟本主题相关的职场情景对话 ☐Be able to introduce the given theme in written form 　能用英语完成主题相关的书面表达
多元文化交流	☐Be able to work in groups to tell the story of China railway role models in English 　能小组合作用英语讲述本主题相关的中国铁路榜样故事

Topic 4　EMU Train Overhaul—With Great Care
主题四　动车组检修——精检细修

Task 1　Learning Objectives 明学习目标

Task Description: Get to know the content and clarify learning objectives.
任务描述：了解学习内容，明确学习目标。

EMU Train Overhaul 动车组检修

- **知识目标**：掌握与"动车组检修"主题相关的行业英语词汇

- **技能目标**：
  1. 能读懂与本主题相关的文章
  2. 能听懂与本主题相关的职场情景对话
  3. 能模拟表演职场情景对话，能用英语讲述中国铁路榜样故事
  4. 能用英语完成与主题相关的书面表达

- **素质目标**：了解"新时代·铁路榜样"动车组地勤机械师马耀锋的榜样故事，学习他敬业、勤奋好学、追求卓越、勇于担当、传承与分享的精神，在未来岗位上热爱工作，不断追求更高的目标，为千千万万旅客的安全出行保驾护航

- **学行业词汇**：overhaul, EMU train, inspection shed, car body, high-voltage traction system, flange, pantograph head stand, skirt board, driving facilities, welding joint, carbon contact strip, etc.

- **习情境案例**：《动车组检修，安全保障》
  1. 动车组检修的重要性和基本知识
  2. 动车组机械师岗位的检修作业要求
  3. 动车组机械师岗位的工作职责与工作态度

- **体验职场情景**：
  - 行业情景会话听说
  - 行业情景会话展示
  - 职业英语写作训练

- **讲中国铁路榜样故事**

新时代·铁路榜样　马耀锋
"动车医生"

Task 2 Lead in 导主题内容

Task Description: Watch the video, complete the following exercises and learn about the English names of eight key components and English expressions for overhaul of an EMU train.

任务描述：观看视频，完成练习，了解动车组八大关键组成部分名称及动车组检修的英文表达。

As a self-powered fixed **consist** car, an **EMU** train consists of powered cars and unpowered cars and it can be driven at both ends.

An EMU train is usually composed of eight key parts and components, including a car body, a bogie, a **high-voltage traction system**, an **auxiliary power supply system**, a brake system, a network system, driving facilities, and in-vehicle devices.

EMU trains drive on the track for a long time. There will be wear and tear between the wheel and the track. And the car body may be affected by wind, frost, rain and snow. So it is very important to check and maintain their **mechanical** parts regularly. Do you know where the overhaul and maintenance of trains are conducted? Yes, they are **conduct**ed in the train **inspection shed**, which is like an **automobile** 4S shop. In the workshop, a mechanist may give a careful examination and detailed repair of parts of the bogie, **high-voltage electrical equipment, traction system equipment**, and driving facilities of the **driver's console**, etc. In this way, components of an EMU train are ensured to be safe and steady.

Task 2.1 Write down the English names of eight key components of an EMU train in the picture.

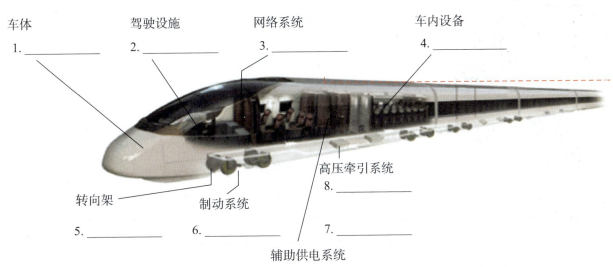

Schematic Diagram of the Composition of an EMU Train

Task 3　Vocabulary Study 学行业词汇

Task Description: Learn the industry vocabulary, complete the following exercises, and master the English expressions for the names and functions of main components of EMU trains.

任务描述：学习行业词汇，完成练习，掌握动车组主要部件名称及其功能的英文表达。

🎧 1. car body

The **car body** is the place where passengers and drivers are accommodated. At the same time, it is also the basis for installing and connecting other equipment and components.

🎧 2. high-voltage traction system

The **high-voltage traction system** provides traction power for EMU trains. Pantograph, main circuit breaker, traction transformer, traction motor and so on are generally included in this system.

🎧 3. auxiliary power supply system

The **auxiliary power supply system** provides electric energy for auxiliary load equipment of EMU trains. It is generally composed of auxiliary AC converter, battery, charging machine, etc.

🎧 4. driving facilities

The **driving facilities** refer to the area and equipment used by EMU drivers to operate and control the train, including the driver's control console, seats, wipers, exterior lighting, etc.

🎧 5. in-vehicle equipment

The **in-vehicle equipment** refers to the accessory devices in the car that serve passengers. It includes air conditioning, lighting, windows, doors, seats, luggage racks and other equipment and systems.

🎧 6. inspection shed

The train **inspection shed** is a building that is specially designed and constructed for train maintenance and repair.

🎧 7. pantograph head stand

The **pantograph head stand** is a device used to support and fix the pantograph head and ensure stable contact between the head and the catenary.

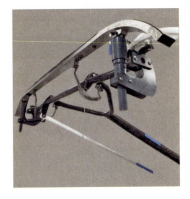

🎧 8. carbon contact strip

The **carbon contact strip** is mainly composed of carbon strips and brackets. It is commonly mounted at the uppermost end of the pantograph and contact with conducting wires of catenary directly.

🎧 9. skirt board

The **skirt board** is generally installed at the lower part of the car body and it is made of aluminum alloy materials through point welding. It is a device used to ensure the airtightness of equipment compartments.

🎧 10. gangway bellows

The **gangway bellows** is a flexible channel between carriages. It prevents air, dust, rainwater and others from entering the carriage and reduces the noise generated during high-speed running.

Task 3.1 Match the words or phrases with the definitions.

1. _____ high-voltage traction system
2. _____ driving facilities
3. _____ inspection shed
4. _____ car body
5. _____ carbon contact strip
6. _____ gangway bellows
7. _____ skirt board
8. _____ in-vehicle equipment

Module 2 Railway Electromechanics 铁道机电

A. the place where passengers and drivers are accommodated
B. the accessory devices in the car that serve passengers
C. a flexible channel between carriages
D. being mounted at the uppermost end of the pantograph and contacting with catenary conducting wires directly
E. the lower part of the car body to ensure the airtightness of equipment compartments
F. a building specially designed and constructed for train maintenance and repair
G. the area and equipment used by EMU drivers to operate and control the train
H. the device which provides traction power for EMU trains

Word Bank

New Words

overhaul /ˌəʊvəˈhɔːl/ v. 彻底检修；n. 大修，彻底检修
consist /kənˈsɪst/ n. 列车编组，(铁路)车列
mechanical /məˈkænɪkl/ adj. 机械(方面)的
conduct /kənˈdʌkt/ v. 实施，进行
automobile /ˈɔːtəməbiːl/ n. 汽车
guarantee /ˌɡærənˈtiː/ v. 确保，保证；n. 保证
negligence /ˈneɡlɪdʒəns/ n. 疏忽，大意
improper /ɪmˈprɒpə/ adj. 不正确的，不适当的
occurrence /əˈkʌrəns/ n. 发生，出现
fundamental /ˌfʌndəˈmentl/ adj. 基本的

stable /ˈsteɪbl/ v. (使)停入，(使)停放
undergo /ˌʌndəˈɡəʊ/ v. 经历，经受
automatic /ˌɔːtəˈmætɪk/ adj. 自动的
accordingly /əˈkɔːdɪŋli/ adv. 相应地，照着
manual /ˈmænjuəl/ adj. 手工的，手动的
procedure /prəˈsiːdʒə/ n. 步骤，程序
standardize /ˈstændədaɪz/ v. 使标准化，使符合标准
error /ˈerə/ n. 错误，差错
scratches /ˈskrætʃɪz/ n. 划痕(scratch的复数)，刮伤
flange /flændʒ/ n. 轮缘，边缘

Phrases & Expressions

EMU (electric multiple unit) train 动车组列车
high-voltage traction system 高压牵引系统
auxiliary power supply system 辅助供电设备
inspection shed 检修库
high-voltage electrical equipment 高压电器设备
traction system equipment 牵引系统设备
driver's console 司机操纵台
car body 车体
driving facilities 驾驶设备
in-vehicle equipment 车内设备
gangway bellows 车端连接风挡

attach great importance to… 高度重视
take…for example 例如,比如说
undergo a thorough cleaning
　　进行彻底清洗
fixed automatic washing machine
　　固定式自动洗车机
EMU depot 动车运用所
senior overhaul 高级检修

machine-based overhaul
　　机检,机器检修
sense of responsibility 责任感
skirt board 裙板
welding joint 焊接接头
pantograph head stand 弓头支架
mounting base 安装底座
carbon contact strip 碳滑板

  Task 4　Passage Study 习情境案例

Task Description：Read the article, complete the following exercises, and learn about the importance and the basic knowledge of EMU training maintenance, as well as the maintenance operation requirements and work attitude of the EMU mechanist.

任务描述：读懂文章,完成练习,了解动车组检修的重要性、基本知识与动车组机械师岗位的检修作业要求与工作态度。

EMU Train Overhaul, Safety Guarantee

Train maintenance is very important for traffic safety. **Negligence** and **improper** maintenance of equipment may lead to safety risk and eventually the **occurrence** of dangerous accidents. Therefore, we must **attach great importance to** train maintenance. Now let's **take** EMU trains **for example** to learn about **fundamental** knowledge of train overhaul.

Before it is **stable**d for maintenance, the EMU train will **undergo a thorough cleaning** by a fixed **automatic** washing machine.

Scheduled overhaul of EMU trains mainly depends on their traveling distance and running time. As long as condition of either traveled distance or running time is met, an overhaul should be conducted **accordingly**. A repair program for EMU trains consists of five levels. At levels 1 and 2, an in-service overhaul is performed in an **EMU depot**, while at levels 3, 4, and 5, a **senior overhaul** is implemented in a qualified overhaul unit.

According to the maintenance and repair program, an overhaul should be conducted after an EMU train has traveled for 5,000 km or 48 hours. Specifically, such an overhaul covers car body safety maintenance and in-vehicle service facilities maintenance. Level 1 overhaul consists of **machine-based overhaul** and **manual** technical overhaul.

An overhaul conducted by the EMU mechanist must follow vehicle inspection **procedure**s and the **standardize**d operating method. The mechanist needs not only the solid professional knowledge and skills, but also a high **sense of responsibility** and professional dedication. They need to work with great care and pay particular attention to details during the maintenance. There is no room for any **error**s.

Task 4.1　Read the passage. Then, choose the correct answers.

1. What is the main purpose of emphasizing train maintenance?
   A. To reduce operating costs.　　　B. To ensure traffic safety.
   C. To increase train speed.　　　　D. To improve passenger comfort.
2. Which of the following factors determine the scheduled overhaul of EMU trains?
   A. Passenger feedback.
   B. Traveled distance and running time.
   C. Weather conditions.
   D. Train model.
3. Why is it important for mechanists to work with great care and pay particular attention to details during maintenance?
   A. To reduce their workload.
   B. To save time.
   C. To ensure the safety of the train and its passengers.
   D. To impress their supervisors.

Task 4.2　Read the sentence pairs. Fill in each blank with the best word or phrase.

1. an EMU depot/a qualified overhaul unit
   A. Lever l and 2 overhaul of EMU trains should be done in _____.
   B. A senior overhaul of EMU trains at levels 3, 4 and 5 is conducted in _____.
2. total running time/in-vehicle service facilities
   A. The scope of an EMU train overhaul specifically includes ensuring car body safety and maintaining _____.
   B. The frequency of these overhauls is largely determined by the trains' accumulated traveling distance and _____.

Task 5　Vocational Situation Experience 演职场情景

Task Description: Experience the situational conversation and complete the following exercises, so as to enhance English application ability related to professional positions.
任务描述：体验岗位情景会话，完成练习，提升与职业岗位相关的英语应用能力。

Task 5.1 Listen to the conversation, and fill in the blanks.

Situation description: A trainee is communicating with the experienced instructor about the inspection results and maintenance precautions of the EMU body, to ensure the safety of train operation and personal safety during the maintenance process.

Instructor: Hi, Xiao Zhang! Have you checked both sides of the car body?

Trainee: Yes. Mr. Wang. We finished checking 1. _____ _____ of the car at the same time, one on each side. All parts such as car body, 2. _____ _____, gangway bellows and couplers are in good condition.

Instructor: That's great. Are there anything wrong with the bogies?

Trainee: Let me check the inspection report. The wheel tread of Carriage 05 is somewhat 3. _____. No defects are found in the **flange**s. And wear conditions are normal.

Instructor: OK. Are there any other problems on the inspection report?

Trainee: When we were checking facilities on the roof, we found that the 4. _____ _____ of the **pantograph head stand** for Carriage 06 cracked.

Instructor: Did you perform a multi-angle visual inspection?

Trainee: Yes. We checked it for several times and confirmed that the welding joint cracked indeed.

Instructor: Well done. It seems that we need to change the **mounting base** of the **carbon contact strip**.

Trainee: OK. I'll get it done right away.

Instructor: Remember to disconnect the power supply before replacing the equipment and pay attention to 5. _____ _____.

Trainee: Thank your for your reminders. We'll take safety measures, and make sure that all parts and components are in normal service before running the train again.

Task 5.2 Listen again and mark the statements as true(T) or false(F).

____ 1. The trainee and his colleague checked both sides of the car simultaneously.
____ 2. A crack was discovered in the welding joint of the pantograph head stand for Carriage 06.
____ 3. The instructor suggested replacing the carbon contact strip mounting base.

Task 5.3 Act out the roles with a partner.

Task 6 Vocational Writing Practice 练职业写作

Task Description: Refer to the table, summarize the standard operation of primary overhaul and master the maintenance procedure, so that you can perform maintenance tasks better and improve work efficiency in future positions.

任务描述：参考表格内容，总结一份动车组一级检修标准作业法，掌握检修流程，以便在未来岗位上更好地执行检修任务。

Standard Operation of Lever 1 Overhaul for EMU Trains

Overhaul Items	Overhaul Objects	Maintainer Arrangement
Inspection of both sides of the car body	① Car body ② **Skirt board** ③ Gangway bellows ④ Bogie ⑤ Coupler	Inspect both sides of car body at the same time, with one person on each side
Inspection in the service pit	① Base plate ② Gangway bellows ③ Bogie	① Each repairman checks in the service pit at the same time from the center line of an EMU train to its both sides ② Turns around and begins to check from both sides to its center line.
Roof equipment inspection	① Windshield ② Antennas on the roof ③ Air conditioning units ④ Gangway bellows ⑤ Pantographs	Completed by a single repairman independently

Task 7 **Telling Stories of China Railway** 讲中国铁路故事

Task Description: Watch the story of railway role models and complete the following exercises to develop the awareness and ability to tell stories of China Railway in English.

任务描述：观看铁路榜样故事，完成练习，培养用英语讲述中国铁路故事的意识和能力。

7.1 How did Ma Yaofeng prepare for the competition when he participated in the National Railway Industry Vocational Skills Competition for the first time?

7.2 Watch the video again and search online for more information about Ma Yaofeng, introduce his personal growth journey and get to know how he grew from a beginner to a national master of skills. Also, share the inspiration and motivation you gained from his spirit. Work in small groups to tell the story of Ma Yaofeng.

Task 8 Topic Test 测章节知识

Task Description: Review this topic and complete the topic test to develop self-testing skills and summarizing analysis skills.

任务描述:复习本章节内容,完成章节测试,培养自我检测和总结分析的能力。

◎ **Choose the correct answers.**

1. What is the first step in preparing an EMU train for maintenance?
   A. Conducting a thorough cleaning. B. Checking the traveled distance.
   C. Assessing the running time. D. Performing a level – 1 overhaul.

2. What kind of overhaul is implemented in a qualified overhaul unit?
   A. Service overhaul. B. Machine-based overhaul.
   C. Senior overhaul. D. Manual technical overhaul.

3. How many kilometers or hours of operation should an EMU train complete before an overhaul is conducted?
   A. 1,000 km or 24 hours. B. 5,000 km or 48 hours.
   C. 10,000 km or 72 hours. D. 15,000 km or 96 hours.

4. Which of the following items are included in the "Inspection of both sides of the car body" during the primary overhaul of EMU trains?
   A. Car body, skirt board, gangway bellows, bogie and coupler.
   B. Base plate, wind shield and bogie.
   C. Windscreens, top antennas and air conditioning units.
   D. Coupler, bogie and wind shield.

5. During the primary overhaul of EMU trains, how is roof equipment inspection arranged?
   A. Each maintainer inspects one specific roof equipment item.
   B. A team of maintainers work together to complete the inspection.
   C. The inspection is completed by a single maintainer independently.
   D. The inspection is the same as the inspection in the service pit.

◎ **Mark the following translations as true(T) or false(F).**

6. Negligence and improper maintenance of equipment may lead to safety risk and eventually the occurrence of dangerous accidents.
   译文:对设备的疏忽以及不恰当的维护,可能带来安全风险,最终导致危险事故的发生。

7. A carbon contact strip is mainly composed of carbon strips and brackets.
   译文:碳滑板主要由碳条、托架等部件组成。

8. As long as condition of either traveled distance or running time is met first, an overhaul

should be conducted accordingly.

译文:只要行驶距离和运行时间都满足,就要进行检修。

9. At levels 1 and 2, an in-service overhaul is performed in an EMU depot, while at levels 3, 4, and 5, a senior overhaul is implemented in a qualified overhaul unit.

译文:一、二级检修为运用检修,在动车运用所进行。三、四、五级检修为中级检修,在具备检修资质的检修单位实行。

10. As a self-powered fixed consist car, an EMU train consists of powered cars and unpowered cars and both ends are driven.

译文:动车组是自带动力的固定编组列车,它由带有动力的车辆和不带动力的车辆组成,两端均可驾驶。

Task 9 Self-assessment 评学习效果

Task Description: Tick the items and self-assess learning outcomes.
任务描述: 勾选选项,自我评估学习效果。

教学目标	评分项目
自主学习完善	☐ Have a good habit of independent learning 有良好的自主学习习惯 ☐ Be clear about learning objectives 明确学习目标 ☐ Know about learning content 了解学习内容 ☐ Complete learning tasks effectively 有效完成学习任务 ☐ Finish the section test consciously 自主进行知识检测
语言思维提升	Master the pronunciation, spelling, definition, and simple usage of the following vocabulary: 掌握下列词汇的发音、拼写、释义及简单应用: ☐ overhaul ☐ EMU train ☐ inspection shed ☐ car body ☐ high-voltage traction system ☐ flange ☐ driver's control console ☐ pantograph head stand ☐ skirt board ☐ scratches ☐ stable ☐ driving facilities ☐ welding joint ☐ mounting base ☐ carbon contact strip
	Be able to read and understand articles related to this topic and talk about them in English: 能读懂本主题相关文章并用英语简单介绍: ☐ The importance of EMU trains maintenance 　动车组检修的重要性 ☐ Basic knowledge of EMU trains maintenance 　动车组检修的基本知识 ☐ Maintenance operation requirements of the position of the EMU trains mechanist 　动车组机械师岗位的检修作业要求 ☐ The job responsibilities and work attitude of the EMU trains mechanist 　动车组机械师岗位的工作职责与工作态度
职场涉外沟通	☐ Be able to understand workplace situational conversations related to this topic 　能听懂本主题相关的职场情景对话 ☐ Be able to simulate workplace situational conversations related to this topic with a partner 　能与搭档一起模拟本主题相关的职场情景对话 ☐ Be able to introduce the given theme in written form 　能用英语完成主题相关的书面表达
多元文化交流	☐ Be able to work in groups to tell the story of China railway role models in English 　能小组合作用英语讲述本主题相关的中国铁路榜样故事

Topic 5　Electrified Railway—Be the Source of Power
主题五　电气化铁路——动力之源

 Task Learning Objectives 明学习目标

Task Description：Get to know the content and clarify learning objectives.
任务描述：了解学习内容，明确学习目标。

Electrified Railway 电气化铁路

- **知识目标**：掌握与"电气化铁路"主题相关的行业英语词汇
- **技能目标**：
  1. 能读懂与本主题相关的文章
  2. 能听懂与本主题相关的职场情景对话
  3. 能模拟表演职场情景对话，能用英语讲述中国铁路榜样故事
  4. 能用英语完成与主题相关的书面表达
- **素质目标**：了解"最美铁路人"接触网工代云华的榜样故事，学习他敬业、勤奋好学、追求卓越、勇于担当和坚韧不拔的精神，在未来岗位上热爱工作，不断追求更高的目标

学行业词汇：electrified railway, traction substation, catenary, skylight pantograph, traction power supply system, catenary maintenance vehicle, high-voltage transmission line, transformer station, alternating current, etc.

习情境案例：《动力之源：电气化铁路三大元件》
1. 电气化铁路的三大元件组成及其运行与维护人员
2. 电气化铁路供电系统的基本原理
3. 接触网维护基本知识

体验职场情景：
- 行业情景会话听说
- 行业情景会话展示
- 职业英语写作训练

讲中国铁路榜样故事：

最美铁路人　代云华
"金牌接触网工"

Module 2　Railway Electromechanics　铁道机电　113

Task 2 Lead in 导主题内容

> **Task Description**: Watch the video, complete the following exercises and master the English expressions about power supply system of the electric locomotive.
>
> **任务描述**：观看视频，完成练习，掌握电力机车供电系统的英文表达。

The railway which uses electric **traction** is called **electrified railway**. The **traction power** of electric locomotives is electric energy. However, electric locomotives do not have power. They rely on the **electricity** provided by the **external power supply system** to move the train forward. Then, how is the external power supply generated? And how is the electric energy **transmit**ted to the electric locomotive? We need to learn about the power supply system of the electric locomotive.

Electricity **generate**d in a **power plant** goes through a step-up transformer and its voltage is thus raised. Then, the electricity is transmitted to **traction substations** along the railway **via high-voltage transmission lines**. In a traction **substation**, a transformer lowers the voltage from 110 kv or 220 kv to 27.5 kv at first and then transmits the electric power to catenaries of the railway lines. Electric locomotives **obtain continuous** and **sufficient** electric energy by contacting the **catenary** with the **pantograph** on the top.

Task 2.1 Write down the English names of supply system for the electric locomotive in the picture.

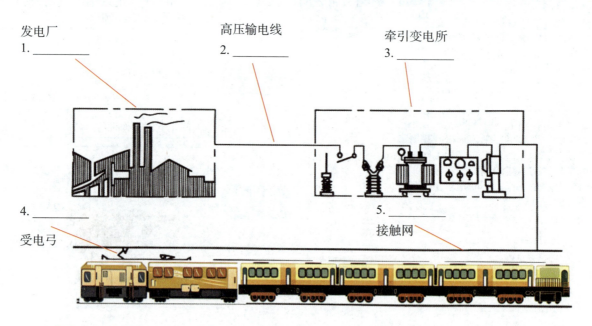

Schematic Diagram of Power Supply System for the Electric Locomotive

Task 3 Vocabulary Study 学行业词汇

Task Description: Learn the industry vocabulary, complete the following exercises, and master the English expressions related to power supply system of electrified railway.

任务描述：学习行业词汇，完成练习，掌握电气化铁路供电系统有关的英文表达。

🎧 1. electrified railway

The **electrified railway** refers to the railway which uses electric traction.

🎧 2. step-up transformer

The **step-up transformer** is a power transformer used for boosting the voltage. It plays an important role in changing the voltage from low to high, and it is one of the key devices used to achieve remote transmission and distribution of power.

🎧 3. high-voltage transmission line

The **high-voltage transmission line** is the power circuit that transmit large amounts of electrical energy from power plants to substations.

🎧 4. traction substation

In a **traction substation**, the electrical energy delivered from the power plant via power transmission lines can be converted into the power suitable for locomotive vehicles, and then transmit it to the catenary.

🎧 5. catenary

The **catenary** refers to a special form of transmission line. It is erected above the electrified railway and supplies power to the electric locomotive.

Module 2 Railway Electromechanics 铁道机电

6. pantograph

The **pantograph** is a device mounted on the roof of a locomotive or an EMU train. It is used to collect electrical energy from the catenary and transmit it to the electric locomotive.

7. traction power supply system

The **traction power supply system** provides the electric locomotive with power sources. It not only enable the electric locomotive to possess traction and braking capabilities, but also provides auxiliary power for other equipment on the vehicle.

8. alternating current

The **alternating current**, or AC for short, is a type of current. When it moves in a conductor, it can change the direction rapidly.

9. maintenance gap

The **maintenance gap** refers to a particular period reserved for construction and maintenance operation when the train is not in operation.

10. catenary maintenance vehicle

The **catenary maintenance vehicle** is an important mechanically powered device. It is used for construction, testing and maintenance, rescue, and cargo transportation of the electrified railway.

Task 3.1 Match the words or phrases with the definitions.

1. _____ catenary
2. _____ traction power supply system
3. _____ alternating current
4. _____ electrified railway
5. _____ high-voltage transmission line
6. _____ maintenance gap
7. _____ catenary maintenance vehicle
8. _____ pantograph

A. the railway which uses electric traction

B. a reserved time for construction and maintenance

C. a kind of transmission line which supplies electric energy to the electric locomotive

D. a system provides auxiliary power for other equipment on the vehicle

E. a current that can change directions

F. a specialized equipment designed for the repair, maintenance, and emergency restoration of the catenary system

G. power lines that transmit large amounts of electrical energy from power plants to substations

H. the equipment that contacts with the catenary and transmits the power to electric locomotives

Word Bank

New Words

traction /ˈtrækʃn/ n. 拉，牵引
electricity /ɪˌlekˈtrɪsəti/ n. 电，电流
external /ɪkˈstɜːnl/ adj. 外部的
transmit /trænzˈmɪt/ v. 传输，传送
generate /ˈdʒenəreɪt/ v. 产生，引起
via /ˈvaɪə/ prep. 经由，经过
voltage /ˈvəʊltɪdʒ/ n. 电压，伏特数
substation /ˈsʌbsteɪʃn/ n. 变电站，配电站
obtain /əbˈteɪn/ v. 得到，获得
continuous /kənˈtɪnjuəs/ adj. 连续不断的，持续的
sufficient /səˈfɪʃnt/ adj. 足够的，充足的
catenary /kəˈtiːnəri/ n. 接触网
pantograph /ˈpæntəɡrɑːf/ n. 受电弓
element /ˈelɪmənt/ n. 要素，元素

acquire /əˈkwaɪə/ v. 获得，学到
convert /kənˈvɜːt/ v. （使）转变，（使）转换
transformer /trænsˈfɔːmə/ n. 变压器
corresponding /ˌkɒrəˈspɒndɪŋ/ adj. 相应的，相关的
scrape /skreɪp/ v. （用小刀等）刮除
disaster /dɪˈzɑːstə/ n. 灾难，灾害
absolute /ˈæbsəluːt/ adj. 完全的，绝对的
screw /skruː/ n. 螺丝
loose /luːs/ adj. 松动的，松脱的
applicable /əˈplɪkəbl/ adj. 能应用的，可适用的
distribution /ˌdɪstrɪˈbjuːʃn/ n. 分配，配送
dispatch /dɪˈspætʃ/ v. 派遣，调度

Phrases & Expressions

electrified railway 电气化铁路
traction power 牵引动力
power supply system 供电系统
power plant 发电厂
step-up transformer 升压变压器
traction substation 牵引变电所
high-voltage transmission line
　　高压输电线
traction power supply system
　　牵引供电系统
anti-freezing oil 防冻油

filling station 加油站
to be concrete 具体来说
alternating current 交流电
tend to… 往往……倾向于……
in the event of… 万一，如果发生
catenary maintenance vehicle
　　接触网检修作业车
in midair 在半空中
transformer station 变电站
electric power circuit workers
　　电力线路工

Module 2　RAILWAY Electromechanics　铁道机电　117

Task 4 Passage Study 习情境案例

Task Description: Read the article, complete the following exercises, and learn about three components of electrified railway and basic knowledge of catenary maintenance.

任务描述：读懂文章，完成练习，了解电气化铁路的三大元件组成与接触网维护的基本知识。

Source of Power: Three Components of Electrified Railway

The electrified railway is composed of an electric locomotive and a traction power supply system. The **traction power supply system** is generally divided into a traction substation and a catenary. Therefore, the electric locomotive, the traction substation and the catenary are commonly known as three major **element**s of the electrified railway.

The electric locomotive directly **acquire**s power from the catenary with the help of a pantograph rising from the roof. Thus, the train can be driven by a traction motor on the locomotive. Each electric locomotive is equipped with one pantograph in the front and the other in the rear. The rising and falling of the pantographs are controlled by the driver. In winter, the repairman applies **antifreezing oil** on joint parts of the pantograph to ensure the smooth rising.

As for the traction substation of the electrified railway, we can compare it to the **filling station. To be concrete**, it **convert**s high-voltage alternating current via a **transformer** into **alternating current** suitable for electric locomotives, and then transmits power to the catenary. Staff in a traction substation needs to inspect, maintain, operate, and monitor **corresponding** power equipment.

At last, the catenary of the electrified railway is a device used to transmit electric energy to electric locomotives. As a power supply device without any protective clothing, it **tend**s **to** be greatly affected by surroundings. Catenary inspection and repair workers for high-speed trains take advantage of the "**maintenance gap**" to fulfill catenary repair and maintenance. For example, they need to **scrape** the ice cover on catenaries **in the event of** freezing rain and snow **disaster**s. In this way, **absolute** safety in train power sources can be fully ensured.

Task 4.1 Read the passage. Then, choose the correct answers.

1. What are the three major components of an electrified railway?
    A. Electric locomotive, traction substation, and staff.
    B. Electric locomotive, traction substation, and catenary.
    C. Catenary, transformer, and electric locomotive.
    D. Traction motor, pantograph, and electric locomotive.
2. What is the catenary in an electrified railway used for?
    A. To transmit electric energy to electric locomotives.

B. To protect the electric locomotives from lightning.

C. To provide shade for passengers.

D. To support the weight of the train.

3. What do catenary inspection and repair workers do in the event of freezing rain and snow disasters?

A. They apply anti-freezing oil on the catenary.

B. They scrape the ice cover on the catenaries.

C. They replace the entire catenary system.

D. They stop all train operations.

Task 4. 2 Read the sentence pairs. Fill in each blank with the best word or phrase.

1. pantograph/catenary

    A. As a power supply device that lacks protective clothing, _____ is often influenced by surroundings.

    B. The rising and falling of the _____ is controlled by the driver.

2. traction substation/electric locomotive

    A. The _____ acquires power directly from the catenary with the help of a pantograph.

    B. Workers in the _____ need to inspect, maintain, operate, and monitor corresponding power equipment.

Task  Vocational Situation Experience 演职场情景

Task Description: Experience the situational conversation and complete the following exercises, so as to enhance English application ability related to professional positions.

任务描述：体验岗位情景会话，完成练习，提升与职业岗位相关的英语应用能力。

Task 5. 1 Listen to the conversation, and fill in the blanks.

Situation description: A trainee is consulting an experienced instructor about the railway power supply system in order to better understand the main functions of the traction power supply system, the role of the catenary maintenance vehicle and the daily work of catenary workers.

Instructor: Hi, Xiao Zhang. I'm Wang Lin.

Trainee: Nice to meet you, Mr. Wang.

Instructor: What do you know about the railway power supply system?

Trainee: Well. A railway power supply system consists of two parts. One is the traction power supply system, and the other is the electric 1. _____ _____ system.

Instructor: You're right. The traction power supply system primarily provides power to electric locomotives. An electric locomotive directly acquires power from a catenary 2. _____ _____ _____ .

Trainee: So, how important the catenary is!

Instructor: Correctly. However, the catenary is easy to be affected by various weather conditions and external forces. 3. _____ of its parts and components often come **loose**.

Trainee: What should I do to ensure its normal service?

Instructor: We have the **catenary maintenance vehicle**. They can be used for 4. _____ and maintenance of catenaries.

Trainee: The car means a lot!

Instructor: Where the car is not **applicable**, a catenary worker needs to 5. _____ _____ _____ and complete maintenance tasks.

Trainee: Catenary workers working at heights need both rich experience and professional skills.

Task 5.2 Listen again and mark the statements as true(T) or false(F).

_____ 1. Railway power supply system only provides power to the traction power supply system.

_____ 2. Because of various weather conditions and external forces, screws of catenary's parts and components may often become loose.

_____ 3. Catenary workers working at heights require both rich experience and professional skills.

Task 5.3 Act out the roles with a partner.

 **Task 6　Vocational Writing Practice 练职业写作**

Task Description：Refer to the table, describe the components, functions and operation and maintenance personnel of electrified railways and master the fundamental principles of the power supply system of electrified railway.

任务描述：参考表格内容，描述电气化铁路组成部分、功能与所需运维人员，掌握电气化铁路供电系统的基本原理。

Compositions, Functions and Basic Operating and Maintenance of the Electrified Railway

Compositions	Description	Functions	Operating and Maintenance Personnel
Electric locomotive	① The pantograph overhead ② To acquire electric energy from the catenary	① To generate traction forces by a motor ② To make the train move ahead	Locomotive drivers (commonly known as train drivers)
Traction substation	① To convert high-voltage alternating current into that suitable for electric locomo-tives ② To feed stable power sources to electric locomotives with the help of catenaries	To ensure steady and high-efficiency operation of electric locomotives	The person on duty for **transformer station** (unavailable now)
Power circuit	① Electric power transmission ② Electric power **distribution**	To supply power for stations, communication, signal and operation **dispatch**ing	**Electric power circuit workers**
Catenary	① A type of high-voltage transmission lines ② Erected above the railroad tracks	To provide power to electric locomotives	Catenary workers

Task 7 Telling Stories of China Railway 讲中国铁路故事

Task Description: Watch the story of railway role models and complete the following exercises to develop the awareness and ability to tell stories of China Railway in English.

任务描述：观看铁路榜样故事，完成练习，培养用英语讲述中国铁路故事的意识和能力。

7.1　How did Dai Yunhua stand out in the skills competition in 2009?

7.2　Watch the video again and search online for more information about Dai Yunhua, introduce his personal growth journey and get to know how he become the strongest in catenary maintenance. Also, share the inspiration and motivation you gained from his spirit. Work in small groups to tell the story of Dai Yunhua.

Task 8 Topic Test 测章节知识

Task Description: Review this topic and complete the topic test to develop self-testing skills and summarizing analysis skills.

任务描述：复习本章节内容，完成章节测试，培养自我检测和总结分析能力。

◎ **Choose the correct answers.**

1. How do electric locomotives obtain continuous and sufficient electric energy?
   A. By generating electricity on their own.
   B. By collecting solar energy from the traction substation directly.
   C. By contacting the catenary with the pantograph on the top.
   D. By receiving wireless electricity transmissions.

2. Who controls the rising and falling of the pantographs on an electric locomotive?
   A. The passengers.   B. The driver.
   C. The maintainer.   D. The station staff.

3. What is the function of a traction substation in an electrified railway?
   A. To convert power transmitted from power plant into that suitable for electric locomotives.
   B. To repair the electric locomotives.
   C. To control the speed of trains.
   D. To provide seating for passengers.

4. Who is responsible for maintaining and operating the catenary system in an electrified railway?
   A. Locomotive driver.
   B. The person on duty for power transformation.
   C. Electric power circuit workers.
   D. Catenary workers.

5. Who is responsible for ensuring the steady and high-efficiency operation of electric locomotives in an electrified railway?
   A. Locomotive driver.
   B. Electric power circuit workers.
   C. Catenary workers.
   D. The person on duty for power transformer station.

◎ **Mark the following translations as true (T) or false (F).**

6. The electrified railway is composed of an electric locomotive and a traction power supply system.
   译文：电气化铁路是由电力机车和牵引供电系统组成的。

7. Each electric locomotive is equipped with one pantograph in the front and the other in the rear.

    译文:每台电力机车的前后各配备一个受电弓。

8. And thus, the train can be driven by a traction motor on the locomotive.

    译文:这样,列车便可以在机车牵引系统的驱动下行驶。

9. To be concrete, it converts high-voltage alternating current via a transformer into alternating current suitable for electric locomotives, and transmits power to the catenary.

    译文:具体来说,牵引变电所通过变压器将高压交流电转换为适合电力机车使用的直流电,并将电力输送到受电弓。

10. Catenary inspection and repair workers for high-speed trains take advantage of the "maintenance gap" to fulfill catenary repair and maintenance.

    译文:高铁接触网检修工人利用"天窗"时间对接触网进行检修和维护。

Task 9 Self-assessment 评学习效果

Task Description: Tick the items and self-assess learning outcomes.
任务描述：勾选选项，自我评估学习效果。

教学目标	评分项目
自主学习完善	☐Have a good habit of independent learning 有良好的自主学习习惯 ☐Be clear about learning objectives 明确学习目标 ☐Know about learning content 了解学习内容 ☐Complete learning tasks effectively 有效完成学习任务 ☐Finish the section test consciously 自主进行知识检测
语言思维提升	Master the pronunciation, spelling, definition, and simple usage of the following vocabulary: 掌握下列词汇的发音、拼写、释义及简单应用： ☐electrified railway ☐traction substation ☐catenary ☐pantograph ☐traction power supply system ☐maintenance gap ☐catenary maintenance vehicle ☐high-voltage transmission line ☐voltage ☐stepup transformer ☐power plant ☐alternating current ☐power circuit ☐electric power circuit workers ☐transformer station
	Be able to read and understand articles related to this topic and talk about them in English: 能读懂本主题相关文章并用英语简单介绍： ☐Three components of electrified railway and their operation and maintenance personnel 　电气化铁路的三大元件组成及其运行与维护人员 ☐Fundamental principles of the power supply system of electrified railway 　电气化铁路供电系统的基本原理 ☐Basic knowledge of catenary maintenance 　接触网维护基本知识
职场涉外沟通	☐Be able to understand workplace situational conversations related to this topic 　能听懂本主题相关的职场情景对话 ☐Be able to simulate workplace situational conversations related to this topic with a partner 　能与搭档一起模拟本主题相关的职场情景对话 ☐Be able to introduce the given theme in written form 　能用英语完成主题相关的书面表达
多元文化交流	☐Be able to work in groups to tell the story of China railway role models in English 　能小组合作用英语讲述本主题相关的中国铁路榜样故事

Module 3
RAILWAY ENGINEERING

铁道工程

Topic 1　Introduction to Posts—Career Planning
主题一　岗位介绍——职业规划

Task 1　Learning Objectives 明学习目标

Task Description: Get to know the learning content and clarify learning objectives.
任务描述：了解学习内容，明确学习目标。

- 知识目标：掌握与"岗位介绍"主题相关的行业英语词汇
  - 学行业词汇：track workshop, rail flaw detector, bridge and tunnel workshop, flaw detection workshop, existing line, comprehensive machine repair workshop, steel rail material, flaw detection data replay, etc.

- 技能目标：
  1. 能读懂与本主题相关的文章
  2. 能听懂与本主题相关的职场情景对话
  3. 能模拟表演职场情景对话，能用英语讲述中国铁路榜样故事
  4. 能用英语完成与主题相关的书面表达
  - 习情境案例：《铁路线上的守护者》
    1. 铁路工务段的主要车间
    2. 工务段每个职位的职责
    3. 各岗位的职业资格证书

- 体验职场情景：
  - 行业情景会话听说
  - 行业情景会话展示
  - 职业英语写作训练

- 素质目标：了解"新时代铁路榜样"中国高铁的平顺大师吕关仁的榜样故事，学习他勤奋钻研、敢于挑战、寻求创新的优秀品质，在未来岗位上做出应有的贡献

- 讲中国铁路榜样故事

中心：Introduction to Posts 岗位介绍

新时代铁路榜样　吕关仁
"中国高铁的平顺大师"

Task 2 Lead in 导主题内容

Task Description: Watch the video, complete the following exercises and learn about the workshops of railway maintenance section.

任务描述：观看视频，完成练习，了解工务段的各个车间。

On the railway lines, there is a group of "**star-chaser**". They work behind the scenes, silently **safeguarding** the safety of trains and passengers with responsibility and dedication. They are railway **maintenance** workers.

As a **grassroots unit** of the railway, the railway maintenance section **undertakes** the important task of maintaining and repairing tracks, bridges, and **tunnels**. It includes the track **workshop**, bridge and tunnel workshop, **flaw** detection workshop, and **comprehensive** machine repair workshop.

The **track workshop** is responsible for the daily maintenance and repair of railway tracks and related equipment, as well as **patrolling** the railway and guarding **railway crossings**. The **bridge and tunnel workshop** handles the maintenance and repair of bridges, tunnels, and **culverts**. The **flaw detection workshop** conducts **non-destructive testing** and maintenance of railway tracks. The **comprehensive machine repair workshop** is in charge of **machine tool** maintenance, parts repair, and **auxiliary processing**.

All the work requires the workers to be hardworking and skillful. They also need to have a high level of **safety awareness** and **team spirit**, strictly **abide by** regulations, and closely cooperate with other departments to ensure the smooth operation of the railway.

Task 2.1 Complete the following mind map.

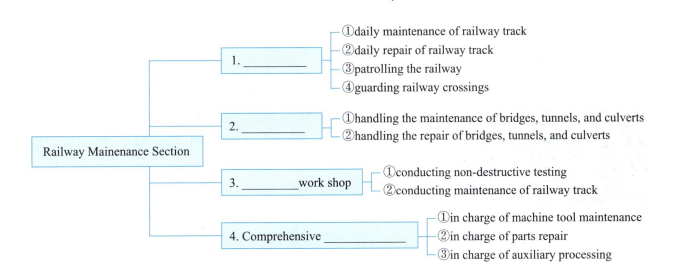

Task 3　Vocabulary Study 学行业词汇

Task Description: Learn the industry vocabulary, complete the following exercises, and master the English expression of the terms related to railway maintenance section.

任务描述:学习行业词汇,完成练习,掌握铁路工务段相关术语的英文表达。

1. rail flaw detector

The **rail flaw detector** is an instrument used to detect internal flaws or tiny surface cracks in rails, especially those covered by **fishplates**.

2. existing line

The **existing line** refers to the railway line that has been constructed and put into operation. A railway line is usually referred to as an existing line when it needs to be modified or upgraded.

3. steel rail material

The **steel rail material** refers to the original rail material that has not been welded. The flaw detection on the steel rail material mainly focuses on the defects of the rail itself.

4. flaw detection data replay

The **flaw detection data replay** is an important step to ensure railway safety. It involves detailed analysis of detection data to identify and prevent potential rail defects.

Task 3.1 Match the words or phrases with the definitions.

1. _____ track workshop   5. _____ existing line
2. _____ rail flaw detector   6. _____ steel rail material
3. _____ bridge and tunnel workshop   7. _____ comprehensive machine repair workshop
4. _____ flaw detection workshop   8. _____ flow detection data replay

A. railway lines that have been constructed and put into in operation
B. an instrument to detect flaws and cracks in rails
C. the original non-welded rail material
D. analyzing detection data to identify and prevent rail defects
E. a workshop for inspecting rail flaws
F. a work shop for the daily maintenance and repair of railway tracks etc.
G. a workshop for machine tool maintenance, parts repair etc.
H. a workshop for maintenance and repair of bridges, tunnels, and culverts

Word Bank

New Words

safeguard /ˈseɪfɡɑːd/ n. 保护措施；
　　　　　　　　　　 v. 保护，护卫
maintenance /ˈmeɪntənəns/ n. 维护，保养
grassroots /ˈɡrɑːsruːts/ adj. 基层的
undertake /ˌʌndəˈteɪk/ v. 承担，从事
tunnel /ˈtʌnl/ n. 隧道
workshop /ˈwɜːkʃɒp/ n. 车间
flaw /flɔː/ n. 缺点，缺陷
comprehensive /ˌkɒmprɪˈhensɪv/ adj.
　　综合性的，全面的
patrol /pəˈtrəʊl/ n. 巡逻，巡查

culvert /ˈkʌlvət/ n. 涵洞
non-destructive adj. 无损的
auxiliary /ɔːɡˈzɪliəri/ adj. 辅助的
fishplate /ˈfɪʃpleɪt/ n. 鱼尾板
guardian /ˈɡɑːdiən/ n. 守卫者，保护者
subgrade /ˈsʌbˌɡreɪd/ n. 路基；地基
turnout /ˈtɜːnaʊt/ n. 道岔
tie /taɪ/ n. 轨枕
ultrasound /ˈʌltrəsaʊnd/ n. 超声，超声波
woodpecker /ˈwʊdpekə/ n. 啄木鸟
spot /spɒt/ n. 地点，场所

Phrases & Expressions

star-chaser
　　星光赶路人（此处指铁路维护工人）
grassroots unit　基层单位
track workshop　线路车间
railway crossing　铁路道口
bridge and tunnel workshop　桥隧车间

flaw detection workshop　探伤车间
non-destructive testing　无损检测
comprehensive machine repair workshop
　　综合修车间
machine tool　机具
auxiliary processing　辅助加工

safety awareness 安全意识	safety helmet 安全帽
team spirit 团队精神	track worker 线路工
abide by 遵守	flaw detection worker 探伤工
rail flaw detector 钢轨探伤仪	bridge and tunnel worker 桥隧工
existing line 既有线	subgrade worker 路基工
steel rail material 钢轨母材	primary doctor 主治医生
flaw detection data replay 探伤数据回放	manual inspection 手动检查
	recruitment advertisement 招聘广告

Task 4　Passage Study 习情境案例

Task Description: Read the article, complete the following exercises, and learn about how the diverse roles in railway maintenance section guard the rail lines.

任务描述：读懂文章，完成练习，了解铁路工务段各岗位人员如何守护铁路线。

Guardians on the Railway Line

When we take the train, we often see some yellow figures wearing orange and yellow vests and **safety helmet**s. They carefully inspect and repair the tracks, ensuring our safe journey with their hard work. They are the maintenance workers, also known as the guardians of the railway.

Railway maintenance workers mainly include **track worker**s, **flaw detection worker**s, **bridge and tunnel worker**s, and **subgrade worker**s.

Railway track workers are called the **primary doctor**s of the railway line. They are mainly responsible for maintaining the tracks. During track inspections, track workers must carefully check **turnout**s, rails, railroad **tie**s, and other equipment. They also need to make maintenance and repair plans, and shoulder the tasks of preventing and addressing track defects.

Flaw detection workers are known as the **ultrasound** doctors of the railway. They are responsible for detecting rail damage. Rail flaw detectors combined with **manual inspection** are employed to check for flaws in rails and connections, inspecting every inch of the rail thoroughly.

Bridge and tunnel workers are the **woodpecker**s of tunnels and bridges. In long, dark tunnels and on high bridges, they need to carefully inspect every corner of bridge and tunnel equipment, leaving no blind **spot**s.

Subgrade workers are called the guardians of the railway subgrade. They are responsible for inspecting and patrolling the railway subgrade to prevent and solve subgrade diseases timely.

No matter how cold or hot it is, railway maintenance workers stay at their posts, protecting the railway from any damage and disease. They dedicate their youth to the railway, demonstrating their strong sense of responsibility and commitment through their sweat.

Task 4.1   Read the passage. Then, choose the correct answers.

1. What is the main idea of the passage?
   A. The importance of regular train travel for commuters.
   B. The challenges faced by railway engineers in designing new tracks.
   C. The dedication and responsibilities of railway maintenance workers in ensuring the safety of railway infrastructure.
   D. The various types of equipment used by railway workers for maintenance tasks.

2. Which of the following statements is TRUE about railway maintenance workers?
   A. They only work in spring and autumn.
   B. They don't need to work in extreme weather.
   C. They safeguard the railway's safety with their hard work.
   D. They don't have any responsibility.

3. What characteristic is emphasized about railway maintenance workers in the passage?
   A. They work only during good weather conditions.
   B. They have a weak sense of responsibility.
   C. They often change jobs frequently.
   D. They are dedicated and committed to their work, regardless of weather conditions.

Task 4.2   Read the sentence pairs. Fill in each blank with the best word or phrase.

1. flaw detection workers/railway track workers
   A. _____ maintain and repair the tracks to ensure smooth and safe train operations.
   B. _____ use specialized equipment to identify and locate defects in railway tracks and structures.

2. bridge and tunnel workers/subgrade workers
   A. _____ construct and maintain the foundation layer of a railway track, known as the subgrade.
   B. _____ maintain and repair bridges and tunnels to ensure safe passage for trains and other vehicles.

Task 5   Vocational Situation Experience 演职场情景

Task Description：Experience the situational conversation and complete the following exercises, so as to enhance English application ability related to professional positions.

任务描述：体验岗位情景会话，完成练习，提升与职业岗位相关的英语应用能力。

Task 5.1 Listen to the conversation, and fill in the blanks.

Situation description: A trainee is about to graduate. He is discussing a railway company's **recruitment advertisement** with his instructor to better understand the job requirements and whether he is suitable for the position.

Trainee: Hello, Mr. Wang. I saw that ABC Railway Company is recruiting. I am very interested in the track worker position. Do you think I'm suitable for this position?

Instructor: The 1. _____ _____ has a good prospect, but the technical requirements are high. Your educational background and major are well-matched with the job requirement. What about practical experience?

Trainee: I have taken up internships for track worker detection and 2. _____ _____ .

Instructor: Very good. By the way, are you ready for the intermediate track worker 3. _____ exam?

Trainee: Yes, I am sure to pass the exam next week.

Instructor: Great. There's one more important thing. You need to be in good health and able to 4. _____ _____ in the wildness or the remote area.

Trainee: Well, I am in sound health and 5. _____ _____ working in various environments.

Instructor: That's good. You are a strong candidate for this position.

Trainee: Thank you, Mr. Wang.

Task 5.2 Listen again and mark the statements as true(T) or false(F).

____ 1. Xiao Zhang will graduate this year, and he is interested in the bridge and tunnel worker position.

____ 2. Xiao Zhang has excellent academic performance and has participated in internships for track worker detection.

____ 3. A track worker should be healthy and can work in various environments.

Task 5.3 Act out the roles with a partner.

Task 6 Vocational Writing Practice 练职业写作

Task Description: Please use the given table as a reference, describe the work tasks of each position and the professional qualification certificates that can be obtained during school and after employment to better plan your career path.

任务描述：根据表格的内容，请描述各专业岗位的工作任务和在校期间与工作后可考取的职业资格证书，以便更好地规划个人职业发展和提升专业技能水平。

Typical Work Tasks of Entry-level Positions and Related Professional Qualification Certificates

Position	Tasks	Professional Qualification Certificates Obtainable During School	Professional Qualification Certificates Obtainable After Employment		
Track Worker	① Railway track: disease inspection and acceptance, maintenance, emergency duty ② Railway subgrade: disease inspection and acceptance, maintenance, patrolling	Intermediate Track Worker Certificate	Advanced Track Worker Certificate	Track Worker Technician Certificate	Track Worker Senior Technician Certificate
Bridge and Tunnel Worker	① Railway bridge and tunnel: maintenance and acceptance, emergency duty ② Railway bridge and tunnel equipment: disease inspection and acceptance, maintenance	Intermediate Bridge and Tunnel Worker Certificate	Advanced Bridge and Tunnel Worker Certificate	Bridge and Tunnel Worker Technician Certificate	Bridge and Tunnel Worker Senior Technician Certificate
Flaw Detection Worker	① Rail weld flaw detection ② Steel rail material flaw detection ③ Flaw detection data replay	Intermediate Flaw Detection Worker Certificate	Advanced Flaw Detection Worker Certificate	Flaw Detection Worker Technician Certificate	Flaw Detection Worker Senior Technician Certificate

Task 3 Topic Test 测章节知识

Task Description: Review this topic and complete the topic test to develop self-testing skills and summarizing study skills.

任务描述：复习本章节内容，完成章节测试，培养自我检测和总结归纳的能力。

◎ **Choose the correct answers.**

1. Which of the following workshops is NOT a part of the railway maintenance section?
   A. Track workshop.

   C. Electrical engineering workshop.
   D. Comprehensive machine repair workshop.

2. What is the main responsibility of the flaw detection workshop?

   B. Machine tool maintenance, parts repair, and auxiliary processing.

3. What are the main responsibilities of the track workshop?
   A. Inspecting and repairing tracks, formulating maintenance and repair plans.
   B. Detecting rail damage using ultrasound equipment.

   D. Inspecting and patrolling the railway subgrade.

4. What is the metaphor used to describe flaw detection workers in the passage?
   A. Primary doctors of the railway line.
   B. Ultrasound doctors of the railway.
   C. Woodpeckers of tunnels and bridges.

5. What is the purpose of the work done by subgrade workers?
   A. To detect rail damage using rail flaw detectors.
   B. To formulate maintenance and repair plans for tracks.
   C. To inspect and patrol the railway subgrade to prevent and address issues.
   D. To repair bridges and tunnels in long, dark tunnels.

◎ **Mark the following translations as true(T) or false(F).**

6. The railway maintenance section is a grassroots unit of the railway.
   译文：铁路工务段是铁路的一个机关单位。

7. They carefully inspect and repair the tracks, ensuring our safe journey with their hard work.

   译文：他们精心检修，用汗水保障着我们的安全之路。

8. Railway track workers are called the primary doctors of the railway line.

   译文：线路工被称为铁路线上的B超大夫。

9. Flaw detection workers are known as the ultrasound doctors of the railway.

   译文：探伤工被称为铁路上的主治大夫。

10. Bridge and tunnel workers are the woodpeckers of tunnels and bridges.

    译文：桥隧工是隧道与桥梁里的啄木鸟。

Task 9 Self-assessment 评学习效果

Task Description: Tick the items and self-assess learning outcomes.
任务描述：勾选选项，自我评估学习效果。

教学目标	评分项目
自主学习完善	☐Have a good habit of independent learning 有良好的自主学习习惯 ☐Be clear about learning objectives 明确学习目标 ☐Know about learning content 了解学习内容 ☐Complete learning tasks effectively 有效完成学习任务 ☐Finish the section test consciously 自主进行知识检测
语言思维提升	Master the pronunciation, spelling, definition, and simple usage of the following vocabulary： 掌握下列词汇的发音、拼写、释义及简单应用： ☐maintenance ☐undertake ☐workshop ☐tunnel ☐flaw ☐comprehensive ☐patrol ☐culvert ☐auxiliary ☐arduous ☐culvert ☐guardian ☐subgrade ☐spot ☐turnout ☐tie Be able to read and understand articles related to this topic and talk about them in English： 能读懂与本主题相关的文章并用英语简单介绍： ☐The main workshops of railway maintenance section 　铁路工务段的主要车间 ☐The duties of each position 　工务段每个职位的职责 ☐The professional qualification certificates of each position 　各岗位的职业资格证书
职场涉外沟通	☐Be able to understand workplace situational conversations related to this topic 　能听懂与本主题相关的职场情境对话 ☐Be able to simulate workplace situational conversations related to this topic with a partner 　能与搭档一起模拟本主题相关的职场情境对话 ☐Be able to introduce the given theme in written form 　能用英语完成主题相关的书面表达
多元文化交流	☐Be able to work in groups to tell the story of China railway role models in English 　能小组合作用英语讲述本主题相关的中国铁路榜样故事

Topic 2　Railway Subgrade—Solid Foundation
主题二　铁路路基——坚如磐石

Task ❶　Learning Objectives 明学习目标

Task Description: Get to know the learning content and clarify learning objectives.
任务描述：了解学习内容，明确学习目标。

知识目标：掌握与"铁路路基"主题相关的行业英语词汇

技能目标：
1. 能读懂与本主题相关的文章
2. 能听懂与本主题相关的职场情景对话
3. 能模拟表演职场情景对话，能用英语讲述中国铁路榜样故事
4. 能用英语完成与主题相关的书面表达

素质目标：了解"最美铁路人"铁路守护者黄伟的榜样故事，学习他的敬业精神、专注精神、创新精神以及奉献精神，在未来岗位上对工作热爱、敬业，不断追求更高的目标

Railway Subgrade 铁路路基

- **学行业词汇**：passenger duty officer, passenger clerk, ticket clerk, train conductor, freight duty officer, freight clerk, station dispatcher, shunting master, coupler, etc.

- **习情境案例**：《强化路基维护：排水与防护并重》
  1. 不同的路基横断面形
  2. 铁路路基的排水与防护
  3. 铁路路基的常见病害与维护措施

- **体验职场情景**：
  - 行业情景会话听说
  - 行业情景会话展示
  - 职业英语写作训练

- **讲中国铁路榜样故事**：

最美铁路人　黄伟
"铁路守护者"

Task 2　Lead in 导主题内容

Task Description: Watch the video, complete the following exercises and learn about the different kinds of subgrade.

任务描述：观看视频，完成练习，了解不同类型的铁路路基。

The speed of high-speed trains depends on track smoothness. The **subgrade**, which serves as the **foundation** of the track, **bear**s the weight and absorbs the impact of passing trains. The quality of the **subgrade** directly affects the overall quality and safety of the railway. Therefore, it must be solid and stable enough to withstand heavy pressures and to ensure safe and smooth railway operations.

Let's get to know the railway subgrade.

To ensure the smoothness of the tracks, railway subgrades are constructed in various ways based on the **terrain** features: when the natural ground is lower than the design **elevation** of the subgrade, filling operations are carried out to form an **embankment**; when the natural ground is higher than the design elevation, **excavation** is performed to form a **cutting**. Additionally, according to different terrain conditions, subgrades also use **semi-embankment**, semi-cutting, half embankment and half cutting, and non-excavation and non-filling forms to **adapt to** the environment and ensure the stability and safety of the railway line.

Task 2.1　Write down the English version of the following terms.

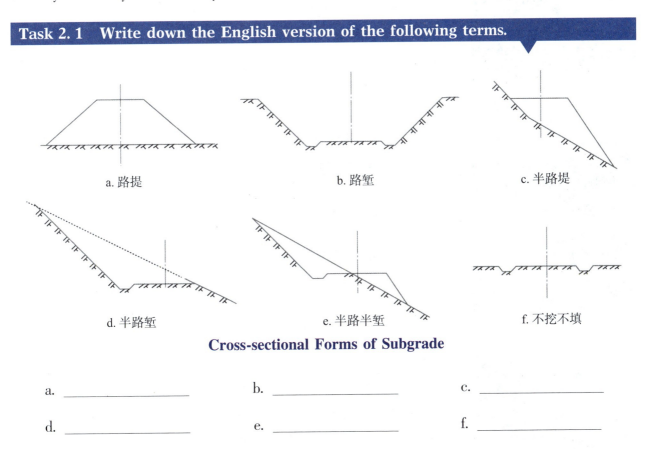

a. 路提　　　　　　　　b. 路堑　　　　　　　　c. 半路堤

d. 半路堑　　　　　　　e. 半路半堑　　　　　　f. 不挖不填

Cross-sectional Forms of Subgrade

a. _____　　b. _____　　c. _____

d. _____　　e. _____　　f. _____

Task 3 Vocabulary Study 学行业词汇

Task Description: Learn the industry vocabulary, complete the following exercises, and master the English expression of titles and responsibilities of posts in railway transportation organization and management.

任务描述:学习行业词汇,完成练习,掌握铁路运输组织与管理各岗位名称及其职责的英文表达。

1. embankment

The **embankment** is the subgrade built by filling with earth and stone materials when the subgrade surface for laying track is higher than the natural ground.

2. cutting

The **cutting** is a subgrade formed by excavation from the ground when the subgrade surface is lower than the natural ground.

3. retaining wall

The **retaining wall** is a structure built on both sides of the line to stabilize the **slope**.

4. drainage ditch

The **drainage ditch** is an open ditch located outside the slope of the embankment, designed to drain the surface water and slope water.

5. side ditch

The **side ditch** is an open ditch close to the shoulder of the cutting to drain water from the subgrade surface and cutting slope.

6. intercepting ditch

The **intercepting ditch** is an open ditch located on the slope platform to intercept and drain water from the upper slope.

7. slope protection

The **slope protection** is a slope engineering built to prevent the subgrade slope from weathering, peeling, sliding, and erosion.

Task 3.1 Match the words or phrases with the definitions.

1. _____ embankment
2. _____ intercepting ditch
3. _____ cutting
4. _____ side ditch
5. _____ retaining wall
6. _____ drainage ditch
7. _____ subgrade
8. _____ slope protection

A. a trench to catch and redirect water
B. a wall that holds back soil or rock
C. a channel for carrying away water
D. a section of ground dug out for a road or railway
E. a raised earthwork
F. measures to prevent slope erosion or collapse
G. the base layer of a road or pavement
H. a ditch alongside a road for drainage

Word Bank

⊙ New Words

foundation /faʊnˈdeɪʃn/ n. 地基,基础
bear /beə/ v. 承担,担负
subgrade /ˈsʌbɡreɪd/ n. 路基
terrain /təˈreɪn/ n. 地形,地域
elevation /ˌelɪˈveɪʃn/ n. 高度,海拔
embankment /ɪmˈbæŋkmənt/ n. 堤岸,路堤
excavation /ˌekskəˈveɪʃn/ n. 挖掘,开挖
cutting /ˈkʌtɪŋ/ n. 路堑
slope /sləʊp/ n. 斜坡,倾斜
peel /piːl/ v. 剥落
slid /slaɪd/ v. 溜坍

erosion /ɪˈrəʊʒn/ n. 侵蚀,腐蚀
drainage /ˈdreɪnɪdʒ/ n. 排水,排水系统
reinforcement /ˌriːɪnˈfɔːsmənt/ n. 加固,加强物
transverse /ˈtrænzvɜːs/ adj. 横向的;横断的
camber /ˈkæmbə/ n. 路拱
longitudinal /ˌlɒŋɡɪˈtjuːdənl/ adj. 纵向的
collapse /kəˈlæpsɪz/ v. 倒塌,崩溃
slip /slɪp/ v. 滑动,滑倒;n. 滑动,滑倒
deformation /ˌdiːfɔːˈmeɪʃn/ n. 变形
crack /kræk/ n. 裂缝

landslide/ˈlændslaɪd/n. [地质]山崩，滑坡
geological/ˌdʒiːəˈlɒdʒɪkl/adj. 地质(学)的

hydrological/ˌhaɪdrəˈlɒdʒɪkəl/adj. 水文学的
monitor/ˈmɒnɪtə/v. 监视；监听

⊙ Phrases & Expressions

semi-embankment　半路堤
semi-cutting　半路堑
adapt to　适应
retaining wall　挡土墙
drainage ditch　排水沟
side ditch　侧沟
intercepting ditch　截水沟

slope protection　边坡防护
shield structure　遮挡建筑物
water accumulation　积水
meteorological department　气象部门
geological and hydrological conditions
　地质与水文条件
semi-annually　每半年一次

Task 4　Passage Study 习情境案例

Task Description: Read the article, complete the following exercises, and learn about the drainage and protection of subgrade.

任务描述：读懂文章，完成练习，了解铁路路基的排水与防护。

Strengthening Subgrade Maintenance: Focusing on Drainage and Protection

The railway line consists of tracks, subgrades, bridge and tunnel structures. The subgrade is the foundation of the tracks and a crucial part of the railway line. It is composed of the subgrade body (such as embankments and cuttings), subgrade **drainage** facilities, and protective **reinforcement** structures.

The solidity and stability of the subgrade are influenced by various factors, among which water damage is a significant one. Therefore, subgrade construction emphasizes drainage functions to maintain the dryness, solidity, and stability of the subgrade. A complete drainage system is installed on the subgrade. To drain surface water, **transverse** drainage is performed through **camber**. In addition, **longitudinal** drainage ditches, side ditches, and intercepting ditches are set up on both sides of the subgrade for effective water drainage. Besides, underground drainage equipment is used to intercept and lower the groundwater level to remove groundwater.

Protective structures such as slope protections and retaining walls are also part of the subgrade. Slope protections aim to prevent the subgrade slopes from weathering, peeling, slipping, and erosion. Common slope protection measures include plant protection, stone slope protection and so on. Additionally, retaining walls or other **shielding structure**s can be set up to enhance protection.

Under the load of trains, the subgrade may suffer from slope **collapse**s, **slip**s, **deformation**s, and other damages due to various reasons. Therefore, subgrade workers need to regularly patrol, maintain, and repair subgrade drainage facilities and protective reinforcement equipment.

Task 4.1 Read the passage. Then, choose the correct answers.

1. Which of the following is NOT a type of slope protection measure mentioned in the passage?
   A. Plant protection.
   B. Stone slope protection.
   C. Concrete sleeper.
   D. Retaining walls.

2. What is the purpose of setting up underground drainage equipment in subgrade construction?
   A. To provide drinking water for railway workers.
   B. To prevent flooding of nearby communities.
   C. To intercept and lower the groundwater level.
   D. To create a scenic water feature.

3. What is the responsibility of subgrade workers in maintaining the subgrade?
   A. To repair the railway tracks.
   B. To repair broken bridges and tunnels.
   C. To regularly patrol, maintain, and repair subgrade drainage facilities and protective reinforcement equipment.
   D. To manage train schedules.

Task 4.2 Read the sentence pairs. Fill in each blank with the best word or phrase.

1. embankment/cutting
   A. An _____ is a raised area of land, often used to support a road or railway.
   B. _____ is a section of a road or railway dug into the side of a hill or mountain.

2. retaining wall/drainage ditches
   A. Regular maintenance of railway _____ is essential to ensure safe train operations during rainy seasons.
   B. To prevent landslides, engineers built a high _____ along the edge of the cliff.

  Task 5 Vocational Situation Experience 演职场情景

Task Description: Experience the situational conversation and complete the following exercises, so as to enhance English application ability related to professional positions.

任务描述：体验岗位情景会话，完成练习，提升与职业岗位相关的英语应用能力。

Task 5.1 Listen to the conversation, and fill in the blanks.

Situation description: A trainee follows his instructor to inspect the railway, learning how to deal with subgrade issues.

Trainee: Xiao Zhang, the rainy season is coming, and the number of subgrade problems is increasing. What should we do?

Instructor: We need to strengthen 1. _____ _____ of the subgrade.

Trainee: Right. Especially after rain, we must check promptly for **water accumulation**, erosion, or cracks.

Instructor: What should we do if we find 2. _____ _____?

Trainee: We need to develop a plan based on the specific issue. For water accumulation, clear ditches for drainage; for erosion, reinforce the slope; for cracks, investigate the cause and address it; for foundation issues, reinforce the subgrade.

Instructor: 3. _____ _____. Besides timely handling, what else can we do to prevent issues?

Trainee: Prevention is also crucial. Checking drainage, protecting slopes, reinforcing the subgrade, and 4. _____ _____ _____ with the **meteorological department** to respond promptly to weather conditions.

Instructor: Thank you, Mr. Wang. I'll remember this and hope the subgrade remains stable through the rainy season.

Trainee: You're welcome, Xiao Zhang. With proper prevention and timely handling, the subgrade will remain 5. _____ _____ _____.

Task 5.2 Listen again and mark the statements as true(T) or false(F).

____ 1. Xiao Zhang mentions that the number of subgrade problems decreases during the rainy season.

____ 2. Mr. Wang suggests strengthening daily inspections of the subgrade.

____ 3. The instructor is unsure of what actions to take if erosion is found on the subgrade.

Task 5.3 Act out the roles with a partner.

Task 6 Vocational Writing Practice 练职业写作

Task Description: Describe common subgrade issues and main remediation measures based on the table, to better understand emergency handling of subgrade issues and ensure the safety and stability of railway operations.

任务描述：根据表格内容描述路基常见病害及主要整治措施，以便更好地掌握路基病害应急处理知识，保障铁路的运行安全与稳定。

Common Subgrade Issues and Maintenance Measures Table

Issue Type	Maintenance Measures	Execution Frequency
Subgrade Settlement	① Strengthen foundation treatment ② Regular inspection and repair ③ Enhance drainage	Quarterly/As needed
Slope Collapse	① Build reinforcing structures ② Drainage and vegetation protection ③ Regular inspections	Monthly/Intensify during rainy season
Landslide	① Reinforce the hillside ② Maintain drainage system ③ Monitor stability ④ Adjust routes if necessary	Semi-annually/Intensify during rainy season
Poor Geological and Hydrological Conditions	① Avoid poor areas, reinforce treatment ② Develop emergency plans, enhance monitoring	Based on changing conditions

_____
_____
_____
_____
_____
_____

Module 3 Railway Engineering 铁道工程

Task 7　Telling Stories of China Railway 讲中国铁路故事

Task Description: Watch the story of railway role models and complete the following exercises to develop the awareness and ability to tell stories of China Railway in English.

任务描述：观看铁路榜样故事，完成练习，培养用英语讲述中国铁路故事的意识和能力。

7.1　What challenges did Huang Wei and his colleagues face during the flood in Lueyang in July 2018?

_____
_____
_____
_____
_____
_____
_____
_____

7.2　What did Huang Wei demonstrate in the face of the disaster, and what was his reaction to the severity of the retaining wall cracks?

_____
_____
_____
_____
_____
_____
_____
_____

Task 8 Topic Test 测章节知识

Task Description: Review this topic and complete the topic test to develop self-testing skills and summarizing analysis skills.

任务描述：复习本章节内容，完成章节测试，培养自我检测和总结分析的能力。

◎ **Choose the correct answers.**

1. What is the foundation of a railway track?
   A. Bridge structures. B. Tunnel structures.
   C. Subgrade. D. Tracks themselves.

2. What is the primary factor that determines the speed of high-speed trains?
   A. The size of the train. B. The quality of the railway subgrade.
   C. The smoothness of the tracks. D. The number of passengers on board.

3. What is the primary function of the railway subgrade?
   A. To provide entertainment for passengers.
   B. To carry the weight and absorb the impact of passing trains.
   C. To generate electricity for the train's power system.
   D. To store water for the train's onboard facilities.

4. What is the main reason subgrade construction emphasizes drainage functions?
   A. To reduce noise.
   B. To increase speed.
   C. To maintain dryness, solidity, and stability.
   D. To improve aesthetics.

5. What are some common slope protection measures?
   A. Tunnel construction. B. Plant protection and stone slope protection.
   C. Train speed limits. D. Underground drainage equipment.

◎ **Mark the following translations as true (T) or false (F).**

6. The subgrade is the foundation of the track and a crucial part of the railway line.
   译文：路堑是轨道的基础，也是铁路线路的重要组成部分。

7. It consists of the subgrade body, subgrade drainage facilities, and protective reinforcement structures.
   译文：路基由路基本体、路基排水设备和防护加固建筑构成。

8. Subgrade construction emphasizes drainage functions to maintain the dryness, solidity, and stability of the subgrade.
   译文：路基构造强调排水功能，以维持铁路的干燥、坚固与安全。

9. Slope protections aim to prevent the subgrade slopes from weathering, peeling, slipping, and erosion.
   译文：护坡旨在防止路基边坡遭受风化、剥落、溜坍及冲刷。

10. Retaining walls or other shielding structures can be set up to enhance protection.
    译文：护坡或其他遮挡建筑物可以强化路基的防护。

Task 9 Self-assessment 评学习效果

Task Description: Tick the items and self-assess learning outcomes.
任务描述：勾选选项，自我评估学习效果。

教学目标	评分项目
自主学习完善	☐Have a good habit of independent learning 有良好的自主学习习惯 ☐Be clear about learning objectives 明确学习目标 ☐Learn about learning content 了解学习内容 ☐Complete learning tasks effectively 有效完成学习任务 ☐Finish the section test consciously 自主进行知识检测
语言思维提升	Master the pronunciation, spelling, definition, and simple usage of the following vocabulary: 掌握下列词汇的发音、拼写、释义及简单应用： ☐subgrade ☐embankment ☐cutting ☐executor ☐terrain ☐elevation ☐drainage ☐reinforcement ☐slope ☐erosion ☐collapses ☐slope protection ☐retaining wall ☐drainage ditch
	Be able to read and understand articles related to this topic and talk about them in English: 能读懂本主题相关文章并用英语简单介绍： ☐Different subgrade cross section form 　不同的路基横断面形 ☐Drainage and protection of railway roadbed 　铁路路基的排水与防护 ☐Common subgrade issues and maintenance measures 　铁路路基的常见病害与维护措施
职场涉外沟通	☐Be able to understand workplace situational conversations related to this topic 　能听懂本主题相关的职场情景对话 ☐Be able to simulate workplace situational conversations related to this topic with a partner 　能与搭档一起模拟本主题相关的职场情景对话 ☐Be able to introduce the given theme in written form 　能用英语完成主题相关的书面表达
多元文化交流	☐Be able to work in groups to tell the story of China railway role models in English 　能小组合作用英语讲述本主题相关的中国铁路榜样故事

Topic 3　Railway Track 1—Seamless Connectivity
主题三　铁路轨道1——无缝连接

Task 1　Learning Objectives 明学习目标

Task Description: Get to know the content and clarify learning objectives.
任务描述：了解学习内容，明确学习目标。

- 知识目标：掌握与"铁路轨道"主题相关的行业英语词汇
- 技能目标：
  1. 能读懂与本主题相关的文章
  2. 能听懂与本主题相关的职场情景对话
  3. 能模拟表演职场情景对话，能用英语讲述中国铁路榜样故事
  4. 能用英语完成与主题相关的书面表达
- 素质目标：了解"京铁工匠"线路工王新春的榜样故事，学习他热爱工作，敬业奉献，专注创新的铁路精神，在未来岗位上不断追求更高的目标

Railway Track1 铁路轨道1

- 学行业词汇：ballastless track, turnout, switch, switch rail, switch machine, frog, check rail, rail gap, track slab, track, ballast bed, sleeper, rail, rail joint fastener, reinforcement equipment, ballasted track, etc.
- 习情境案例：《铁路轨道，铸就平顺线路》
  1. 铁路轨道的组成部件名称
  2. 铁路轨道各部件的功能
  3. 线路工岗位的工作职责与工作态度
- 体验职场情景：
  - 行业情景会话听说
  - 行业情景会话展示
  - 职业英语写作训练
- 讲中国铁路榜样故事

"京铁工匠" 王新春
铁路养护维修"守护者"

Task ❷ Lead in 导主题内容

Task Description: Watch the video, complete the following exercises and learn about the English expressions for the main components of railway turnout.

任务描述：观看视频，完成练习，了解铁路道岔主要部件的英文表达。

Unlike cars and ships, trains do not have **steering wheel**s. So how does a train change **track**s on complex railway lines?

The special railway equipment can help trains change their tracks, which is called a **turnout**. A common **single turnout** is composed of a **switch**, a **frog**, **check rails**, and connecting parts, enabling the **rolling stock** to transfer from one track to another. The switch is the key equipment of turnout, including two **switch rail**s, two **stock rail**s and a **switch machine**. Operating switch machine can change the position of switch rails, and determine the opening direction of turnout. In this way, the train can move from **straight track** to **diverging track**, or from diverging track to straight track.

Task 2.1 Write down the English expressions of components of a common single turnout in the picture.

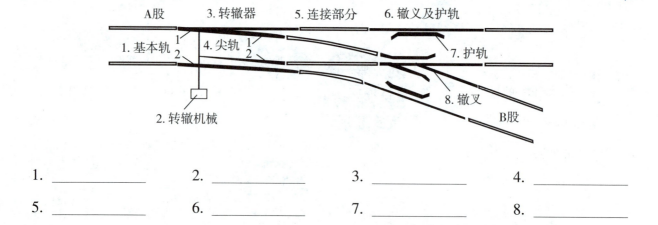

1. _____ 2. _____ 3. _____ 4. _____
5. _____ 6. _____ 7. _____ 8. _____

Task ❸ Vocabulary Study 学行业词汇

Task Description: Learn the industry vocabulary, complete the following exercises, and master the English expression and function of main components of railway track.

任务描述：学习行业词汇，完成练习，掌握铁路轨道的组成名称及其功能的英文表达。

1. track

The **track** is a component of the railway line. It is above the **formation** and below the **rail** and is used to guide the operation of trains.

2. turnout

The **turnout** is a connection device of line that enables the rolling stock to move from one track to another.

3. switch rail

The **switch rail** is the movable part in a turnout that guides the train onto the desired track.

4. switch machine

The **switch machine** is an **electric mechanical equipment** used to move the switch rail in a turnout.

5. frog

The **frog** is the crossing device in a turnout that allows the train wheels to change from one track to another.

6. check rail

The **check rail** is a rail located inside the running rail in a turnout, **serves to** prevent train wheels from **derail**ing.

🎧 7. ballast bed

The **ballast bed** is a **layer** below sleeper and above the formation. The **ballasted track** is **laid** with **graded gravel**(**ballast**), while **ballastless track** use **track slab**s made of **concrete** or **asphalt** materials(**monolithic bed**).

🎧 8. sleeper

The **sleeper** is a component that supports **rail**. According to the different materials, it can be classified into **wooden sleeper** and **concrete sleeper**.

🎧 9. rail

The **rail** is a component of track, which can directly bear huge pressure of wheels and guide the running direction of the wheels.

🎧 10. rail joint fasteners

The **rail joint fasteners** refer to the joint components used to connect rails, including **fishplate**, **bolt**, **nut**, and so on.

🎧 11. rail gap

The **rail gap** is the gap left at the rail **joint**s to allow for the free **expansion** and **contraction** of the rail with temperature changes.

🎧 12. creep of track

Due to the longitudinal force during train operation, the rail will experience longitudinal movement, which is known as **creep of track**.

🎧 13. reinforcement equipment

The **reinforcement equipment** is the component used to reinforce **weak points** of the track.

🎧 14. ballasted track

The **ballasted track** is a track structure with the ballast bed of graded gravel(ballast).

🎧 **15. ballastless track**

The **ballastless track** is a track structure laid with track slabs made of concrete or asphalt material.

Task 3.1 Match the words or phrases with the definitions.

1. _____ sleeper
2. _____ switch rail
3. _____ creep of track
4. _____ rail gap
5. _____ turnout
6. _____ ballastless track
7. _____ frog
8. _____ switch machine

A. a connection device of railway line that enables the rolling stock to move from one track to another.

B. a component which supports rail

C. the movable part in a turnout that guides the train onto the desired track

D. crossing device in a turnout that allows the train wheels to change from one track to another

E. the longitudinal movement of the rail as a result of the longitudinal force during train operation

F. the gap left at the rail joints to allow for the free expansion and contraction of the rail with temperature changes

G. an electric mechanical equipment used to move the switch rail in a turnout

H. a track structure laid with track slabs made of concrete or asphalt material

Word Bank

⊙ New Words

track /træk/ n. 轨道
turnout /ˈtɜːnaʊt/ n. 道岔
switch /swɪtʃ/ n. 转辙器
frog /frɒg/ n. 辙叉
formation /fɔːˈmeɪʃn/ n. 路基面
electric /ɪˈlektrɪk/ adj. 电子的
mechanical /məˈkænɪkl/ adj. 机械的
derail /diːˈreɪl/ v. (使)脱轨，出轨

layer /ˈleɪə/ n. 层，垫层
lay /leɪ/ v. 铺设、安装
ballast /ˈbæləst/ n. 道砟
concrete /ˈkɒŋkriːt/ n. 混凝土
asphalt /ˈæsfælt/ n. 沥青
sleeper /ˈsliːpə/ n. 轨枕
rail /reɪl/ n. 钢轨
fishplate /ˈfɪʃˌpleɪt/ n. 夹板，鱼尾板

bolt /bəʊlt/ n. 螺栓
nut /nʌt/ n. 螺母
joint /dʒɔɪnt/ n. 接合处、接缝
expansion /ɪkˈspænʃn/ n. 扩大；膨胀
contraction /kənˈtrækʃn/ n. 收缩，缩小
reinforcement /ˌriːɪnˈfɔːsmənt/ n. 加强，加固
constitute /ˈkɒnstɪtjuːt/ v. 构成
integral /ˈɪntɪɡrəl/ adj. 完整的
gauge /ɡeɪdʒ/ n. 轨距
transfer /trænsˈfɜː/ v. (使)转移
fastener /ˈfɑːsnə/ n. 扣件(中间连接零件)

secure /sɪˈkjʊə/ v. 固定
maintenance /ˈmeɪntənəns/ n. 维护，保养
promptly /ˈprɒmptli/ adv. 迅速地；立即
geological /ˌdʒiːəˈlɒdʒɪkl/ adj. 地质的，地质学的
terrain /təˈreɪn/ n. 地形，地势
steep /stiːp/ adj. (路、山等)陡峭的
slope /sləʊp/ n. 斜坡，坡度
vibration /vaɪˈbreɪʃn/ n. 震动，颤动
elasticity /ˌiːlæˈstɪsəti/ n. 弹性，灵活性
lifespan /ˈlaɪfspæn/ n. 寿命；使用期
workload /ˈwɜːkləʊd/ n. 工作量，工作负荷

⊙ Phrases & Expressions

steering wheel　方向盘
single turnout　单开道岔
check rail　护轨
rolling stock　车辆
switch machine　转辙机
switch rail　尖轨
stock rail　基本轨
straight track　直轨，直股
diverging track　弯轨，曲股
electric mechanical equipment　电动机械设备
serve to...　起到……的作用，用于……
ballast bed　道床
graded gravel　级配碎石
ballasted track　有砟轨道
track slab　轨道板
ballastless track　无砟轨道

monolithic bed　整体道床
wooden sleeper　木质轨枕
concrete sleeper　混凝土轨枕
rail joint fasteners　接头连接零件
rail gap　轨缝
creep of track　轨道爬行
reinforcement equipment　加强设备
anti-creeper　防爬器
anti-creeping strut　防爬撑
I-beam steel rail　工字形钢轨
rail head　轨头
rail web　轨腰
rail base　轨底
track worker　线路工
track defect　轨道病害
water permeability　透水性

Task 4　Passage Study 习情境案例

Task Description: Read the article, complete the following exercises, and learn about the basic components and functions of railway track, as well as the job responsibilities of track workers.

任务描述：读懂文章，完成练习，了解铁路轨道的基本构成及其功能和线路工岗位的工作职责。

Railway Track, Creating a Smooth Track

The track is an essential component of the railway line. It constitutes an integrated engineering structure, consisting of ballast bed, sleepers, rails, fastening parts, reinforcement equipment, and turnout.

Ballast bed is a layer laid on the formation. It is used to fix and support sleepers, prevent them from moving, **transmit** the pressure from the upper parts of the sleepers to the subgrade evenly, and maintain track stability.

Sleepers are laid on the ballast bed. The primary function is to support and fix the rails in place, maintain their direction and position, ensure the proper **gauge**, as well as **transfer** the pressure from the rails to the ballast bed.

Rails are on the top of the sleepers. The function of rails is to bear the huge pressure of the wheels and guide the train's moving direction. Rail typically use I-beam steel rail, consisting of the **rail head**, **rail web**, and **rail base**.

Fastening parts connect rail to sleeper, which are classified into two types: **fasteners** and rail joint fasteners. Fasteners secure the rail to the sleeper, to ensure the rail in the correct position. Rail joint fasteners are used to connect the joints between rails. In conventional railway, the joints between rails must maintain a specific gap, known as a rail gap. Rail joint is one of the three weak points in the track and it is a key object for track maintenance task.

Reinforcement equipment can prevent creep of track and ensure the stability of track structure. This equipment includes anti-creeper and anti-creeping strut.

Turnout is a connection device of line that enables rolling stock to move from one track to another.

The railway **track worker** is responsible for inspecting and **maintain**ing the track, **promptly** finding **track defect**s to prevent accidents and to ensure safe and smooth train operation.

Task 4.1　Read the passage. Then, choose the correct answers.

1. What is the main purpose of the article?
   A. Describe the components and functions of a railway track system.
   B. Compare different types of railway tracks and their advantages.
   C. Advocate for the use of modern track reinforcement equipment.
   D. Warn about potential safety hazards associated with railway tracks.

2. What is the function of reinforcement equipment in a railway track?

   A. To connect the joints between rails.

   B. To support the rail and fix it in place.

   C. To prevent track creeping and ensure the stability of the track structure.

   D. To enable rolling stock to move from one track to another.

3. What is the responsibility of the track worker?

   A. To design new railway tracks.

   B. To inspect and maintain the track, and promptly find track defects.

   C. To operate the trains.

   D. To build new turnouts.

Task 4.2　Read the sentence pairs. Fill in each blank with the best word or phrase.

1. sleeper/track

   A. A _____ can support the rails.

   B. The _____ is an essential component of the railway line.

2. turnout/ballastless track

   A. The _____ is used in the construction of high-speed railway lines.

   B. The _____ is crucial for directing trains onto different tracks.

Task 5　Vocational Situation Experience 演职场情景

Task Description: Experience the situational conversation and complete the following exercises, so as to enhance English application ability related to professional positions.

任务描述：体验岗位情景会话，完成练习，提升与职业岗位相关的英语应用能力。

Task 5.1　Listen to the conversation, and fill in the blanks.

Situation description: A trainee is consulting instructor about the two type of tracks, ballasted track and ballastless track, and their differences.

Instructor: Xiao Zhang, we're standing on a standard ballasted track. Do you know the differences between ballasted track and ballastless track used in high-speed railway?

Trainee: Of course, Mr. Wang. Beneath the ballasted tracks is paved with 1._____ _____, while there's no gravel in 2._____ _____.

Instructor: Yes, the gravel can spread the pressure generated when the train passes, especially suitable for areas with complex **geological** conditions or

156　铁路行业英语

Trainee: **variable terrain.** It's also easier to be constructed and maintained.

Trainee: I remember that the Y-shaped railway designed by Mr. Zhan Tianyou also used 3. _____ _____, successfully solved the difficulties of **steep slope** and complex terrain.

Instructor: That's correct. Mr. Zhan Tianyou's design is really admirable. However, with the development of technology, ballastless track is gradually being used for high-speed railway.

Trainee: Instead of graded gravel beneath the track, ballastless track uses 4. _____ _____ made of concrete or asphalt materials.

Instructor: Yes. This design can greatly improve the smoothness and precision of the track, and reduces the 5. _____ _____ _____ during the operation of the train.

Trainee: I see. It seems that with the development of technology, railway construction is also making progress continuously!

Task 5.2   Listen again and mark the statements as true(T) or false(F).

_____ 1. Ballasted tracks and ballastless tracks both use graded gravel beneath the track.

_____ 2. The Y-shaped railway designed by Mr. Zhan Tianyou overcame steep slopes and complex terrain by using ballastless tracks.

_____ 3. Ballasted track is made of concrete or asphalt materials and is designed to enhance track smoothness, precision, and reduce noise and vibration during the operation of the train.

Task 5.3   Act out the roles with a partner.

Task 6 Vocational Writing Practice 练职业写作

Task Description: Refer to the following table, describe the characteristics, advantages and disadvantages of ballasted track and ballastless track.

任务描述：参考下列表格信息，阐述有砟轨道与无砟轨道各自的特点、优点及不足。

Characteristics, Advantages and Disadvantages of Ballasted Track and Ballastless Track

Type	Characteristics	Advantages	Disadvantages
Ballasted Track	① Laid with graded gravel (ballast) ② Include rails, sleepers, ballast bed, fastening parts, etc.	① Good **elasticity** ② Shock absorption, noise reduction, **water permeability** ③ High load-bearing capacity ④ Easy to pave and low cost ⑤ Easy to replace and adjust	① Ballast wearing or missing, affecting track elasticity and rail support ② Heave maintenance **workload** ③ Not suitable for high-speed rail
Ballastless Track	① Use track slabs made of concrete or asphalt materials ② Includes rails, fasteners, track slabs, bases, etc.	① Good rigidity ② Stable structure ③ Reduced vibration and high ride comfort ④ Long **lifespan** and low maintenance workload	① High construction cost ② High technical requirements ③ Difficult to adjust once constructed

Task 7　Telling Stories of China Railway 讲中国铁路故事

Task Description：Watch the story of railway role models and complete the following exercises to develop the awareness and ability to tell stories of China Railway in English.

任务描述：观看铁路榜样故事,完成练习,培养用英语讲述中国铁路故事的意识和能力。

7.1　How did Wang Xinchun solve the deviation problem of turnout?

_____
_____
_____
_____
_____
_____
_____
_____
_____

7.2　Watch the video again and search online for more information about Wang Xinchun. Please introduce his major achievements and share the spiritual qualities you can learn from him. Work in small groups to tell the story of Wang Xinchun.

_____
_____
_____
_____
_____
_____
_____
_____
_____

Task 8 Topic Test 测章节知识

Task Description: Review this topic and complete the topic test to develop self-testing skills and summarizing analysis skills.

任务描述：复习本章节内容，完成章节测试，培养自我检测和总结分析能力。

◎ **Choose the correct answers.**

1. Which part of the railway track structure supports and fixes the rails, maintaining their direction and position?
    A. The ballast bed.   B. The sleepers.
    C. The rail connectors.   D. The turnouts.

2. What is the main function of the ballast bed in a railway track?
    A. To support the weight of the trains.
    B. To fix and support sleepers, prevent them from moving, and maintain track stability.
    C. To guide the direction of the trains.
    D. To connect the rail to the sleeper.

3. Which part of the railway track structure supports and fixes the rails, maintaining their direction and position?
    A. The ballast bed.   B. The sleepers.
    C. The turnout.   D. The fastening parts.

4. What is the term used to describe the gap maintained between rails at a joint?
    A. Rail gap.   B. Joint.   C. Sleep.   D. Gauge.

5. What is the primary purpose of fasteners in a railway track?
    A. To connect adjacent rails at the joints.
    B. To secure the rail to the sleeper and ensure its correct position.
    C. To prevent track creeping.
    D. To enable the track to withstand extreme weather conditions.

◎ **Mark the following translations as true(T) or false(F).**

6. Ballast bed is a layer laid on the formation.
   译文：道床是铺设在道砟上的垫层。

7. Rail typically use I-beam steel rail, consisting of the rail head, rail web, and rail base.
   译文：钢轨通常采用"工"字形钢轨，由轨头、轨腰和轨底组成。

8. Rail joint fasteners are used to connect the joints between rails.
   译文：扣件用来连接钢轨与钢轨之间的接头。

9. The function of rails is to bear the huge pressure of the wheels and guide the train's moving direction.
   译文：钢轨的功能是承受车轮的巨大压力并引导列车的行驶方向。

10. The track worker is responsible for inspecting and maintaining the track, promptly finding track defects.
    译文：铁路线路工负责检查和维护轨道，及时发现轨道病害。

Task 9 Self-assessment 评学习效果

Task Description: Tick the items and self-assess learning outcomes.
任务描述：勾选选项，自我评估学习效果。

教学目标	评分项目
自主学习完善	☐Have a good habit of independent learning 有良好的自主学习习惯 ☐Be clear about learning objectives 明确学习目标 ☐Know about learning content 了解学习内容 ☐Complete learning tasks effectively 有效完成学习任务 ☐Finish the section test consciously 自主进行知识检测
语言思维提升	Master the pronunciation, spelling, definition, and simple usage of the following vocabulary： 掌握下列词汇的发音、拼写、释义及简单应用： ☐track ☐ballast bed ☐sleeper ☐rail ☐rail joint fastener ☐reinforcement equipment ☐ballasted track ☐ballastless track ☐turnout ☐switch ☐switch rail ☐switch machine ☐frog ☐check rail ☐rail gap ☐track slab ☐gauge Be able to read and understand articles related to this topic and talk about them in English： 能读懂本主题相关文章并用英语简单介绍： ☐The name of railway track components 　铁路轨道的组成部件名称 ☐Function of each railway track component 　铁路轨道各部件的功能 ☐The job responsibilities and work attitude of track workers 　线路工岗位的工作职责与工作态度
职场涉外沟通	☐Be able to understand workplace situational conversations related to this topic 　能听懂本主题相关的职场情景对话 ☐Be able to simulate workplace situational conversations related to this topic with a partner 　能与搭档一起模拟本主题相关的职场情景对话 ☐Be able to introduce the given theme in written form 　能用英语完成主题相关的书面表达
多元文化交流	☐Be able to work in groups to tell the story of China railway role models in English 　能小组合作用英语讲述本主题相关的中国铁路榜样故事

Topic 4　Railway Track 2—Precise Maintenance
主题四　铁路轨道2——严检慎修

Task ❶　Learning Objectives 明学习目标

Task Description: Get to know the content and clarify learning objectives.
任务描述：了解学习内容，明确学习目标。

掌握与"铁路轨道"主题相关的行业英语词汇

知识目标

1. 能读懂与本主题相关的文章
2. 能听懂与本主题相关的职场情景对话
3. 能模拟表演职场情景对话，能用英语讲述中国铁路榜样故事
4. 能用英语完成与主题相关的书面表达

技能目标

了解"最美铁路人"钢轨神探黄涛的榜样故事，学习他的敬业精神、专注精神、创新精神以及奉献精神，在未来岗位上热爱工作，不断追求更高的目标。

素质目标

Railway Track 2 铁路轨道2

学行业词汇：continuous welded rail, rolling contact fatigue, crazing, shoulder damage, mud pumping, tongue lipping, grinding, alignment, clearing, maintenance gap, transverse fissure, etc.

习情境案例：《守护铁路安全：解析轨道病害》
1. 铁路轨道各部件的常见病害
2. 铁路轨道常见病害的主要整治措施
3. 探伤工岗位的工作职责与工作态度

体验职场情景：
行业情景会话听说
行业情景会话展示
职业英语写作训练

讲中国铁路榜样故事

最美铁路人　黄涛
"钢轨神探"

Task 2 Lead in 导主题内容

Task Description: Watch the video, complete the following exercises and learn about the English expressions of the remarkable characteristics of ballastless track and continuous welded rail.

任务描述：观看视频，完成练习，了解无砟轨道和无缝钢轨的显著特点的英文表达。

The high-speed train runs rapidly but a coin stands still. It **benefits from** the "double-no" design, namely ballastless track and **continuous welded rail**.

Compared to ballasted tracks, ballastless tracks avoid the "**splattering**" of ballast, providing better smoothness and **stability**, thus ensuring the fast and smooth operation of high-speed trains. Unlike **conventional** tracks with **joints** every 25 meters, high-speed train rails have no obvious joints and can extend for several kilometers or even hundreds of kilometers. This type of rail allows high-speed trains to run at extremely high speed without **bump** and noise.

Certainly, the smooth operation of high-speed train also **depends on** the daily **meticulous** and careful track inspection, maintenance, and repair work carried out by our railway track workers. From ballasted tracks to ballastless tracks, and from jointed rails to continuous welded rails, these represent a technological **leap** in China's railway tracks, and a powerful **demonstration** of China's speed.

Task 2.1 Choose appropriate expressions to describe the following pictures.

| ballastless track | continuous welded rail |
| ballasted track | jointed rail |

1. _____
2. _____
3. _____
4. _____

Task 3 Vocabulary Study 学行业词汇

Task Description: Learn the industry vocabulary, complete the following exercises, and learn about the English names of common track defects and corrective measures.

任务描述：学习行业词汇，完成练习，掌握铁路轨道常见病害及整治措施的英文表达。

1. continuous welded rail

The **continuous welded rail**（**CWR**）, also known as jointless rail or seamless rail, refers to a long and jointless rail which is formed by welding standard-length rails.

2. rolling contact fatigue

The **rolling contact fatigue** is a damage, which appears on the surface or inside of rails. It is caused by repeated contact between rails and wheels, as well as the heavy pressure from trains.

3. crazing

The **crazing** refers to fine cracks on the surface of railroad ties. It generally appears at the end and middle parts of sleepers.

4. shoulder damage

The **shoulder damage** is a damage to the shoulders of railroad ties. It is caused by damaged pads or horizontal pressure from fasteners.

5. mud pumping

The **mud pumping** is one of the common track defects. It means that the clayey soil in the railway subgrade is **diluted** into **slurry** by water, and the slurry is **squeezed** upwards through the ballast. This situation indicates that the ballast bed is dirty and the drainage is poor.

6. tongue lipping

The **tongue lipping** is one of the common rail defects. It is the **extrusion** towards both sides of rail surface caused by stress, often accompanied by flaking of the rail.

🎧 7. grinding

The **grinding** is one of the track maintenance tasks. It refers to grind the rail surface to remove the damage on the rail surface and **restore** the rail to its original shape.

🎧 8. alignment

The **alignment** refers to the task of adjusting the gauge and the rate of gauge change to specified standards.

🎧 9. clearing

The **clearing** is one of the track maintenance tasks. It means to remove debris, dust, sand, and fine particles such as coal ash from the ballast to keep it clean.

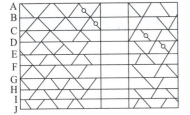

🎧 10. maintenance gap

The **maintenance gap** refers to a particular period reserved for construction and maintenance operation when the train is not in operation.

🎧 11. rail lifting

The **rail lifting** is the operation of raising the rail along with the railroad ties to a certain height.

🎧 12. tamping

The **tamping** is the operation of compacting the ballast under the railroad ties to enhance the stability of tracks.

🎧 13. lining

The **lining** refers to the process of moving the rail to restore it to its correct position when it has shown **abnormality**, such as irregular bending.

Module 3　Railway Engineering　铁道工程　165

Task 3.1 Match the words or phrases with the definitions.

1. _____ rolling contact fatigue
2. _____ shoulder damage
3. _____ grinding
4. _____ tongue lipping
5. _____ crazing
6. _____ mud pumping
7. _____ tamping
8. _____ rail lifting

A. a common track defect indicates that the ballast bed is dirty and the drainage is poor
B. a damage to the rail caused by repeated contact between rails and wheels
C. a common rail defect often accompanied by flaking of the rail
D. fine cracks on the surface of railroad ties
E. a damage to the shoulders caused by damaged pads or horizontal pressure from fasteners
F. raising the rail along with the railroad ties to a certain height
G. polishing the rail surface to remove the damage on the rail surface
H. compacting the ballast under the railroad ties

Word Bank

New Words

splatter /ˈsplætə/ v. 泼溅，溅落
stability /stəˈbɪləti/ n. 稳定(性)，稳固(性)
conventional /kənˈvenʃənl/ adj. 普通的，常规的
joint /dʒɔɪnt/ n. 接头，接缝
bump /bʌmp/ n. 颠簸，碰撞
meticulous /məˈtɪkjələs/ adj. 一丝不苟的，注意细节的
leap /liːp/ n. 跳跃，飞跃，激增
demonstration /ˌdemənˈstreɪʃn/ n. 证实，表达，演示
dilute /daɪˈluːt/ v. 稀释，冲淡
slurry /ˈslʌri/ n. 泥浆；悬浮液
squeeze /skwiːz/ v. 挤压，捏
extrusion /ɪkˈstruːʒn/ n. 挤出；喷出
restore /rɪˈstɔː/ v. 使复原，整修
abnormality /ˌæbnɔːˈmæləti/ n. 异常；畸形

defect /ˈdiːfekt/ n. 缺点，缺陷
address /əˈdres/ v. 处理，设法解决
emerge /ɪˈmɜːdʒ/ v. 浮现，出现，显露
susceptible /səˈseptəbl/ adj. 易受影响的，易得病的
fissure /ˈfɪʃə/ n. (细小)裂缝
corrosion /kəˈrəʊzn/ n. 腐蚀，侵蚀
poor /pʊə/ adj. 差的，不合理的
transverse /ˈtrænzvɜːs/ adj. 横向的；横断的
longitudinal /ˌlɒŋgɪˈtjuːdənl/ adj. 纵向的，纵观的
crack /kræk/ n. 裂缝，裂纹
crazing /ˈkreɪzɪŋ/ n. 破裂，龟裂
chipping /ˈtʃɪpɪŋ/ n. 剥落，碎石
dirtiness /ˈdɜːtinəs/ n. 肮脏；污秽
settlement /ˈsetlmənt/ n. 下沉，下陷
prone /prəʊn/ adj. 有……倾向的，易于……的

alignment /əˈlaɪnmənt/ n. 协调,一致,排成直线
hazard /ˈhæzəd/ n. 危险,危害,风险
corrective /kəˈrektɪv/ adj. 修正的,矫正的
eliminate /ɪˈlɪmɪneɪt/ v. 消除,排除,淘汰
grind /graɪnd/ v. 磨碎,打磨
clearing /ˈklɪərɪŋ/ n. 清除,清理
implement /ˈɪmplɪment/ v. 执行,贯彻

grinding /ˈgraɪndɪŋ/ n. 打磨,磨光
inject /ɪnˈdʒekt/ v. 注入;投入
grout /graʊt/ n. 水泥浆 v. 灌浆
replacement /rɪˈpleɪsmənt/ n. 代替,更换
insufficient /ˌɪnsəˈfɪʃnt/ adj. 不充分的,不够重要的
tamping /ˈtæmpɪŋ/ n. 捣固
lining /ˈlaɪnɪŋ/ n. 衬砌,拨道

⊙ Phrases & Expressions

benefit from… 从……中获得好处或利益
continuous welded rail 无缝线路,连续焊接钢轨
depend on 依赖,取决于……
be susceptible to 易受影响,易受伤害
rolling contact fatigue 滚动接触疲劳
transverse fissure 横裂缝
shoulder damage 挡肩破损
mud pumping 翻浆冒泥
weak point 薄弱环节

be prone to 倾向于,易于……
suffer from 遭受……
flaw detection worker 钢轨探伤工
flaw detector 钢轨探伤仪
manual inspection 人工检测
tongue lipping 肥边,毛刺
maintenance gap 天窗
keep…in mind 牢记,铭记……
rail lifting 起道
wear and tear 损耗,磨损

Task 4 Passage Study 习情境案例

Task Description: Read the article, complete the following exercises, and learn about the common track defects and corrective measures, as well as the job responsibilities and work attitude of flaw detection workers.

任务描述：读懂文章，完成练习，了解铁路轨道常见病害及整治措施和探伤工岗位的工作职责与工作态度。

Guarding Railway Safety: Analysis of Track Defects

Rails, sleepers, ballast beds, turnouts, fastening parts, and track reinforcement devices are the main components of railway tracks. These parts will produce various **defects** because of the effect of train travel and natural conditions. The track workers need to **address** them regularly. Do you understand these common track defects? Let's learn more about them.

Defect issues gradually **emerge** during the long-term use of facilities of railway track. The common defects mainly include the followings. Rails **are susceptible to rolling contact fatigue fissures**, wear, **corrosion**, and **poor** track gauge. Concrete ties can develop **transverse fissures** and **longitudinal cracks**, **crazing**, **shoulder damage**, and **chipping** of bottom edge. Ballast beds may suffer from **mud pumping**, **dirtiness**, **settlement** and so on. Turnouts, as one of the three **weak points** in railway tracks, they **are prone to** various problems. For example, poor **alignment**, poor contact between switch blades and stock rails, and wear on the frog and wing rails. Fastening parts and track reinforcement devices may also **suffer from** damage or failure, etc.

One of the most common track defects is the fissures which appear on the surface or inside of rails. Therefore, **flaw detection workers** need to combine the use of the **flaw detector** with **manual inspection**, applying professional knowledge and skills to conduct thorough and regular "check-ups" of the rails. This ensures that they can find the potential safety **hazards** of the rail in time, and take various **corrective** measures to **eliminate** defects.

Task 4.1 Read the passage. Then, choose the correct answers.

1. What is the passage mostly about?
    A. The function of different components of railway tracks.
    B. The introduction to common defects of railway tracks.
    C. The analysis of corrective measures to the common track defects.
    D. The introduction to the daily work of track workers.
2. What are the common defects of concrete ties?
    A. Rolling contact fatigue fissures, wear, corrosion.
    B. Crazing, shoulder damage, and chipping of bottom edge.
    C. Mud pumping, dirtiness, settlement.
    D. Poor alignment, wear on the frog and wing rails.
3. How do flaw detection workers conduct regular "check-ups" on the rails?
    A. Combining the use of the flaw detector with drone inspection.
    B. Combining the use of large machinery with manual inspection.
    C. Combining the use of the flaw detector with manual inspection.
    D. Combining the use of large machinery with drone inspection.

Task 4.2 Read the sentence pairs. Fill in each blank with the best word or phrase.

1. lining/alignment
    A. We need to perform _____ when the rail is in improper alignment.
    B. We need to perform _____ to adjust the gauge of rails.
2. grinding/clearing
    A. There is a lot of dirt on the ballast, so the track workers need to perform _____ .
    B. The track workers perform _____ to restore the rail to its original shape.

Task 5 Vocational Situation Experience 演职场情景

Task Description: Experience the situational conversation and complete the following exercises, so as to enhance English application ability related to professional positions.

任务描述：体验岗位情景会话，完成练习，提升与职业岗位相关的英语应用能力。

Task 5.1 Listen to the conversation, and fill in the blanks.

Situation description: A trainee is conducting track inspection under the guidance of his instructor. His instructor asks him about the problems found during the inspection and provides suggestions for corrections.

Instructor: Did you find any problems after inspecting the track?

Trainee: Yes, the track is in 1. _____ _____ overall, but there are some defects in the rails and ballast.

Instructor: Oh, what are they?

Trainee: The rail surface has some scratches and small 2. _____ _____ .

Instructor: Then we need to **grind** the rails. Are there any other problems with the rails?

Trainee: Yes, the 3. _____ between the two rails exceeds the standard gauge of 1,435mm.

Instructor: In that case, we need to perform alignment work. What's the matter with the ballast?

Trainee: Some sections of the ballast are mixed with a lot of clay, dead leaves, and even some garbage.

Instructor: We must do **clearing** as soon as possible. Otherwise, it will cause 4. _____ _____ in the track bed.

Trainee: Ok, I have recorded all these tasks and will **implement** them in the afternoon.

Instructor: Remember to work during the 5. _____ _____ to ensure safety.

Trainee: Sure, we will definitely **keep** all the requirements of work safety **in mind** to ensure the safety of driving and personnel.

Task 5.2 Listen again and mark the statements as true(T) or false(F).

____ 1. The rails of this section of track is in good condition.
____ 2. The alignment work needs to be carried out to restore the gauge to the standard one.
____ 3. The ballast of this section of track needs to be cleared as quickly as possible.

Task 5.3 Act out the roles with a partner.

Task 6 Vocational Writing Practice 练职业写作

Task Description: to the table, get familiar with the common track defects and major corrective measures in order to better perform track maintenance and repair in the future position and ensure the safe operation of railway track.

任务描述：参考表格内容，熟悉轨道常见的病害及主要整治措施，以便在未来岗位上更好地执行轨道养护与维修的任务，确保铁路轨道的安全运行。

Overview of Common Track Defects and Main Corrective Measures

Basic Track Components	Common Defects	Main Corrective Measures
Rails	① Cracks, wear ② Corrosion ③ Poor track gauge ④ Excessive or insufficient joints	① **Grinding**, welding, replacement ② Rail rust prevention ③ **Rail lifting**, alignment ④ Adjusting joints
Sleepers	① Transverse fissure and longitudinal cracks, crazing ② Shoulder damage ③ Chipping of bottom edge	① **Injecting grout, replacement** ② Repairing shoulders, replacing pads ③ Repairing or replacing ties
Ballast Bed	① Mud pumping ② Dirtiness ③ Settlement, **insufficient** ballast	① Repairing drainage facilities ② Clearing ③ Replacing or adding ballast, **tamping**
Turnout	① Poor alignment ② Poor contact between parts ③ Structural **wear and tear**	① **Lining**, adjusting the spacing ② Tightening, adjusting ③ Grinding, replacement

____
____
____

Task 7 Telling Stories of China Railway 讲中国铁路故事

Task Description: Watch the story of railway role models and complete the following exercises to develop the awareness and ability to tell stories of China Railway in English.

任务描述：观看铁路榜样故事，完成练习，培养用英语讲述中国铁路故事的意识和能力。

7.1 How did Huang Tao accurately judge the grade of rail damage?

7.2 Watch the video again and search online for more information about Huang Tao. Please introduce his major achievements and share the spiritual qualities you can learn from him. Work in small groups to tell the story of Huang Tao.

Module 3 Railway Engineering 铁道工程

Task 8 Topic Test 测章节知识

Task Description: Review this topic and complete the topic test to develop self-testing skills and summarizing analysis skills.

任务描述：复习本章节内容，完成章节测试，培养自我检测和总结分析的能力。

◎ **Choose the correct answers.**

1. What is the main reason that a coin can stand still on a running high-speed train according to this topic?
   A. The strong control of the train's interior.
   B. The dynamic design of the train's body.
   C. The application of ballastless tracks and continuous welded rails.
   D. The weight distribution inside the train.

2. What kind of defects can railway tracks produce over time?
   A. Only aesthetic defects like discoloration.
   B. Defects in all components of track.
   C. Defects only in the ballast beds and turnouts.
   D. Defects only in the rails and sleepers.

3. What are some common defects that can appear in concrete ties?
   A. Only dirtiness and settlement.
   B. Transverse fissures and shoulder damage.
   C. Rusting and corrosion.
   D. Wear from train wheels.

4. Why are turnouts considered one of the three weak points in railway tracks?
   A. Because they are located at the ends of tracks.
   B. Because they are prone to various issues.
   C. Because they are used less frequently than other parts of the track.
   D. Because they are made of weaker materials.

5. How do flaw detection workers detect the rails?
   A. By relying on automated flaw detectors.
   B. By conducting regular manual inspections without using any tools.
   C. By repairing defects immediately without conducting any inspections first.
   D. By combining the use of flaw detectors with manual inspection and applying professional knowledge.

◎ **Mark the following translations as true(T) or false(F).**

6. These parts will produce various defects because of the effect of train travel and natural conditions.

   译文:这些部件受火车运行和自然条件的影响,会产生诸多病害。

7. Rails are susceptible to rolling contact fatigue fissures, wear, corrosion, and poor track gauge.

   译文:钢轨容易发生滚动接触疲劳裂纹、磨损、掉块、轨向轨距不良的问题。

8. Concrete ties can develop transverse fissures and longitudinal cracks.

   译文:混凝土轨枕会产生横纵向裂缝。

9. Turnouts, as one of the three weak points in railway tracks, they are prone to various issues.

   译文:道岔,作为铁路轨道的三大薄弱环节之一,容易出现各种问题。

10. Flaw detection workers need to combine the use of flaw detectors with manual inspection.

    译文:钢轨探伤工需要将使用轨检小车和手工检查结合起来。

Task 9 Self-assessment 评学习效果

Task Description: Tick the items and self-assess learning outcomes.
任务描述: 勾选选项，自我评估学习效果。

教学目标	评分项目
自主学习完善	☐Have a good habit of independent learning 有良好的自主学习习惯 ☐Be clear about learning objectives 明确学习目标 ☐Learn about learning content 了解学习内容 ☐Complete learning tasks effectively 有效完成学习任务 ☐Finish the section test consciously 自主进行知识检测
语言思维提升	Master the pronunciation, spelling, definition, and simple usage of the following vocabulary: 掌握下列词汇的发音、拼写、释义及简单应用： ☐continuous welded rail ☐rolling contact fatigue ☐crazing ☐shoulder damage ☐mud pumping ☐tongue lipping ☐grinding ☐alignment ☐clearing ☐maintenance gap ☐rail lifting ☐tamping ☐lining ☐transverse fissure ☐rolling contact fatigue Be able to read and understand articles related to this topic and talk about them in English: 能读懂本主题相关文章并用英语简单介绍： ☐Common defects of various components of railway tracks 　铁路轨道各部件的常见病害 ☐Major corrective measures for common track defects 　铁路轨道常见病害的主要整治措施 ☐The job responsibilities and work attitude of flaw detection workers 　探伤工岗位的工作职责与工作态度
职场涉外沟通	☐Be able to understand workplace situational conversations related to this topic 　能听懂本主题相关的职场情景对话 ☐Be able to simulate workplace situational conversations related to this topic with a partner 　能与搭档一起模拟本主题相关的职场情景对话 ☐Be able to introduce the given theme in written form 　能用英语完成主题相关的书面表达
多元文化交流	☐Be able to work in groups to tell the story of China railway role models in English 　能小组合作用英语讲述本主题相关的中国铁路榜样故事

Topic 5　Railway Bridge & Tunnel—Broad Thoroughfares

主题五　铁路桥隧——通衢广陌

 Task ❶　Learning Objectives 明学习目标

Task Description：Get to know the learning content and clarify learning objectives.
任务描述：了解学习内容，明确学习目标。

```
掌握与"铁路桥隧"主题相关        知识
的行业英语词汇                  目标

1. 能读懂与本主题相关的文章
2. 能听懂与本主题相关的职场      技能
   情景对话                     目标
3. 能模拟表演职场情景对话，能
   用英语讲述中国铁路榜样故事
4. 能用英语完成与主题相关的书
   面表达

了解守护铁路桥隧的追梦人——
通化工务段桥隧车间第一维修     素质
小组的榜样故事，学习他们心     目标
系桥梁隧道，创造卓越以确保安
全的优秀品质，在未来岗位上做
出应有的贡献
```

Railway Bridge & Tunnel 铁路桥隧

- 学行业词汇：tunnel water damage, bridge span structure, support system, refuge bay, beam bridge, arch bridge, substructure, cable duct, tunnel portal, etc.

- 习情境案例：《桥梁与隧道维护：确保铁路安全与顺畅》
  1. 铁道桥隧的常见分类与组成部件
  2. 铁道桥隧常见病害的主要整治措施
  3. 桥隧工岗位的工作职责与工作态度

- 体验职场情景：
  - 行业情景会话听说
  - 行业情景会话展示
  - 职业英语写作训练

- 讲中国铁路榜样故事

通化工务段桥隧车间第一维修小组
守护铁路桥隧的追梦人

Module 3　Railway Engineering　铁道工程　175

Task ❷ Unit Content 导主题内容

Task Description: Watch the video, complete the following exercises and learn about the characteristics of railway bridge and tunnels, as well as maintenance requirements to ensure the long-term safety and smooth transportation.

任务描述：观看视频，完成练习，了解铁道桥隧特点和维修要求，以确保铁道桥梁和隧道的长期安全和畅通运输。

When building railways, it is often necessary to cross rivers, valleys, highways, or **intersect with** another railway. To overcome these geographical obstacles, railway bridges are constructed.

Railway bridges are designed specially for trains. They must **bear** the heavy loads of railway vehicles. The **span** and width of the bridges are limited, and the railway line requires a high level of **smoothness**. Therefore, various factors must be considered for the standard design, construction, maintenance, and repair of bridges to ensure they meet the demands of railway transportation and safety requirements.

Railway bridges **come in** various forms and types. According to the construction materials, there are steel bridges, reinforced concrete bridges, and stone bridges. Based on structural forms, the main types are beam bridges, arch bridges, cable-stayed bridges, and suspension bridges.

Unlike bridges, railway tunnels are mostly built through mountains. They are structures built to **avoid** deep cuttings when the railway line crosses mountains.

Bridges and tunnels enable the railway to achieve **continuity** and smoothness. They allow trains to reach their **destinations** without being blocked by **terrain.**

Task 2.1 Complete the following mind map.

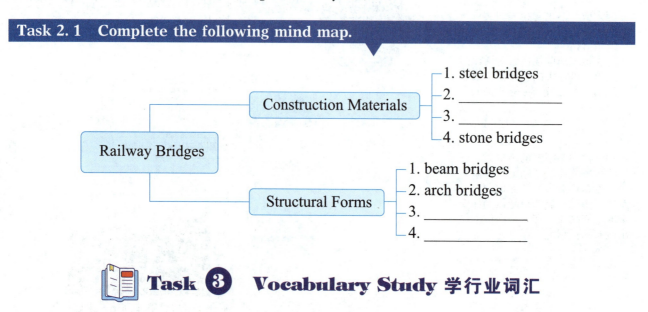

Task ❸ Vocabulary Study 学行业词汇

Task Description: Learn the industry vocabulary, complete the following exercises, and master the classification of railway bridge and tunnel, as well as the English expression of main components.

任务描述：学习行业词汇，完成练习，掌握铁道桥隧分类与主要部件的英文表达。

🎧 1. reinforced concrete bridge

The **reinforced concrete bridge** is a bridge made primarily of reinforced concrete.

🎧 2. beam bridge

The **beam bridge** also known as a flat bridge or a **span** beam bridge. It uses a bending-resistant main beam as the primary **load-bearing component**.

🎧 3. arch bridge

The **arch bridge** is a bridge with an arch as the main load-bearing component. The **vertical load** is **transferred** to the abutments through the arch.

🎧 4. cable-stayed bridge

The **cable-stayed bridge** is a special bridge structure where the main beam is directly **held up by** numerous cables attached to the bridge towers.

🎧 5. suspension bridge

The **suspension bridge i**s also known as a hanging bridge. It is characterized by using cables suspended from towers and anchored at both ends (or to the sides of the bridge) as the main load-bearing components.

🎧 6. tunnel portal

The **tunnel portal** is the **support** structure at the tunnel entrance. It is built with masonry and architectural decoration, and marks the tunnel's entrance and exit.

🎧 7. cut-and-cover tunnel

The **cut-and-cover tunnel** is a tunnel constructed using the Open-Cut method. It's usually built at the entrance and exit of a tunnel.

Module 3　Railway Engineering　铁道工程

🎧 8. refuge bay

The **refuge bay** is a chamber built into the sidewalls of tunnels. It's used to **avoid** running trains and ensure the safety of pedestrians, maintenance workers, and equipment.

🎧 9. cable duct

The **cable duct is** used for laying cables for lighting, communication, signal and power. It is made of concrete.

🎧 10. tunnel water damage

The **tunnel water damage** refers to water interference and damage encountered during the construction or operation of a tunnel.

🎧 11. bridge span structure

The **bridge span structure** is the load-bearing part of the bridge above the supports, spanning the arch.

🎧 12. support system

The **support system** refers to facilities set at the junctions of the bridge span structure and **bridge piers** or **abutments** to **transmit loads.**

🎧 13. bridge pier

The **bridge pier** refers to structures in the river that support the superstructure of the bridge spans, located between two abutments.

🎧 14. bridge abutment

The **bridge abutment** refers to structures on the shore supporting the superstructure of the bridge spans, located at both ends of the bridge.

15. major overhaul

Major overhaul usually refers to **comprehensive maintenance**, reinforcement, and **defect treatment** of the entire bridge or tunnel structure according to their **health status.**

Task 3.1 Match the words or phrases with the definitions.

1. _____ tunnel water damage
2. _____ support system
3. _____ beam bridge
4. _____ cable duct
5. _____ bridge span structure
6. _____ refuge bay
7. _____ substructure
8. _____ tunnel portal

A. the load-bearing part of the bridge above the supports, spanning the arch.
B. chambers built into the sidewalls of tunnels, when a train passes through.
C. to support the superstructure of the bridge spans on both sides in the river.
D. the support structure at the tunnel entrance.
E. facilities set at the junctions of the bridge span structure and bridge piers.
F. using a bending-resistant main beam as the primary load-bearing component.
G. the water interference and damage encountered during the construction or operation of a tunnel.
H. used for laying lighting, communication, signal, and power cables, made of concrete.

Word Bank

New Words

intersect /ˌɪntəˈsekt/ v. 交叉,相交
bear /beə/ v. 承受,忍受
span /spæn/ n. 跨度,跨距
smoothness /ˈsmuːðnəs/ n. 平滑,流畅
avoid /əˈvɔɪd/ v. 避开,回避
continuity /ˌkɒntɪˈnjuːəti/ n. 连续性
destination /ˌdestɪˈneɪʃn/ n. 目的地,终点
terrain /təˈreɪn/ n. 地形,地势
transfer /ˈtrænsfəːr/ v. 转移,传递
support /səˈpɔːt/ v. 支持,支撑
substructure /ˈsʌbstrʌktʃə/ n. 下部结构,基础结构

auxiliary /ɔːgˈzɪliəri/ adj. 辅助的,附加的
identification /aɪˌdentɪfɪˈkeɪʃn/ n. 识别,鉴定
dim /dɪm/ adj. 暗淡的,模糊的
humidity /hjuːˈmɪdəti/ n. 湿度,湿气
endanger /ɪnˈdeɪndʒə/ v. 危及,危害
foundation /faʊnˈdeɪʃn/ n. 基础,地基
railing /ˈreɪlɪŋ/ n. 栏杆,扶手
crack /kræk/ n. 裂缝,裂纹
extend /ɪkˈstend/ v. 延长,扩展
conduct /kənˈdʌkt/ v. 进行,实施

⊙ Phrases & Expressions

intersect with	与……相交	bridge abutment	桥台
come in	起作用,发挥作用	major overhaul	大修
reinforced concrete bridge	钢筋混凝土桥	comprehensive maintenance	综合检查
beam bridge	梁桥	defect treatment	病害整治
load-bearing component	承重构件,承载荷载的部件	health status	健康状态
arch bridge	拱桥	drainage facility	排水设备
vertical load	垂直荷载	ventilation equipment	通风设备
cable-stayed bridge	斜拉桥	circuit shorts	电路短路
be held up by…	被……阻碍	expansion joints	伸缩缝
suspension bridge	悬索桥	bridge deck paving	桥面铺装
tunnel portal	洞门	bridge deck deterioration	桥面破损
cut-and-cover tunnel	明洞	railing fractures	栏杆断裂
refuge bay	避车洞	expansion joint failures	伸缩缝损害
cable duct	电缆槽	load-bearing capacity	荷载能力
tunnel water damage	隧道水害	service life	使用寿命
bridge span structure	桥跨结构	construction materials	建造材料
support system	支座系统	adapt to	适应……
bridge pier	桥墩	external forces	外力
transmit loads	传递荷载	local cracks	局部裂缝

Task 4 Passage Study 习情境案例

Task Description: Read the article, complete the following exercises, and understand the classification and components of railway bridges and tunnels, as well as common defects.

任务描述: 读懂文章,完成练习,了解铁道桥隧分类和部件构成以及常见病害。

Bridge and Tunnel Maintenance: Ensuring Railway Safety and Smoothness

Railway tunnels consist of two main parts: the main structure and the **auxiliary** structure. The main structure of the tunnel is built to maintain the tunnel's stability. It includes the tunnel body structure, tunnel portal, and cut-and-cover tunnel. Some auxiliary structures need to be built to ensure the normal use of the tunnel and the safe operation of trains. They include **drainage facilities**, refuge bays, cable ducts, **ventilation equipment**, and so on. For easy **identification**, the location of refuge bays is marked with white arrows on the **dim** tunnel walls, guiding the steps of the protectors.

The most common form of tunnel damage is water damage. Tunnel water damage not only increases **humidity** inside the tunnel, causing **circuit shorts** and other accidents, but also **endangers** train operation.

Bridges generally consist of the superstructure, substructure, and auxiliary structure. The superstructure, also known as the bridge span structure, is used to span the bridge openings. The superstructure is composed of the bridge span structure and support system. The substructure is composed of bridge piers, bridge abutments, and **foundations**. It supports the bridge span structure and transfer the loads from the superstructure, along with its own weight and external forces, to the foundation below. Auxiliary components mainly include **expansion joints**, lighting, **bridge deck paving**, drainage systems, **railings**, and so on.

Crack is one of the biggest damages to bridge structures. Damages such as **bridge deck deterioration**, **railing fractures**, **expansion joint failures**, and cracks severely affect the **load-bearing capacity** and **service life** of the bridge.

Bridge and tunnel workers need to inspect, maintain, repair, and overhaul bridge and tunnel equipment to maintain their normal and good condition, **extend** their service life, and ensure the safety and smoothness of railway transportation.

Task 4.1 Read the passage. Then, choose the correct answers.

1. What are the two main parts of a railway tunnel?
   A. The superstructure and the substructure.
   B. The main structure and the auxiliary structure.
   C. The tunnel body and the tunnel portal.
   D. The drainage system and the ventilation equipment.

2. What is marked with white arrows on the tunnel walls for easy identification?
   A. The location of drainage facilities.
   B. The location of ventilation equipment.
   C. The location of refuge bay.
   D. The cable ducts.

3. Which of the following is NOT mentioned as a common damage to bridge structures?
   A. Cracks.
   B. Bridge deck deterioration.
   C. Expansion joint failures.
   D. Tunnel water damage.

Task 4.2 Read the sentence pairs. Fill in each blank with the best word or phrase.

1. main structure/superstructure
   A. The _____ of the tunnel is built to maintain the tunnel's stability.

B. The _____ is composed of the bridge span structure and support system.

2. water damage/crack

A. The most common form of tunnel damage is _____ .

B. _____ is one of the biggest damages to bridge structures.

Task 5 Vocational Situation Experience 演职场情景

Task Description: Experience the situational conversation and complete the following exercises, so as to enhance English application ability related to professional positions.

任务描述：体验岗位情景会话，完成练习，提升与职业岗位相关的英语应用能力。

Task 5.1 Listen to the conversation, and fill in the blanks.

Situation description: A trainee is seeking guidance from experienced instructor on different **construction materials** and the maintenance practices for high-speed railway bridges.

Trainee: Mr. Wang, according to different 1. _____ _____ we have steel bridges, reinforced concrete bridges, and stone bridges. What materials are most high-speed railway bridges made of?

Instructor: Most high-speed railway bridges are made of 2. _____ .

Trainee: Why is concrete mainly used to build bridges?

Instructor: On one hand, concrete is relatively inexpensive. Besides, the 3. _____ _____ _____ _____ for concrete bridges are relatively less.

Trainee: Then, what are the disadvantages of steel bridges?

Instructor: Steel bridges may rust and develop 4. _____ _____ . The inspection, maintenance, and repair work later on will consume a lot of manpower and resources.

Trainee: Does it mean that the maintenance work for concrete bridges on high-speed railways is relatively easy?

Instructor: Not exactly. Concrete bridges of high-speed railways are often built on the bridge piers over ten meters or even dozens of meters high. It is not easy to **conduct** 5. _____ _____ at such high bridge piers.

Trainee: Oh, working at heights is really not an easy job!

Instructor: Most bridge and tunnel workers need to work at heights. You should slowly **adapt to** it and overcome the fear of heights. It is also a test of courage and patience.

Task 5.2 Listen again and mark the statements as true(T) or false(F).

____ 1. Most high-speed railway bridges are made of steel.

____ 2. Concrete is used to build bridges mainly because it is expensive and requires frequent maintenance.

____ 3. The maintenance work for concrete bridges on high-speed railways is very easy.

Task 5.3 Act out the roles with a partner.

Task 6 Vocational Writing Practice 练职业写作

Task Description: Describe the structure and main functions of bridges and tunnels based on the table to master basic knowledge of bridge and tunnel maintenance and to do a better job in future position.

任务描述: 根据表格描述桥梁与隧道的结构和主要功能,以便更好地掌握桥隧维修基本知识,以胜任未来的职业岗位。

Overview of Bridge and Tunnel Structures, Main Functions, and Basic Maintenance Tasks

Name	Structure		Functions	Maintenance Tasks
Bridge	Superstructure	① Bridge span structure ② Support system	Spanning the bridge opening	① Inspection, maintenance, repair, overhaul ② Maintaining the good condition of bridge and tunnel equipment ③ Extending service life
	Substructure	① Bridge piers ② Bridge abutments ③ Foundation	① Supporting the structure of bridge span ② Transferring the loads of the superstructure, its own weight, and **external forces** to the foundation	
	Auxiliary Structure	① Expansion joints ② Lighting ③ Bridge deck paving ④ Drainage system ⑤ Railings	① Protecting the structure of bridge ② Provide basic lighting ③ Protect the bridge deck ④ Drain water ⑤ Safety protection	

Module 3 Railway Engineering 铁道工程 183

Continued

Name	Structure		Functions	Maintenance Tasks
Tunnel	Main Structure	① Tunnel body structure ② Tunnel portal ③ Cut-and-cover tunnel	Maintaining tunnel stability	
	Auxiliary Structure	① Drainage facilities ② Refuge bays ③ Cable ducts ④ Ventilation equipment	① Reducing water accumulation in the tunnel ② Ensuring the safety of maintenance personnel and pedestrians ③ Protecting cables ④ Improving air quality	

Task 7 **Telling Stories of China Railway 讲中国铁路故事**

Task Description: Watch the story of railway role models and complete the following exercises to develop the awareness and ability to tell stories of China Railway in English.

任务描述：观看铁路榜样故事，完成练习，培养用英语讲述中国铁路故事的意识和能力。

7.1 What is the core principle and sacred responsibility that the First Maintenance Team of the Tonghua Bridge and Tunnel Workshop holds in their work?

7.2 Watch the video again and search online for more information about the selfless dedication of bridge and tunnel workers. Please introduce their main achievements and share the spiritual qualities you have learned from them. Work in a group to tell the story of the bridge and tunnel workers.

Task 8 Topic Test 测章节知识

Task Description: Review this topic and complete the topic test to develop self-testing skills and summarizing analysis skills.

任务描述：复习本章节内容，完成章节测试，培养自我检测和总结分析能力。

◎ **Choose the correct answers.**

1. Which part of a bridge is responsible for spanning the bridge opening?
   A. Superstructure.   B. Substructure.
   C. Auxiliary Structure.   D. Foundation.

2. What is the primary function of the tunnel body structure?
   A. To provide basic lighting. B. To maintain tunnel stability.
   C. To protect cables.   D. To improve air quality.

3. What is are the maintenance tasks for the bridge and tunnel equipment?
   A. Drain water.
   B. Reduce water accumulation.
   C. Inspect, maintain, repair, and overhaul.
   D. Ensure the safety of maintenance personnel.

4. What structure of a bridge transfers the loads from the superstructure to the foundation?
   A. Expansion joints.   B. Substructures.
   C. Bridge deck paving.   D. Lighting.

5. Which of the following is an auxiliary structure of a tunnel that helps to improve air quality?
   A. Drainage facilities.   B. Refuge bays.
   C. Cable ducts.   D. Ventilation equipment.

◎ **Mark the following translations as true(T) or false(F).**

6. The main structure of the tunnel is built to maintain the tunnel's stability.
   译文：隧道的主体结构是为了保持隧道的稳定而修建的。

7. Some auxiliary structures need to be built to ensure the normal use of the tunnel and the safe operation of trains.
   译文：为了使隧道正常使用，保证列车安全运行，无须修建一些附属结构。

8. The superstructure is composed of the bridge span structure and support system.
   译文：桥梁上部结构不是由桥跨结构、支座系统组成。

9. Bridges generally consist of the superstructure, substructure, and auxiliary structure.
   译文：桥梁一般由上部结构、下部结构和附属结构组成。

10. Crack is one of the biggest damages to bridge structures.
    译文：裂缝不是桥梁结构上最大的病害之一。

Task 9 Self-assessment 评学习效果

Task Description：Tick the items and self-assess learning outcomes.
任务描述：勾选选项，自我评估学习效果。

教学目标	评分项目
自主学习完善	☐Have a good habit of independent learning 有良好的自主学习习惯 ☐Be clear about learning objectives 明确学习目标 ☐Know about learning content 了解学习内容 ☐Complete learning tasks effectively 有效完成学习任务 ☐Finish the section test consciously 自主进行知识检测
语言思维提升	Master the pronunciation, spelling, definition, and simple usage of the following vocabulary： 掌握下列词汇的发音、拼写、释义及简单应用： ☐reinforced concrete bridge ☐tunnel portal ☐tunnel water damage ☐cut-and-cover tunnel ☐refuge bay ☐bridge span structure ☐support system ☐substructure ☐bridge pier ☐bridge abutment ☐major overhaul ☐defect treatment ☐health status grade ☐bridge deck deterioration ☐local cracks ☐comprehensive inspections
	Be able to read and understand articles related to this topic and talk about them in English： 能读懂本主题相关文章并用英语简单介绍： ☐Classifications and various components of railway bridges and tunnels 　铁道桥隧的常见分类与组成部件 ☐Major corrective measures for common bridges defects 　铁道桥隧常见病害的主要整治措施 ☐The job responsibilities and work attitude of railway bridge and tunnel workers 　桥隧工岗位的工作职责与工作态度
职场涉外沟通	☐Be able to understand workplace situational conversations related to this topic 　能听懂本主题相关的职场情景对话 ☐Be able to simulate workplace situational conversations related to this topic with a partner 　能与搭档一起模拟本主题相关的职场情景对话 ☐Be able to introduce the given theme in written form 　能用英语完成主题相关的书面表达
多元文化交流	☐Be able to work in groups to tell the story of China railway role models in English 　能小组合作用英语讲述本主题相关的中国铁路榜样故事

Module 4
Railway Telecommunications

铁道电信

Topic 1　Introduction to Posts—Career Planning
主题一　岗位描述——职业规划

Task 1　Learning Objectives 明学习目标

Task Description: Get to know the content and clarify learning objectives.
任务描述：了解学习内容，明确学习目标。

- 知识目标：掌握与"岗位描述"主题相关的行业英语词汇
- 技能目标：
  1. 能读懂与本主题相关的文章
  2. 能听懂与本主题相关的职场情景对话
  3. 能模拟表演职场情景对话，能用英语讲述中国铁路榜样故事
  4. 能用英语完成与主题相关的书面表达
- 素质目标：了解"最美铁路人"信号达人起明的榜样故事，学习他的敬业精神、专注精神、创新精神以及奉献精神，在未来岗位上对工作热爱、敬业，不断追求更高的目标

Introduction to Posts 岗位描述

- 学行业词汇：railway telecommunication department, signal section, communication section, railway signalman, railway communication worker, onboard signalman, etc.
- 习情境案例：《各司其职，信号保通畅》
  1. 铁路信号工及其职责
  2. 铁路通信工及其工作职责
  3. 岗位的工作职责与素养要求
- 体验职场情景：行业情景会话听说 / 行业情景会话展示 / 职业英语写作训练
- 讲中国铁路榜样故事

最美铁路人　起明
"信号达人"

188　铁路行业英语

Task 2　Lead in 导主题内容

Task Description：Watch the video, complete the following exercises and learn about the Signal Section and the Communication Section, as well as various job titles within these two departments.

任务描述：观看视频，完成练习，了解电务段和通信段以及这两个部门的各种岗位名称。

When you travel by train across vast lands, no matter day or night, there is always a "**guardian**" silently ensuring the safe operation of the train, and that is the **railway telecommunication department**.

Railway telecommunication department includes the **Signal Section** and the **Communication Section**. The Signal Section is mainly responsible for managing and maintaining various signal equipment for train operations. In simple terms, they serve as the "traffic lights" for train operations. The representative job in this section is the **railway signalman**. The Communication Section is mainly responsible for maintaining the railway communication network, ensuring smooth information contact across the railway. In simple terms, they are responsible for "connecting and maintaining the network". The **representative** job in this section is the **railway communication workers**.

Dear fellow students, do you know what job positions you will take up after graduation?

Based on the professional direction, graduates of the Signal major can work in the signal section as **station and section signalman**, **onboard signalman**, **maintenance signal man** and so on. Graduates of the communication major can work in the communication section as **line maintenance communication workers**, **wireless maintenance communication workers**, **indoor equipment maintenance communication workers**, and other positions, etc.

Task 2.1　Please list the various job titles in the Signal Section and Communication Section.

Railway Telecommunication Department		
Section	Signal Section	Communication Section
Responsibilities	Manage and maintain signal equipment for train operations.	Maintain the railway communication network for smooth information contact.
Representative job	Railway signalman	Railway communication worker
Job positions	1. _____ 2. _____ 3. _____	4. _____ 5. _____ 6. _____

Module 4　Railway Telecommunications　铁道电信　189

Task 3 Vocabulary Study 学行业词汇

Task Description: Learn the industry vocabulary, complete the following exercises, and master the English expression of two types of occupations in Railway Telecommunication, including the names and responsibilities of positions within each occupation.

任务描述：学习行业词汇，完成练习，掌握铁路电务的两个工种及工种的各岗位名称及职责的英文表达。

🎧 1. railway signalman

A **railway signalman** is a job role mainly **responsible for** the **installation** and **maintenance** of railway signal equipment.

🎧 2. railway communication worker

A **railway communication worker** is a job role in railway transportation that involves **transmitting** information and technical processing using various communication method.

🎧 3. station and section signalman

A **station and section signalman** is responsible for maintenance signaling equipment in station and sections including **switch**, **track circuits**, signal, etc.

🎧 4. onboard signalman

An **onboard signalman** is responsible for the daily maintenance of onboard equipment, such as **LKJ** (**Train Operation Monitoring Device**) and other **auxiliary** equipment.

🎧 5. maintenance signalman

A **maintenance signalman** is responsible for testing and maintenance of various signaling devices such as relays and **switch machines**.

🎧 6. line maintenance communication worker

A **line maintenance communication worker** is responsible for the repair and construction of communication **optical cables**, **electrical cables** and their auxiliary equipment.

🎧 **7. wireless maintenance communication worker**

A **wireless maintenance communication worker** is maintaining wireless communication equipment such as **CIR**（**Cab Integrated Radio communication equipment**）, **wireless train dispatching** and so on.

🎧 **8. indoor equipment maintenance communication worker**

An **indoor equipment maintenance communication worker** is using advanced monitoring technology to **remotely** monitor all equipment in the section and promptly identifying and **addressing** communication equipment faults.

Task 3.1 Match the words or phrases with the definitions.

1. _____ indoor equipment maintenance communication worker
2. _____ railway signalman
3. _____ station and section signalman
4. _____ maintenance signalman
5. _____ onboard signalman
6. _____ wireless maintenance communication worker
7. _____ line maintenance communication worker
8. _____ railway communication worker

A. in charge of maintaining signaling equipment in station and sections

B. a job role that involves transmitting information and technical processing using various communication methods

C. remotely oversee equipment, detecting and resolving communication faults

D. in charge of the regular upkeep of onboard equipment

E. a job role focused on installing and upkeeping railway signaling systems

F. responsible for repairing and constructing optical and electrical cables

G. responsible for testing and upkeep of different signaling devices

H. maintaining wireless communication equipment

word Bank

◉ **New Words**

guardian [ˈɡɑːdiən] n. 守护者；保护者

representative [ˌreprɪˈzentətɪv] n. 代表；adj. 典型的；有代表性的

installation [ˌɪnstəˈleɪʃn] n. 安装

maintenance [ˈmeɪntənəns] n. 维护；维修
transmit [trænzˈmɪt] v. 传输；使通过；传送
switch [swɪtʃ] n. 道岔
relays [ˈriːleɪz] n. 继电器
auxiliary [ɔːgˈzɪliəri] adj. 辅助的
device [dɪˈvaɪs] n. 装置；设备
remotely [rɪˈməʊtli] adv. 远程地
nervous [ˈnɜːvəs] adj. 焦虑的；神经系统的
neurologist [njʊəˈrɒlədʒɪst] n. 神经科医生

surgeons [ˈsɜːdʒənz] n. 外科医生
All-in-One [ˌɔːl ɪn ˈwʌn] n. 一体化；万灵通
address [əˈdres] vt. 设法解决
meticulousness [məˈtɪkjələsnəs] adj. 一丝不苟
dedication [ˌdedɪˈkeɪʃn] n. 奉献；
lubricate [ˈluːbrɪkeɪt] vt. 润滑；给……上润滑油；
components [kəmˈpəʊnənts] n. 部件；成分

⊙ Phrases & Expressions

railway telecommunication department
　铁路电务
signal section　电务段
communication section　通信段
railway signalman　铁路信号工
railway communication worker
　铁路通信工
station and section signalman
　车站与区间信号工
onboard signalman　车载信号工
maintenance signalman　检修信号工
line maintenance communication worker
　线务维护通信工
wireless maintenance communication worker
　无线维护通信工
indoor equipment maintenance communication worker　室内设备维护通信工
responsible for　负责
track circuits　轨道电路
LKJ：Train Operation Monitoring Device
　列车运行监控记录装置
switch machines　转辙器
optical cables　光缆
electrical cables　电缆
CIR：Cab Integrated Radio communication equipment　机车综合无线通信设备
wireless train dispatching　无线列调
microcomputer monitoring　微机监测
microcomputer interlocking　微机联锁
TDCS：Train Dispatch Command System
　铁路列车调度指挥系统
entry-level positions　初级岗位
ATP：Automatic Train Protection System
　列车自动防护系统
GSM-R：Global System for Mobile Communications-Railway
　铁路移动通信系统
mainline signalman　正线信号工
depot signalman　车辆段信号工
ATS signalman ATS　信号工

Task 4　Passage Study 习情境案例

Task Description: Read the article, complete the following exercises, and learn about the job responsibilities of various positions in Railway Telecommunication.

任务描述: 读懂文章,完成练习,了解铁路电务各种岗位的工作职责。

Each Performs Its Role, Ensuring Smooth Signals

Railway signalmen are known as "eye doctors", as they are responsible for maintaining signal equipment to ensure that trains are always "sharp-eyed and keen-eared". Station and section signalmen act as the "health doctors" of signal equipment, ensuring that the signal system operates safely at stations and section. Onboard signalmen are the "brain doctors" for the safe operation of locomotives, ensuring the normal operation of onboard signal systems to prevent accidents.

The communication networks serve as the "**nervous** system" of trains, and railway communication workers act as the "**neurologists**" of trains. Line maintenance communication workers are the "**surgeons**", mainly engaged in the maintenance of optical and electrical cables along the railway line. Indoor equipment maintenance communication workers are the "**All-in-One**" responsible for maintaining indoor communication equipment, monitoring the communication system's operation, and promptly addressing fault.

Although they hold different positions, they perform duties with the same dedication. Railway signalmen and railway communication workers ensure the safe operation of equipment with **meticulousness** and **dedication**, guaranteeing the safe and smooth operation of railway transportation.

Task 4.1　Read the passage. Then, choose the correct answers.

1. Why are railway signal workers called "eye doctor"?
   A. The communication networks serve as the "nervous system" of trains.
   B. They are mainly engaged in the maintenance of optical and electrical cables.
   C. They are responsible for maintaining signal equipment ensuring that trains always have a sharp eye and a keen ear.
   D. They are maintaining indoor communication equipment.

2. Who is responsible for maintaining the signal equipment on trains to prevent accidents?
   A. Station and section signalmen.
   B. Onboard signalmen.
   C. Line maintenance communication workers.
   D. Indoor equipment maintenance communication workers.

3. Who is responsible for monitoring the communication system's operation, and promptly addressing fault?

   A. Station and section signalmen.

   B. Onboard signalmen.

   C. Line maintenance communication workers.

   D. Indoor equipment maintenance communication workers.

Task 4.2 Read the sentence pairs. Fill in each blank with the best word or phrase.

1. onboard signalmen/station and section signalmen

   A. _____ act as the "health doctors" of signal equipment.

   B. _____ are the "brain doctors" of locomotive safety.

2. line maintenance communication workers/indoor equipment maintenance communication workers

   A. _____ responsible for maintaining indoor communication equipment.

   B. _____ mainly engaged in the maintenance of optical and electrical cables along the railway line.

Task 5 Vocational Situation Experience 演职场情景

Task Description: Experience the situational conversation, complete the following exercises, so as to enhance English application ability related to professional position.

任务描述：体验岗位情景会话，完成练习，提升与职业岗位相关的英语应用能力。

Task 5.1 Listen to the conversation, and fill in the blanks.

Situation description: A trainee is consulting the experienced instructor on how signalmen and communication workers maintain signal and communication equipment during winter.

Trainee: Mr. Chen, can you tell me how do signalmen protect 1. _____ _____ during winter?

Instructor: Sure. Signalmen will adjust the 2. _____, clean the contacts and motors of switch machines, **lubricate** the various **components**, and cover the switch machine housings with "small quilts" to protect them from the cold.

Trainee: Got it. What are the indoor signaling and communication equipment that need 3. _____?

194 铁路行业英语

Instructor: We need to inspect **microcomputer monitoring**, **microcomputer interlocking**, 4. _____, and other equipment to ensure they meet winter 5. _____ _____.

Trainee: I've learned a lot, thank you, Mr. Chen.

Task 5.2 Listen again and mark the statements as true(T) or false(F).

____ 1. The trainee wants to know how do Line maintenance communication workers protect the signaling equipment during winter?

____ 2. Cover the switch machine housings with "small quilts" to protect them from the cold.

____ 3. Microcomputer monitoring, microcomputer interlocking and TDCS are indoor signaling and communication equipment.

Task 5.3 Act out the roles with a partner.

Task 6 Vocational Writing Practice 练职业写作

Task description: Please describe the main entry-level positions in this field and the related work tasks to better plan personal career development.

任务描述：请描述本专业主要初级岗位以及相关工作任务，以便更好地规划个人职业发展。

Main Entry-level Positions and Job Tasks of Each Major

Students	Main Entry-level Positions	Job Responsibilities
Railway communication and information technology major students	Station and section signalman	Maintenance of station and section signal equipment
	Onboard signalman	Maintenance of locomotive signal equipment, LKJ, and **ATP** equipment
	Maintenance signalman	Maintenance of relays and switch machines
Urban rail transit communication signal technology major students	Line maintenance communication worker	Construction and maintenance of optical and electrical cables
	Wireless maintenance communication worker	① Maintenance of locomotive comprehensive wireless equipment ② Maintenance of **GSM-R** wireless communication equipment

Continued

Students	Main Entry-level Positions	Job Responsibilities
Urban rail transit communication signal technology students	On-site Comprehensive Maintenance com-munication worker	① Maintenance of GSM-R section equipment ② Comprehensive maintenance of on-site equipment ③ Maintenance of station equipment ④ Maintenance of train broadcasting equipment
	Indoor equipment Maintenance commun-ication worker	① Maintenance of transmission and access networks ② Maintenance of dedicated communication systems ③ Maintenance of power supply systems
	Mainline signalman	Maintenance of mainline signal equipment
	Depot signalman	Maintenance of depot signal equipment
	Onboard signalman	Maintenance of onboard signal equipment
	ATS signalman	Maintenance of ATS signal equipment

Task 7 Telling Stories of China Railway 讲中国铁路故事

Task Description: Watch the story of railway role models and complete the following exercises to develop the awareness and ability to tell stories of China Railway in English.

任务描述：观看铁路榜样故事，完成练习，培养用英语讲述中国铁路故事的意识和能力。

7.1 What kind of abilities and spirit are needed for Qi Ming to lead the team to overcome such a huge challenge like the major mudslide disaster on the Chengdu-Kunming Railway in 2016？

7.2 Watch the video again and search online for more information about Qi Ming, introduce his major achievements and get to know how did he achieve extraordinary performance in an ordinary position and ensure the safe operation of the trains. Also, share the inspiration and motivation you gained from his spirit. Work in small groups to tell the story of Qi Ming.

Module 4 Railway Telecommunications 铁道电信

Task 8 Topic Test 测章节知识

Task Description: Review this topic and complete the topic test to develop self-testing skills and summarizing analysis skills.

任务描述：复习本章节内容，完成章节测试，培养自我检测和总结分析的能力。

◎ **Choose the correct answers.**

1. What role do railway signalmen play in ensuring safe railway transportation?
   A. Maintaining communication networks.
   B. Monitoring locomotive safety systems.
   C. Operating communication equipment.
   D. Ensuring trains are visually and audibly alert.

2. How are station and section signalmen described in the passage?
   A. Brain doctors.   B. Eye doctors.   C. Health doctors.   D. Surgeons.

3. How are railway communication workers likened in the passage?
   A. Neurologists.   B. All-in-One.   C. Surgeons.   D. Eye doctors.

4. According to the passage, what is the primary duty of line maintenance communication workers?
   A. Monitoring communication systems.
   B. Ensuring station operation.
   C. Maintaining optical and electrical cables.
   D. Addressing faults promptly.

5. Which of the following best summarizes the main idea of the passage?
   A. The importance of dedication in ensuring railway safety.
   B. The different roles of railway signalmen and railway communication workers.
   C. The challenges faced by railway safety workers.
   D. The history of railway transportation systems.

◎ **Mark the following translations as true(T) or false(F).**

6. Railway signalmen are known as "eye doctors", as they are responsible for maintaining signal equipment.
   译文：铁路信号工被称为"眼科医生"，主要负责维护列车的通信网络。

7. Onboard signalmen are the "brain doctors" for the safe operation of locomotives, ensuring the normal operation of onboard signal systems to prevent accidents.
   译文：车载信号工是机车安全上线的"脑科医生"，确保车载信号系统正常运行，防止事故发生。

198 铁路行业英语

8. Line maintenance communication workers are the "**surgeons**", mainly engaged in the maintenance of optical and electrical cables along the railway line.

   译文：线务维护通信工是"手术医生"，主要从事维护列车内部信号系统的工作。

9. Station and section signalmen act as the "health doctors" of signal equipment, ensuring that the signal system operates safely at station and section.

   译文：车站与区间信号工是信号设备的"保健医生"，确保信号系统在车站与区间安全可靠地运行。

10. Indoor equipment maintenance communication workers are the "**All-in-One**" responsible for maintaining indoor communication equipment, monitoring the communication system's operation, and promptly addressing fault.

    译文：室内设备维护通信工不是"万灵通"，不用负责室内通信设备的维护和保养，仅负责监控通信系统的运行情况。

Task 9 Self-assessment 评学习效果

Task Description: Tick the items and self-assess learning outcomes.
任务描述: 勾选选项，自我评估学习效果。

教学目标	评分项目
自主学习完善	☐Have a good habit of independent learning 有良好的自主学习习惯 ☐Be clear about learning objectives 明确学习目标 ☐Learn about learning content 了解学习内容 ☐Complete learning tasks effectively 有效完成学习任务 ☐Finish the section test consciously 自主进行知识检测
语言思维提升	Master the pronunciation, spelling, definition, and simple usage of the following vocabulary: 掌握下列词汇的发音、拼写、释义及简单应用： ☐railway telecommunication department ☐signal section ☐communication section ☐railway signalman ☐railway communication worker ☐station and section signalman ☐onboard signalman ☐maintenance signalman ☐line maintenance communication worker ☐wireless maintenance communication worker ☐indoor equipment maintenance communication worker
	Be able to read and understand articles related to this topic and talk about them in English: 能读懂本主题相关文章并用英语简单介绍： ☐Railway railway signalman and their responsibilities 　铁路信号工及其职责 ☐Railway communication workers and their job responsibilities 　铁路通信工及其工作职责 ☐Job responsibilities and quality requirements for positions 　岗位的工作职责与素养要求
职场涉外沟通	☐Be able to understand workplace situational conversations related to this topic 　能听懂本主题相关的职场情景对话 ☐Be able to simulate workplace situational conversations related to this topic with a partner 　能与搭档一起模拟本主题相关的职场情景对话 ☐Be able to introduce the given theme in written form 　能用英语完成主题相关的书面表达
多元文化交流	☐Be able to work in groups to tell the story of China railway role models in English 　能小组合作用英语讲述本主题相关的中国铁路榜样故事

Topic 2　Railway Signaling—Be Safe and Reliable
主题二　铁路信号——安全可靠

 Task **Learning Objectives 明学习目标**

Task Description：Get to know the content and clarify learning objectives.
任务描述：了解学习内容，明确学习目标。

掌握与"铁路信号"主题相关的行业英语词汇 — 知识目标

1. 能读懂与本主题相关的文章
2. 能听懂与本主题相关的职场情景对话
3. 能模拟表演职场情景对话，能用英语讲述中国铁路榜样故事
4. 能用英语完成与主题相关的书面表达
— 技能目标

了解新时代铁路榜样叶琛林的榜样故事，学习他挥洒青春汗水，辛勤耕耘，厚德敬业，实干先行的精神品质，在未来岗位上作出应有的贡献 — 素质目标

Railway Signaling 铁路信号

学行业词汇：interlocking, single track ABS, block, insulated joint, safe braking distance, through signal, double track ABS, bond, signal light, etc.

习情境案例：《缩短行车间隔的关键技术：自动闭塞系统》
1. 铁路信号设备的基本组成部分
2. 自动闭塞系统的工作原理
3. 单线自动闭塞系统和双线自动闭塞系统的区别
4. 信号显示的含义

体验职场情景：行业情景会话听说　行业情景会话展示　职业英语写作训练

讲中国铁路榜样故事：
新时代铁路榜样　叶琛林
心怀匠心追逐高铁梦

Module 4　Railway Telecommunications　铁道电信　201

Task 2　Lead in 导主题内容

Task Description: Watch the passage, complete the following exercises and learn about the main components of railway signaling system and types of block system.

任务描述：观看视频，完成练习，了解铁路信号系统和闭塞系统的主要组成部分和类型的英文表达。

When trains race along the tracks, how do these huge moving vehicles avoid each other? Behind this is a complex and fascinating railway signaling system. Railway signals are like **elegant** dancers, guiding trains when to go ahead and when to stop with the language of red, yellow, and green lights.

Railway signaling equipment is the general term for railway signals, station **interlocking** equipment, and section blocking equipment, etc., including signals, **track circuits**, **switches**, and so on. These devices are used to control and **command** train operation.

How can we prevent **rear-end collisions** and improve railway operations and **efficiency**? We can use technological means to separate train operation sections—block system. Depending on different **principles**, the **block** system can be divided into various types, such as **telephone blocking**, **semi-automatic blocking**, and **automatic blocking**.

Automatic blocking system uses the status of the track circuit to automatically change the **signal lights**, coordinating with the train operation control systems to ensure trains operate safely and at high speeds in the section.

Task 2.1　Please list the components of railway signaling system and types of block system.

Railway Signaling System	
Purpose	Ensure safe and efficient train operations.
Components	1. _____ 2. _____ 3. _____ Station interlocking equipment

Block System	
Purpose	Prevent rear-end collisions and improve railway operations and efficiency
Types	4. _____ Semi-automatic blocking 5. _____

Task 3 Vocabulary Study 学行业词汇

Task Description: Learn the industry vocabulary, complete the following exercises, and master the English names and functions of main components of block system.

任务描述：学习行业词汇，完成练习，掌握闭塞系统主要部件名称及其功能的英文表达。

1. interlocking

The **interlocking** is a system that establishes a mutually restrictive relationship between signals, switches, and train routes to ensure safe train operations at stations.

2. automatic blocking

The **automatic blocking** is an advanced block system that automatically changes signal indication based on train operation and the status of blocks, allowing drivers to operate trains according to signal indication.

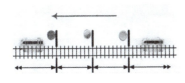

3. block

The main track of the section between two adjacent stations is divided into several segments, which are called **blocks**.

4. through signal

The **through signal** indicates whether the train can enter the protected block or inter-post section.

5. safe braking distance

The **safe braking distance** is the distance a train needs to completely stop before reaching an obstruction.

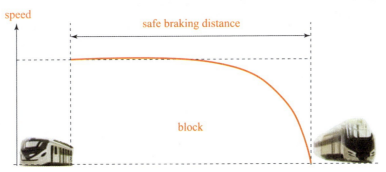

Module 4 Railway Telecommunications 铁道电信

6. double track ABS

The **double track ABS** is the most common form of ABS used on lines with two parallel tracks. It mainly adopts the mode of single-direction train operation, where one line only allows up-train operation, while the other line only allows down-train operation.

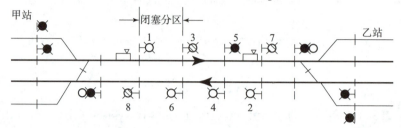

7. single track ABS

The **single track ABS** is a form of ABS used on lines with a single track. It not only prevents head on collision of two trains in reverse directions running into the same section simultaneously, but also avoids rear-end collision of two trains running in the same direction.

8. insulated joint

The **insulated joint** is used to divide the track into sections in track circuits.

9. track circuit

The **track circuit** is an electrical circuit. It utilizes two rails as conductors, with insulated joints separating the two ends and connecting the middle rail gaps by bonds. One end of the rail sends electricity while the other end receives it.

10. bond

The **bond** is a conductive connector used to maintain circuit continuity for track circuits and electrified tracks.

Task 3.1 Match the words or phrases with the definitions.

1. _____ interlocking
2. _____ block
3. _____ safe braking distance
4. _____ double track ABS
5. _____ single track ABS
6. _____ insulated joint
7. _____ through signal
8. _____ bond

A. the distance a train needs to a complete stop
B. a mutual constraint between the signal and the switches
C. used to divide the track into sections
D. a segment of the main track used to separate trains
E. to indicate whether the train can enter the protected block
F. to avoid head-on collisions and rear-end collision
G. a conductive connector
H. to ensure the safety of train operation in the single-direction

Word Bank

New Words

elegant /ˈelɪɡənt/ adj. 高雅的, 举止优雅的
interlocking /ˌɪntəˈlɒkɪŋ/ n. 联锁
circuit /ˈsɜːkɪt/ n. 电路
switch /swɪtʃ/ n. （铁路的）转辙器, 道岔
command /kəˈmɑːnd/ n. 命令, 指示
efficiency /ɪˈfɪʃnsi/ n. 效率, 效能
principle /ˈprɪnsəpl/ n. 准则, 原则
block /blɒk/ n. 闭塞分区
automatic /ˌɔːtəˈmætɪk/ adj. 自动的
segment /ˈseɡmənt/ n. 部分, 片段
braking /ˈbreɪkɪŋ/ v. 制动；刹车
insulated /ˈɪnsjuleɪtɪd/ adj. 绝缘的

joint /dʒɔɪnt/ n. 接头
conductor /kənˈdʌktə/ n. 导体
bond /bɒnd/ n. 接续线
current /ˈkʌrənt/ n. 电流
detect /dɪˈtekt/ v. 检测
intact /ɪnˈtækt/ adj. 完好无损的
transmit /trænzˈmɪt/ v. 播送, 传输
potential /pəˈtenʃl/ adj. 潜在的, 可能的
hazard /ˈhæzəd/ n. 危险, 危害
liaison /liˈeɪzn/ n. 沟通；联络人
registration /ˌredʒɪˈstreɪʃn/ n. 登记, 注册
proceed /prəˈsiːd/ v. 行进, 前往

Phrases & Expressions

track circuit   轨道电路
rear-end collision   追尾
telephone blocking   电话闭塞
semi-automatic blocking   半自动闭塞
automatic blocking   自动闭塞

signal light   信号灯
train intervals   行车间隔
peak travel times   客流高峰期
safe braking distance   安全制动距离
double track ABS   双线自动闭塞系统

single track ABS　单线自动闭塞系统
head-on collision　正面碰撞
insulated joint　绝缘节

restricted speed　限速
specified speed　规定的速度

Task 4　Passage Study 习情境案例

Task Description: Read the article, complete the following exercises, and learn about the function, types, composition of automatic block signaling system, as well as the job responsibilities and work attitude of station and section signalman.

任务描述：读懂文章，完成练习，了解自动闭塞系统的功能、类型以及组成，了解车站与区间信号工岗位的工作职责与工作态度。

Key Technology to Shorten Train Intervals: Automatic Blocking System

During **peak travel times**, how to shorten the train intervals while ensuring safe train operations? The answer is automatic blocking. The main track of the section between two stations is divided into several **segments** known as blocks. Through signals are set up at the entrances to blocks. They tell drivers whether their train can enter the block, thereby maintaining a **safe braking distance** between trains.

The **double track ABS** is suitable for double-track sections, maintaining a safe distance between trains running in the same direction. Single-track sections require a **single track ABS**. It is more complex because it also has to prevent **head-on collisions** between trains.

In the automatic block system, rails are divided into several blocks by **insulated joints**. Each block constitutes a separate track circuit. The rails are used as **conductors**, covered with insulated joints at both ends, **and** connecting the middle rail gaps by **bonds**. Then the electric **current** will pass from one end to another.

The track circuit can **detect** and monitor whether the track is occupied and whether the rails are **intact**. By **transmitting** train operation information through the track circuit, the display of each signal is determined, providing commands to ensure safe train operations.

As the "health doctors" of blocks, station and section signalman can identify **potential** safety **hazards** by inspecting track circuits, signals and other equipment.

Task 4.1　Read the passage. Then, choose the correct answers.

1. What is the passage mainly about?
   A. The history of railroad automatic block systems.
   B. How automatic block systems work.
   C. A comparison of manual and automatic block systems.
   D. Common problems experienced in automatic block systems.

2. What can you infer about automatic block systems?
   A. Single track systems have through signals facing in opposite directions.
   B. They were impossible to make before electrified rails were developed.
   C. They reduce the minimum safe braking distance between trains.
   D. Lines with more than two tracks use different signal systems.
3. How are single track ABSs more complicated than double track ABSs?
   A. Their tracks need multiple track circuits running in opposite directions.
   B. Their tracks have more switches and signals per interlocking.
   C. They are divided into smaller blocks and use more through signals.
   D. They must maintain distances between trains in two directions.

Task 4.2 Read the sentence pairs. Fill in each blank with the best word or phrase.

1. single track ABS/double track ABS
   A. A _____ maintains distances between trains in one direction.
   B. A _____ must prevent trains from colliding head-on.
2. track circuit/bonds
   A. A(n) _____ determines if a train occupies a particular set of tracks.
   B. _____ continue track circuits and connect blocks.

 Task **Vocational Situation Experience 演职场情景**

Task Description: Experience the situational conversation and complete the following exercises, so as to enhance English application ability related to professional positions.
任务描述：体验岗位情景会话，完成练习，提升与职业岗位相关的英语应用能力。

Task 5.1 Listen to the conversation, and fill in the blanks.

Situation description: A trainee who works as a station and section signalman is discussing daily maintenance work with the instructor.

Trainee: Can we go on 1. _____ after we prepare the maintenance tools?

Instructor: Not yet. After preparing, we need to 2. _____ _____ and wait for the station **liaison** officer to complete the relevant procedures.

Trainee: Understood.
(Five minutes later, the station liaison officer completes the contact and **registration** procedures.)

Instructor: Let's go. The 3. _____ _____ is our main inspection focus tonight.

Trainee: What is the function of the track circuit?

Instructor: It automatically and continuously detects whether this section of track is occupied by vehicles and transmits 4. _____ _____ information to ensure safety.

Trainee: I see, we must 5. _____ it thoroughly.

Task 5.2 Listen again and mark the statements as true(T) or false(F).

____ 1. The station and section signalman can immediately go on track after preparing the maintenance tools.

____ 2. The supervisor instructs the signalman to wait for the station liaison officer to complete procedures before proceeding on track.

____ 3. The function of the track circuit is only to check if a section of track is occupied by vehicles.

Task 5.3 Act out the roles with a partner.

Task 6　Vocational Writing Practice 练职业写作

Task Description：Please introduce the various displays of the four-aspect automatic blocking section through signal and their meanings to better understand the working principles of this system and the theoretical knowledge required for the safe operation of trains.

任务描述：请介绍四显示自动闭塞区段通过信号机的各种显示以及其显示的意义,以便更好地掌握该系统的工作原理和列车的安全行驶所需理论知识,确保列车安全运行。

The Signal Indication and Its Meaning

Signal Indication	The meaning of signal indication
Red Light	① Stop before this signal ② The block ahead is occupied or there is a track fault
Yellow Light	① **Proceed** at a **restricted speed** ② One block ahead is clear
Green-Yellow Light	① Proceed at the **specified speed** ② Two blocks ahead are clear
Green Light	① Proceed at the specified speed ② At least three blocks ahead are clear

_____

_____

_____

_____

Task 7 Telling Stories of China Railway 讲中国铁路故事

Task Description: Watch the story of railway role models and complete the following exercises to develop the awareness and ability to tell stories of China Railway in English.

任务描述：观看铁路榜样故事，完成练习，培养用英语讲述中国铁路故事的意识和能力。

7.1 What maintenance method did Ye Chenlin summarize for high-speed railway switches, and how did it benefit the operation of the equipment?

7.2 Watch the video again and search online for more information about Ye Chenlin, introduce his major achievements. Also, share the inspiration and motivation you gained from his spirit. Work in small groups to tell the story of Ye Chenlin.

Task 8 Topic Test 测章节知识

Task Description: Review this topic and complete the topic test to develop self-testing skills and summarizing analysis skills.

任务描述：复习本章节内容，完成章节测试，培养自我检测和总结分析的能力。

◎ **Choose the correct answers.**

1. What is the main purpose of an automatic blocking system in train operations?
   A. To increase the speed of trains during peak travel times.
   B. To ensure safe braking distances between trains.
   C. To reduce the number of signals on the tracks.
   D. To simplify the operation of train drivers.

2. How does a double track ABS differ from a single track ABS?
   A. Double track ABS is more complex than single track ABS.
   B. Single track ABS is used for trains running in opposite directions.
   C. Double track ABS maintains safe distances between trains in the same direction.
   D. Single track ABS requires fewer signals to operate.

3. What role do signals play in the automatic block system?
   A. They control the speed of trains within each block.
   B. They inform drivers about the weather conditions.
   C. They let drivers know if their train can enter a block safely.
   D. They communicate with other stations to coordinate schedules.

4. How are rails divided and monitored in the automatic block system?
   A. Rails are divided into separate circuits using insulated joints.
   B. Rails are continuously electrified to prevent collisions.
   C. Rails are inspected by station attendants every hour.
   D. Rails are covered with sensors to detect potential hazards.

5. Who plays the role of "health doctors" in monitoring the safety of blocks in the automatic blocking system?
   A. Train drivers.　　　　　　　　　B. Station and section signalmen.
   C. Track maintenance crews.　　　D. Automatic control systems.

◎ **Mark the following translations as true (T) or false (F).**

6. During peak travel times, how to shorten the train intervals while ensuring safe train operations?
   译文：客流高峰期，如何在确保列车行车安全的情况下缩短行车间隔？

7. The main track of the section between two stations is divided into several segments known as blocks.

   译文：两个车站之间的轨道区段划分成若干个被称为联锁的小段。

8. Single track ABS is more complex because it also has to prevent head-on collisions between trains.

   译文：单线自动闭塞系统还要防止列车发生正面碰撞，因此更为复杂。

9. In the automatic block system, rails are divided into several blocks by insulated joints.

   译文：自动闭塞系统中，钢轨被绝缘节分成若干个小段。

10. The track circuit can detect and monitor whether the track is occupied and whether the rails are intact.

    译文：轨道电路可以检查和监督轨道是否有车占用及钢轨是否完整。

Task 9 Self-assessment 评学习效果

Task Description：Tick the items and self-assess learning outcomes.
任务描述：勾选选项，自我评估学习效果。

教学目标	评分项目
自主学习完善	☐Have a good habit of independent learning 有良好的自主学习习惯 ☐Be clear about learning objectives 明确学习目标 ☐Know about learning content 了解学习内容 ☐Complete learning tasks effectively 有效完成学习任务 ☐Finish the section test consciously 自主进行知识检测
语言思维提升	Master the pronunciation, spelling, definition, and simple usage of the following vocabulary： 掌握下列词汇的发音、拼写、释义及简单应用： ☐interlocking ☐block ☐bond ☐automatic blocking ☐through signal ☐safe braking distance ☐single track ABS ☐double track ABS ☐insulated joint ☐track circuit ☐signal light ☐head-on collision ☐rear-end collision ☐restricted speed ☐specified speed
	Be able to read and understand articles related to this topic and talk about them in English： 能读懂本主题相关文章并用英语简单介绍： ☐The basic parts of a railway signaling equipment 　铁路信号设备的基本组成部分 ☐The working principle of automatic block system 　自动闭塞系统的工作原理 ☐The difference between single track ABS and double track ABS 　单线自动闭塞系统和双线自动闭塞系统的区别 ☐The meaning of signal indication 　信号显示的含义
职场涉外沟通	☐Be able to understand workplace situational conversations related to this topic 　能听懂本主题相关的职场情景对话 ☐Be able to simulate workplace situational conversations related to this topic with a partner 　能与搭档一起模拟本主题相关的职场情景对话 ☐Be able to introduce the given theme in written form 　能用英语完成主题相关的书面表达
多元文化交流	☐Be able to work in groups to tell the story of China railway role models in English 　能小组合作用英语讲述本主题相关的中国铁路榜样故事

Topic 3　Train Control System (TCS) — Be Precise and Stable

主题三　列车运行控制系统（TCS）——精准平稳

Task 1　Learning Objectives 明学习目标

Task Description: Get to know the content and clarify learning objectives.
任务描述：了解学习内容，明确学习目标。

Train Control System 列车运行控制系统

- **知识目标**：掌握与"列车运行控制系统"主题相关的行业英语词汇

- **技能目标**：
  1. 能读懂与本主题相关的文章
  2. 能听懂与本主题相关的职场情景对话
  3. 能模拟表演职场情景对话，能用英语讲述中国铁路榜样故事
  4. 能用英语完成与主题相关的书面表达

- **素质目标**：了解"中老铁路跨境动车组"车载设备信号工的榜样故事，学习她们严于律己、忠诚担当、无私奉献的铁路精神，在未来岗位上对工作热爱、敬业，不断追求更高的目标

- **学行业词汇**：transmission, overspeed, deceleration, balise, abnormal, emergency braking distance, automatic train stop device, train overspeed protection system, automatic train deceleration system, automatic train operation system, etc.

- **习情境案例**：《列车安全的隐形守护者：列车控制系统》
  1. 列车运行控制系统和列车速度控制系统的组成
  2. CTCS-3系统的优势
  3. 车载信号工岗位的工作职责与工作态度

- **体验职场情景**：
  - 行业情景会话听说
  - 行业情景会话展示
  - 职业英语写作训练

- **讲中国铁路榜样故事**：

"95后"的"萌妹子"
中老铁路的"绿巨人大脑"守护者

Task 2 Lead in 导主题内容

Task Description: Watch the video, complete the following exercises and learn about the components of Train Control System.

任务描述：观看视频，完成练习，了解列车运行控制系统的组成部分。

When a train runs at 200 km/h, it requires an **emergency braking distance** of 2,000 meters. At 350 km/h, the emergency braking distance should increase to 6,500 meters. When the train is running at high speed, if the driver completely relies on his eyesight to observe the ground signal and drive the train, it is impossible to ensure the safety of the train. Therefore, when the speed of the train **exceeds** 160 km/h, a train control system must be equipped.

The train control system includes onboard equipment and ground equipment. It uses ground **transmission** equipment to **transmit** various information to the moving train, so that the driver can understand the state of the ground line and control the speed of the train. Only by this way, can the safety of the train operation be guaranteed.

The train control system comprises **locomotive signals**, **automatic train stop devices**, and train speed control systems. The train speed control system **consists of** the **train overspeed protection system**, **automatic train deceleration system**, and **automatic train operation system**.

Task 2.1 Please list the components of train control system and train speed control system.

Train Control System	
Purpose	Utilizes ground transmission equipment for information exchange Aimed at ensuring train safety
Components	1. _____ 2. _____ 3. _____

Train Speed Control System	
Purpose	1. Control the direction, spacing, and speed of train operation. 2. Aimed at ensuring the safe operation of trains and improving operational efficiency.
Components	3. _____ 4. _____ 5. _____

Module 4 Railway Telecommunications 铁道电信

Task 3　Vocabulary Study 学行业词汇

Task Description: Learn the industry vocabulary, complete the following exercises, and master the English names and functions of main components of train control system.

任务描述: 学习行业词汇,完成练习,掌握列车运行控制系统的主要组成部件的名称及其功能的英文表达。

1. locomotive signal

The **locomotive signal** is the signal in the driver's cab indicating the train's running conditions ahead.

2. automatic train stop device

The **automatic train stop device** is a device that automatically **implement** emergency brakes if the driver fails to confirm and execute deceleration or stop measure after receiving such signals.

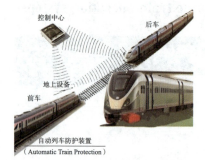

3. train overspeed protection system

The **train overspeed protection system** is an advanced technological device using sensors, computers, and control devices to monitor and control the train's speed and automatically take measures to decelerate when the train exceeds the speed limit.

4. automatic train deceleration system

The **automatic train deceleration system** is a speed control system that automatically reduces the train's speed to below the specified value when the train needs to decelerate, according to the dispatch, track, and operating conditions.

5. automatic train operation system

The **automatic train operation system** is a subsystem of automatic train control that achieves automatic speed adjustment and station stopping control.

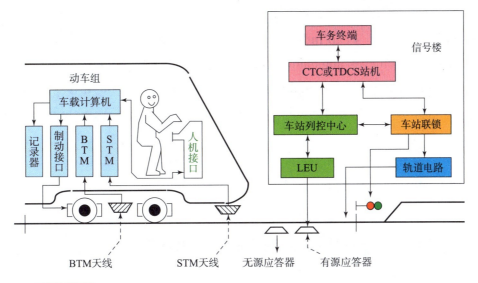

6. balise

The **balise** is a point-based device that achieves high-speed data transmission between train and ground based on the principle of **electromagnetic coupling**. It is used to transmit message information to the train on specific ground, and achieve train positioning.

7. radio block center

The **radio block center**, short for RBC, is a signal control system based on a fault-safe computer platform, serving as the core ground equipment for the CTCS – 3 level system.

Task 3.1 Match the words or phrases with the definitions.

1. _____ locomotive signal
2. _____ automatic train stop device
3. _____ automatic train deceleration system
4. _____ automatic train operation system
5. _____ train overspeed protection system
6. _____ balise
7. _____ radio block center

A. a signal control system based on a fault-safe computer platform
B. a point-based device which is used to transmit messages to trains in a specific place to realize train location

Module 4 Railway Telecommunications 铁道电信

C. signals in the driver's cab **indicating** the train's running conditions ahead
D. a system that achieves automatic speed adjustment and station stopping control
E. a device that automatically implement emergency brakes if the driver fails to confirm
F. a speed control system that automatically reduces the train's speed to below the specified value
G. a device using advanced technologies to monitor and control the train's speed and automatically take measures to decelerate when the train exceeds the speed limit

Word Bank

New Words

exceed /ɪkˈsiːd/ v. 超过,超出
transmission /trænzˈmɪʃn/ n. 发送,传递
transmit /trænzˈmɪt/ v. 传输,传递
overspeed /ˌoʊvərˈspiːd/ n. 超速
implement /ˈɪmplɪmənt/ v. 执行,贯彻
indicate /ˈɪndɪkeɪt/ v. 表明,指示
deceleration /ˌdiːseləˈreɪʃn/ n. 减速
balise /ˈbəliːz/ n. 应答器

electromagnetic /ɪˌlektroʊmæɡˈnetɪk/ adj. 电磁的
coupling /ˈkʌplɪŋ/ n. [电]耦合;结合,联结
navigator /ˈnævɪɡeɪtər/ n. 导航仪,领航员
diagnose /ˌdaɪəɡˈnoʊs/ v. 诊断;找出原因
abnormal /æbˈnɔːrml/ n. 异常的,反常的

Phrases & Expressions

emergency braking distance 紧急制动距离
consist of 由……组成
locomotive signal 机车信号
automatic train stop device 列车自动停车装置
train overspeed protection system 列车超速防护系统
automatic train deceleration system 列车自动减速系统
automatic train operation system 列车自动运行系统
evolve from...to 从……演变成……

intellectual property rights 知识产权
range from...to... 范围从……到……
temporary speed restriction server 临时限速服务器
computer-based interlocking 计算机联锁
GSM-R mobile switching center GSM-R 移动交换中心
train operation command center 行车指挥中心
state-of-the-art 最先进的;达到最高水准的
the target distance 目标距离

Task 4 Passage Study 习情境案例

Task Description: Read the article, complete the following exercises, and learn about China's train control systems as well as the job responsibilities and work attitude of onboard signalman.

任务描述：读懂文章，完成练习，了解中国的列车控制系统和车载信号工岗位的工作职责与工作态度。

The Invisible Guardians of Train Safety: Train Control Systems

With the development of high-speed railways in China, the train control system has **evolved from** locomotive signals (mainly based-on signals) and train operation monitoring recording devices to CTCS Level 2 and Level 3. The latters are mainly based on board signal system with overspeed protection functions.

The CTCS Level 2 and Level 3 control systems are developed in China and possess independent **intellectual property rights**. The CTCS Level 2 control system is suitable for high-speed railways with speeds **ranging from** 200 to 250 km/h, while the CTCS Level 3 control system meets the operational requirements of high-speed railways with speeds ranging from 300 to 350 km/h.

The CTCS-3 control system includes onboard equipment and ground equipment. The onboard equipment acts as the "**navigator**" of the train. It includes a human-machine interface display unit, onboard safety computer, GSM-R wireless communication unit, speed and distance measurement unit, balise information transmission module, and track circuit information reader.

Ground equipments are divided into trackside equipment and indoor equipment. Trackside equipment mainly includes ZPW-2000 track circuits, balises, and GSM-R wireless base stations. Indoor equipment primarily consists of the radio block center (RBC), train control center (TCC), **temporary speed** restriction server, **computer-based interlocking**, **GSM-R mobile switching center**, and **train operation command center**.

The onboard signalman, who performs comprehensive "health checks" on the onboard signal equipment, is called the "brain surgeon" of onboard signals. Each time, they complete nearly a hundred inspection and testing projects, analyze thousands of data points, accurately **diagnose** and handle **abnormal** information, to safeguard the safety of the train silently.

Task 4.1 Read the passage. Then, choose the correct answers.

1. What is the primary distinguishing factor between earlier train control systems and China's CTCS Level 2 and Level 3 systems?
   A. They are based on GPS signals.
   B. They utilize onboard signal-based system with overspeed protection functions.
   C. They rely solely on ground-based visual signals.
   D. They require manual input from train operators.

2. Which speed ranges do the CTCS Level 2 and Level 3 systems respectively support for high-speed railways in China?
   A. Level 2:100 – 150 km/h, Level 3:200 – 250 km/h.
   B. Level 2:150 – 200 km/h, Level 3:250 – 300 km/h.
   C. Level 2:200 – 250 km/h, Level 3:300 – 350 km/h.
   D. Level 2:300 – 350 km/h, Level 3:400 – 450 km/h.

3. Which of the following is NOT a key onboard equipment that comprises the CTCS – 3 system's "navigator" for the train?
   A. Human-machine interface display unit.
   B. GSM-R wireless communication unit.
   C. Speed and distance measurement unit.
   D. Track circuit information unit.

Task 4.2   Read the sentence pairs. Fill in each blank with the best word or phrase.

1. train overspeed protection system/train automatic deceleration system
   A. When the train exceeds the speed limit, _____ can slow down the train.
   B. _____ can automatically reduce the train's speed according to the running state of the train.

2. trackside equipment/indoor equipment
   A. _____ includes ZPW – 2000 track circuits, balises, and GSM – R wireless base stations.
   B. _____ consists of the radio block center (RBC), train control center (TCC), temporary speed restriction server, computer-based interlocking, GSM – R mobile switching center, and train operation command center.

 Task  Vocational Situation Experience 演职场情景

> **Task Description**: Experience the situational conversation and complete the following exercises, so as to enhance English application ability related to professional positions.
>
> 任务描述:体验岗位情景会话,完成练习,提升与职业岗位相关的英语应用能力。

Task 5.1   Listen to the conversation, and fill in the blanks.

Situation description: A trainee is consulting the experienced instructor about the CTCS – 3 control.

    Trainee: Mr. Li, I'm quite fascinated by China's high-speed rail. What is the maximum operating speed of China's high-speed rail?

Instructor: The maximum operating speed has reached 350 kilometers per hour, which is quite remarkable.

Trainee: Impressive indeed. And what kind of 1. _____ _____ _____ do you use to ensure safe operation at such high speeds?

Instructor: We rely on the CTCS – 3 control system, which is a **state-of-the-art** technology independently developed in China. It's specifically 2. _____ _____ high-speed rail operations.

Trainee: I'd love to know more about the advantages of this CTCS – 3 system.

Instructor: Well, its most notable advantage is its ability to 3. _____ large amounts of continuous information. It provides the train with crucial data like **the target distance** up to 32 kilometers ahead and the 4. _____ _____ on the line. This significantly enhances both safety and operational efficiency.

Trainee: It seems your high-speed rail technology is truly 5. _____ .

Task 5.2 Listen again and mark the statements as true(T) or false(F).

____ 1. China's high-speed rail can reach speed up to 300 kilometers per hour.

____ 2. The CTCS – 3 system used in China's high-speed rail was developed in collaboration with international partners.

____ 3. The CTCS – 3 system provides critical data such as target distance and permitted speed for safe operation of high-speed trains.

Task 5.3 Act out the roles with a partner.

Task 6 Vocational Writing Practice 练职业写作

Task Description: Please compare the CTCS-2 and CTCS-3 systems in terms of application speed, equipment composition, and equipment functions, and summarize the advantages of the CTCS-3 system to master the theoretical knowledge of railway train operation control systems.

任务描述：请从应用时速、设备构成、设备功能这三个方面比较 CTCS-2 和 CTCS-3 系统的差异，并总结 CTCS-3 系统的优势，以便更好地掌握铁路列车运行控制系统理论知识。

Comparison of CTCS-2 and CTCS-3 Systems

Aspect	CTCS-2	CTCS-3
Application Speed	200-250 km/h	Above 300 km/h
Equipment Composition	① Station control centers ② Track circuits ③ Balises	① Temporary speed restriction server ② Radio Block Center (RBC) ③ GSM-R communication interface equipment
Equipment Functions	① Train occupancy check ② Sending train authorization information to onboard equipment	① Train authorization generated by ground equipment RBC ② Driving commands transmitted by GSM-R communication interface equipment
Advantages	① Fast operating speed ② High safety performance	① Faster operating speed ② Higher safety performance

 **Task 7 Telling Stories of China Railway 讲中国铁路故事**

Task Description: Watch the story of railway role models and complete the following exercises to develop the awareness and ability to tell stories of China Railway in English.

任务描述：观看铁路榜样故事，完成练习，培养用英语讲述中国铁路故事的意识和能力。

7.1 What qualities or traits can we learn from these young on-board signalwomen as railway professionals?

7.2 Watch the video again and search online for more information about these young on-board signalwomen, introduce their main work, understand how they undertake the critical task of maintaining the train control on-board equipment of CRH EMUs, and ensure the safe and stable operation of the China-Laos Railway. Also, share the inspiration and motivation you gained from their spirit. Work in small groups to tell the story of the young on-board signalwomen team.

Task 8 Topic Test 测章节知识

Task Description: Review this topic and complete the topic test to develop self-testing skills and summarizing analysis skills.

任务描述:复习本章节内容,完成章节测试,培养自我检测和总结分析的能力。

◎ **Choose the correct answers.**

1. What are the primary functions of the CTCS Level 2 and Level 3 control systems in China?
    A. Monitor passenger behavior.
    B. Ensure train safety and overspeed protection.
    C. Provide onboard entertainment services.
    D. Control ticketing and reservations.

2. What type of wireless communication unit is included in the onboard equipment of the CTCS – 3 control system?
    A. 4G.　　　　B. Bluetooth.　　　　C. GSM – R.　　　　D. Wi-Fi.

3. Which type of ground equipment includes ZPW – 2000 track circuits and balises?
    A. Radio Block Center(RBC).　　B. Train Control Center(TCC).
    C. GSM – R wireless base stations.　　D. Trackside equipment.

4. Which of the following is NOT mentioned as an indoor equipment in the text?
    A. Radio Block Center(RBC).
    B. Temporary Speed Restriction Server.
    C. GSM – R Mobile Switching Center.
    D. Wayside Signaling System.

5. What nickname is given to the onboard signalman who performs health checks on the onboard signal equipment?
    A. Brain Surgeon.　　　　B. Data Analyst.
    C. Signal Master.　　　　D. Safety Guardian.

◎ **Mark the following translations as true(T) or false(F).**

6. The train control system has evolved from locomotive signals(mainly based-on signals) and train operation monitoring recording devices to CTCS Level 2 and Level 3 system.
    译文:列车运行控制系统已由车载信号(以地面信号为主)、列车运行监控记录装置发展为 CTCS – 2 级和 CTCS – 3 级列控系统。

7. The CTCS – 3 control system includes onboard equipment and ground equipment.
    译文:CTCS – 3 级列控系统包括地面设备和车载设备。

8. Ground equipment are divided into trackside equipment and indoor equipment.
    译文:地面设备分为轨旁设备和室内设备。

9. Trackside equipment mainly includes ZPW – 2000 track circuits, balises, and GSM – R wireless base stations.

译文:轨旁设备主要有 ZPW – 2000 轨道电路、测速测距单元、GSM – R 无线基站。

10. The onboard signalman, who performs comprehensive "health checks" on the onboard signal equipment, is called the "brain surgeon" of onboard signals.

译文:对车载信号设备做全方位"体检"的车载设备信号工被称为车载信号"脑科医生"。

Task 9 Self-assessment 评学习效果

Task Description: Tick the items and self-assess learning outcomes.
任务描述: 勾选选项，自我评估学习效果。

教学目标	评分项目
自主学习完善	☐Have a good habit of independent learning 有良好的自主学习习惯 ☐Be clear about learning objectives 明确学习目标 ☐Know about learning content 了解学习内容 ☐Complete learning tasks effectively 有效完成学习任务 ☐Finish the section test consciously 自主进行知识检测
语言思维提升	Master the pronunciation, spelling, definition, and simple usage of the following vocabulary: 掌握下列词汇的发音、拼写、释义及简单应用: ☐transmission ☐overspeed ☐implement ☐indicate ☐bogie ☐deceleration ☐balise ☐diagnose ☐abnormal ☐emergency braking distance ☐automatic train stop device ☐train overspeed protection system ☐automatic train deceleration system ☐automatic train operation system
	Be able to read and understand articles related to this topic and talk about them in English: 能读懂本主题相关文章并用英语简单介绍: ☐The components of train control system and train speed control system. 　列车运行控制系统和列车速度控制系统的组成 ☐The advantages of the CTCS–3 system 　CTCS–3 系统的优势 ☐The job responsibilities and work attitude of onboard signalman 　车载信号工岗位的工作职责与工作态度
职场涉外沟通	☐Be able to understand workplace situational conversations related to this topic 　能听懂本主题相关的职场情景对话 ☐Be able to simulate workplace situational conversations related to this topic with a partner 　能与搭档一起模拟本主题相关的职场情景对话 ☐Be able to introduce the given theme in written form 　能用英语完成主题相关的书面表达
多元文化交流	☐Be able to work in groups to tell the story of China railway role models in English 　能小组合作用英语讲述本主题相关的中国铁路榜样故事

Topic 4　Railway Communication—Be Connected and Smooth

主题四　铁道通信——连通畅通

Task ❶　Learning Objectives 明学习目标

Task Description：Get to know the content and clarify learning objectives.
任务描述：了解学习内容，明确学习目标。

知识目标
掌握与"铁道通信"主题相关的行业英语词汇

技能目标
1. 能读懂与本主题相关的文章
2. 能听懂与本主题相关的职场情景对话
3. 能模拟表演职场情景对话，能用英语讲述中国铁路榜样故事
4. 能用英语完成与主题相关的书面表达

素质目标
了解"最美铁路人"光缆守护者钱锋的榜样故事，学习他的敬业精神、专注精神、创新精神以及奉献精神，在未来岗位上对工作热爱、敬业，不断追求更高的目标

Railway Communication 铁道通信

学行业词汇
railway communication, wired communication, wireless communication, satellite communication, optical cable, radio communication, mobile communication, etc.

习情境案例
《铁路运输的"神经网络"——光、电缆》
1. 铁路通信的作用以及分类
2. 铁路通信光、电缆的作用和分类
3. 线务维护通信工的职责和工作态度

体验职场情景
行业情景会话听说
行业情景会话展示
职业英语写作训练

讲中国铁路榜样故事

最美铁路人　钱锋
"光缆守护者"

Module 4　Railway Telecommunications　铁道电信　227

Task 2 Lead in 导主题内容

Task Description: Watch the video, complete the following exercises and learn about the English expressions related to the functions and classification of railway communication.

任务描述：观看视频，完成练习，了解铁路通信的功能以及分类的英文表达。

Railway communication is like the wings and ears of trains, silently **safeguarding** every journey along the lines. As trains speed along, communication equipment acts like a magician, maintaining smooth communication between stations and drivers through **waves** and signals.

Railway communication covers all aspects of communication between trains, trains and **dispatch center**, trains and crew members, as well as crew members and dispatch centers. Its functions include **dispatching and command**, safety monitoring, passenger services and **fault alarms**. The technologies used in this system include **wired communication** technologies (such as telephone, electric cable, **optical fiber**, etc.) and **wireless communication** technologies (such as **satellite communication**, **radio communication**, **mobile communication**, etc.).

Through advanced technologies and equipment, railway communication ensures the safety, efficiency, and stability of train operations.

Task 2.1 Please list the technologies used in railway communication.

Railway communication			
Functions	Communication links	Technologies used	
Dispatching and command Safety monitoring Passenger services Fault alarms	Trains < – > Dispatch center Trains < – > Crew members Crew members < – > Dispatch center	1. _____ Telephone—electric cable 3. _____	2. _____ Satellite communication 4. _____ Mobile communication

 # Task 3   Vocabulary Study 学行业词汇

Task Description: Learn the industry vocabulary, complete the following exercises, and master the English expression of the definition, function, classification of railway communication and railway communication equipment.

任务描述：学习行业词汇，完成练习，掌握铁路通信的定义、功能分类以及铁路通信设备的英文表达。

🎧 **1. railway communication**

The **railway communication** refers to the communication technology and equipment used in the railway transportation system for information transmission and personnel communication.

🎧 2. wired communication

The **wired communication** refers to telecommunication that uses media such as cables and optical fibers to transmit information.

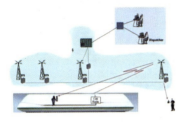

🎧 3. wireless communication

The **wireless communication** is a communication method that uses **electromagnetic** waves to send and receive information through the air.

🎧 4. satellite communication

The **satellite communication** is a communication method that uses communication satellites to relay signals.

🎧 5. radio communication

The **radio communication** is also known as radio transmission, it uses radio waves to transmit information.

🎧 6. mobile communication

The **mobile communication** is communication between mobile **entities** or between a mobile entity and a fixed entity.

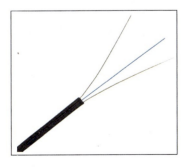

🎧 7. optical cable

An **optical cable** is a communication line composed of a certain number of optical fibers arranged in a specific way, encased in a protective **sheath**, and used for transmitting optical signals.

Module 4　Railway Telecommunications　铁道电信

8. electrical cable

An **electrical cable** is a conductor or group of conductors insulated and protected by an outer layer, used to transmit electricity or information from one place to another.

9. GSM – R handheld terminal

A **GSM – R handheld terminal** is a handheld mobile device that can realize or obtain GSM – R communication services within the GSM – R digital mobile communication network.

Task 3.1 Match the words or phrases with the definitions.

1. _____ optical cable
2. _____ electrical cable
3. _____ satellite communication
4. _____ wired communication
5. _____ wireless communication
6. _____ radio communication
7. _____ GSM – R handheld terminal

A. a group of conductors insulated and protected by an outer layer, used to transmit electricity or information

B. uses communication satellites for signal transmission

C. uses electromagnetic waves to transmit information through the air

D. uses cables and optical fibers to transmit information

E. uses radio waves to transmit information

F. a handheld mobile device that can realize or obtain GSM – R communication services

G. a communication line composed of a certain number of optical fibers, used for transmitting optical signals

Word Bank

● New Words

safeguard ['seɪfɡɑːd] v. 保障；保护；n. 安全设施
stability [stə'bɪləti] n. 稳定（性）
electromagnetic [ɪˌlektrəʊmæɡ'netɪk] adj. 电磁的
waves [weɪvz] n. 波
entity ['entəti] n. 实体
sheath [ʃiːθ] n. 护套；护皮
criteria [kraɪ'tɪəriə] n. 标准

metallic [mə'tælɪk] adj. 金属的
crucial ['kruːʃl] adj. 关键的
medium ['miːdiəm] adj 中等的；n. 介质
enthusiastic [ɪnˌθjuːzi'æstɪk] adj. 热情的
publicity [pʌb'lɪsəti] n. 宣传
inspection [ɪn'spekʃn] n. 检查
reliable [rɪ'laɪəbl] adj. 可信赖的
challenging ['tʃælɪndʒɪŋ] adj. 挑战性的
collaborating [kə'læbəreɪtɪŋ] v. 合作

● Phrases & Expressions

railway communication　铁路通信
dispatch center　调度中心
dispatching and command　调度指挥
fault alarms　故障告警
optical fiber　光纤
wired communication　有线通信
wireless communication　无线通信
satellite communication　卫星通信
radio communication　无线电通信
mobile communication　移动通信
be classified into　分类为
be divided into　分为

pipeline cable　管道电缆
optical cable　光缆
optical fiber cable　光纤电缆
overhead cable　架空电缆
pipeline cables　管道电缆
fault handling　故障处理
GSM – R handheld terminal　手持终端
station PA intercom equipment
　站场扩音对讲设备
on-board intercom equipment
　车载对讲设备（无线列调）
radio alarm device　无线电报警装置

 Task Passage Study 习情境案例

Task Description: Read the article, complete the following exercises, and learn about Railway-Communication Optical and Electric Cables and responsibilities of line maintenance communication workers.

任务描述：读懂文章，完成练习，了解铁路通信光、电缆以及线务维护通信工的职责。

The "Natural Network" of Railway-Communication Optical and Electric Cables

Along the railway lines, there are some small posts appearing at regular intervals. These are special markers, indicating the presence of railway communication optical and electrical cables

 Module 4　RAILWAY Telecommunications　铁道电信

(optical cables, electrical cables) buried below.

Railway communication optical and electric cables are used to transmit optical and electrical signals, enabling high-speed and long-distance information transmission. They can **be classified into** different types based on various criteria. According to the transmission medium, they can **be divided into metallic** cables and **optical fiber cables**. According to the laying method, they can be divided into **overhead cables**, **pipeline cables**, etc.

As an important information transmission **medium** in the railway system, railway communication optical and electric cables are responsible for train operation control, dispatching and command, and safety monitoring, forming the "natural network" that ensures the orderly operation of railway transportation. Therefore, the safety and maintenance of optical and electric cables are **crucial**. Regular inspections and timely repairs are important measures to ensure their performance.

In daily maintenance, line maintenance communication workers should be "**enthusiastic** in line protection **publicity**, meticulous in inspection work, careful in fault handling, and dedicated in learning business skills", ensuring the safe and reliable operation of railway communication optical cables.

Task 4.1 Read the passage. Then, choose the correct answers.

1. What are the two main types of railway communication cables mentioned in the passage?
   A. Pipeline cables and overhead cables.
   B. Metallic cables and pipeline cables.
   C. Electrical cables and metallic cables.
   D. Optical cables and electrical cables.

2. What is the railway communication optical and electric cables responsible for in the railway system?
   A. Passenger ticketing and onboard entertainment.
   B. Train operation control, dispatch command, and safety monitoring.
   C. Station decoration and landscaping.
   D. Freight transport optimization and scheduling.

3. Which of the following best describes the qualities expected of line maintenance communication workers?
   A. Passionate, reckless, tired, careless.
   B. Reckless, careless, indifferent, eager.
   C. Enthusiastic, meticulous, careful, dedicated.
   D. Indifferent, imprecise, cautious, diligent.

Task 4.2 Read the sentence pairs. Fill in each blank with the best word or phrase.

1. pipeline cables/optical fiber cables
   A. According to the transmission medium, they can be divided into metallic cables and

_____.

B. According to the laying method, they can be divided into overhead cables and, _____ etc.

2. railway communication optical and electric cables/line maintenance communication workers

A. _____ act as the "natural network" of railway.

B. _____ must perform daily inspections and maintenance, keeping track of changes around the cables.

 Task Vocational Situation Experience 演职场情景

Task Description: Experience the situational conversation, complete the following exercises, so as to enhance English application ability related to professional position.

任务描述：体验岗位情景会话，完成练习，提升与职业岗位相关的英语应用能力。

Task 5.1　Listen to the conversation, and fill in the blanks.

Situation description: A trainee is asking his instructor about the required skills for becoming a line maintenance communication worker.

Trainee: Miss Wang, may I ask you some questions?

Instructor: Of course.

Trainee: What skills do I need to become a line maintenance 1. _____ _____?

Instructor: You should be familiar with 2. _____ and maintaining communication equipment. Strong problem-solving skills and a/an 3. _____ ability are also crucial.

Trainee: It sounds quite challenging. Fault handling and 4. _____ _____ are important, right?

Instructor: Exactly. Promptly identifying faults and collaborating with other departments to 5. _____ resolve problems are crucial.

Trainee: Got it. Thank you. Miss Wang. I'll **strive** to **exce**l in this position in the future!

Task 5.2 Listen again and mark the statements as true(T) or false(F).

____ 1. Only strong problem-solving skills is crucial for a line maintenance communication worker.

____ 2. Fault handling and emergency response are important for a line maintenance communication worker.

____ 3. The student wants to be an excellent signalman.

Task 5.3 Act out the roles with a partner.

Task 6 Vocational Writing Practice 练职业写作

Task Description: Please introduce the types of railway communication, equipment, and summarize the roles of two communication methods to better grasp railway communication theory and ensure the safe operation of trains.

任务描述：请介绍铁路通信的种类、设备，并概述两种通信方式的作用，以便更好地掌握铁路通信理论知识，确保列车安全运行。

Types, Equipment, and Functions of Railway Communication

Type	Equipment Name	Functions
Wired Communication	① Station telephone ② **Station PA intercom equipment** ③ Passenger station broadcasting equipment	Fixed communication ① Operational command within the station ② Business contact
Wireless Communication	① **GSM – R handheld terminal** ② **On-board intercom equipment** (wireless train dispatching) ③ Train radio communication ④ In-station radio communication ⑤ **Radio alarm device**	Mobile communication ① Communication between trains ② Communication between trains and the dispatch center

Task **Telling Stories of China Railway 讲中国铁路故事**

Task Description: Watch the story of railway role models and complete the following exercises to develop the awareness and ability to tell stories of China Railway in English.

任务描述：观看铁路榜样故事，完成练习，培养用英语讲述中国铁路故事的意识和能力。

7.1 What is Qian Feng's innovative achievements? What qualities have you learned from him?

7.2 Watch the video again and search online for more information about Qian Feng, introduce his major achievements and get to know how he protected millions of communication optical cables with passion, perseverance, and wisdom. Also, share the inspiration and motivation you gained from his spirit. Work in small groups to tell the story of Qian Feng.

Task 8　Topic Test 测章节知识

Task Description：Review this topic and complete the topic test to develop self-testing skills and summarizing analysis skills.

任务描述：复习本章节内容，完成章节测试，培养自我检测和总结分析的能力。

◎ **Choose the correct answers.**

1. What is railway communication optical cables and electric cables called in the railway system?

    A. Brain.　　　B. Bones.　　　C. Heart.　　　D. Nervous system.

2. The functions of the small posts along the railway line are ____ .

    A. marking railway mileage.

    B. indicating the locations for burying communication optical cables and electric cables.

    C. marking safety warning information.

    D. locating the direction of train travel.

3. What is the main purpose of railway communication optical and electric cables?

    A. To provide internet access to passengers.

    B. To regulate train schedules.

    C. To power the lights along the railway tracks.

    D. To enable high-speed, long-distance information transmission for train operation control and safety monitoring.

4. How can railway communication optical and electric cables be classified based on the transmission medium?

    A. By color-coding.　　　　　　　B. By laying method.
    C. By signal frequency.　　　　　D. By metallic cables and optical fiber cables.

5. Why are regular inspections and timely repairs important for railway communication optical and electric cables?

    A. To maintain their performance and safety.

    B. To ensure passenger comfort.

    C. To prevent train delays.

    D. To improve train speed.

◎ **Mark the following translations as true(T) or false(F).**

6. These are special markers, indicating the presence of railway communication optical and electrical cables(optical cables, electrical cables) buried below.

    译文：它们是铁路通信专用标桩，表示下方埋设有火车站的位置的标志。

7. Railway communication optical and electric cables are used to transmit optical and electrical signals.

   译文:铁路通信光缆和电缆仅用于传输光信号。

8. According to the transmission medium, they can be divided into metallic cables and optical fiber cables.

   译文:按传输介质可分为金属线缆和架空纤缆两种。

9. Railway communication optical and electric cables are responsible for train operation control, dispatching and command, and safety monitoring.

   译文:铁路通信光、电缆负责列车运行控制、调度指挥、安全监控等。

10. Regular inspections and timely repairs are important measures to ensure their performance.

    译文:定期巡检和及时维修是保障其性能的重要措施。

Task 9 Self-assessment 评学习效果

Task Description: Tick the items and self-assess learning outcomes.
任务描述: 勾选选项，自我评估学习效果。

教学目标	评分项目
自主学习完善	☐Have a good habit of independent learning 有良好的自主学习习惯 ☐Be clear about learning objectives 明确学习目标 ☐Learn about learning content 了解学习内容 ☐Complete learning tasks effectively 有效完成学习任务 ☐Finish the section test consciously 自主进行知识检测
语言思维提升	Master the pronunciation, spelling, definition, and simple usage of the following vocabulary: 掌握下列词汇的发音、拼写、释义及简单应用: ☐railway communication ☐wired communication ☐wireless communication ☐satellite communication ☐optical cable ☐radio communication ☐mobile communication ☐electrical cable
	Be able to read and understand articles related to this topic and talk about them in English: 能读懂本主题相关文章并用英语简单介绍: ☐The functions and classification of railway communication 　铁路通信的作用以及分类 ☐The functions and classification of railway communication optical and electrical cables 　铁路通信光、电缆的作用和分类 ☐The job responsibilities and work attitude the positions of line maintenance communication workers 　线务维护通信工的职责和工作态度
职场涉外沟通	☐Be able to understand workplace situational conversations related to this topic 　能听懂本主题相关的职场情景对话 ☐Be able to simulate workplace situational conversations related to this topic with a partner 　能与搭档一起模拟本主题相关的职场情景对话 ☐Be able to introduce the given theme in written form 　能用英语完成主题相关的书面表达
多元文化交流	☐Be able to work in groups to tell the story of China railway role models in English 　能小组合作用英语讲述本主题相关的中国铁路榜样故事

Topic 5　Train Dispatching Command System— Be Efficient and Intelligent

主题五　列车调度指挥系统——高效智能

 Task 1 **Learning Objectives 明学习目标**

Task Description: Get to know the content and clarify learning objectives.
任务描述: 了解学习内容，明确学习目标。

- **知识目标**: 掌握与"列车调度指挥系统"主题相关的行业英语词汇

- **技能目标**:
  1. 能读懂与本主题相关的文章
  2. 能听懂与本主题相关的职场情景对话
  3. 能模拟表演职场情景对话，能用英语讲述中国铁路榜样故事
  4. 能用英语完成与主题相关的书面表达

- **素质目标**: 了解安顺西通信车间通信工吕一丹的榜样故事，学习她认真负责、勇于担当、不断学习、团结协作和积极向上的精神品质，在未来岗位上作出应有的贡献

TDCS 列车调度指挥系统

- **学行业词汇**: Central Local Area Network, Station base Level Network, Train Dispatching Center, Station Train Log, Dispatch Order, Cloud Computing, real-time information, dispatch order, etc.

- **习情境案例**: 《铁路运输的"最强大脑"：列车调度指挥系统》
  1. 列车运行调度指挥系统的先进技术
  2. TDCS的主要功能和具体作用
  3. 室内设备维修通信岗位的工作职责与工作态度

- **体验职场情景**:
  - 行业情景会话听说
  - 行业情景会话展示
  - 职业英语写作训练

- **讲中国铁路榜样故事**:

安顺西通信车间　吕一丹
全国铁路先进女职工

Module 4　RAILWAY Telecommunications　铁道电信　239

Task 2 Lead in 导主题内容

Task Description: Watch the video, complete the following exercises and learn about the function and advanced technologies of train dispatching command system.

任务描述：观看视频，完成练习，了解列车调度指挥系统的功能和先进技术。

In China, over 4,000 high-speed trains run on **approximately** 45,000 kilometers of high-speed railway lines every day. As the world's fastest high-speed railway, the Beijing-Shanghai High-Speed Railway has a minimum **departure interval** of just 3 minutes. How to ensure the safe, **punctual**, and efficient operation of so many trains? The answer is the **train dispatching command system** (**TDCS**).

The train operation dispatching command system acts like a wise **commander**, ensuring the safe and punctual operation of every train. TDCS is a large-scale computer network system that **integrate**s advanced communication, signaling, computer networks, data transmission, and multimedia technologies. It has achieved scientific and modernized railway transportation organization, greatly increasing railway transportation capacity and reducing the workload of dispatch personnel.

Task 2.1 Please list the function and advanced technologies of train operation dispatching command system.

Train operation dispatching command system	
Function	Ensure safe, 1._____, 2._____ and efficient operation of high-speed trains
Advanced technologies	3._____ 4._____ 5._____ 6._____ Multimedia technologies

Task 3 Vocabulary Study 学行业词汇

Task Description: Learn the industry vocabulary, complete the following exercises, and master the English names related to train dispatching and command systems.

任务描述：学习行业词汇，完成练习，掌握与列车调度指挥系统相关的英文名称。

🎧 **1. central LAN**

The **central LAN** (central local area network) is a local area network established at each

railway bureau location, connected via **dedicated lines** to the China Railway Corporation and its **subordinate** dispatch centers for information exchange.

🎧 2. station base level network

The **station base level network** is the foundation of the TDCS, including station terminal equipment and network transmission equipment. It is responsible for real-time **supervision** and control of train operations within the station.

🎧 3. train dispatching center

The **train dispatching center** is established within railway transportation departments. Its core tasks include directing train operations, **freight loading** and **unloading**, planning and organizing of train operation, as well as **adjusting train flows**.

🎧 4. dispatch order

The **dispatch order** is an instruction issued by train dispatchers during the dispatch command process, requiring relevant personnel to comply and complete the tasks.

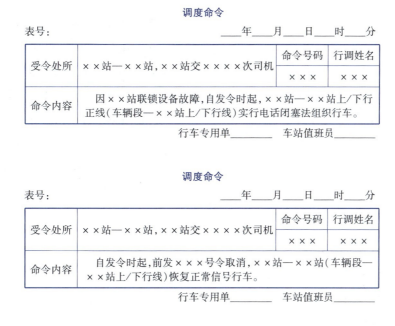

🎧 5. cloud computing

The **cloud computing** is an internet-based computing model.

🎧 6. station train log

Station train log is the original records of train operations kept by each station.

Task 3.1　Match the words or phrases with the definitions.

1. _____ central local area network
2. _____ station base level network
3. _____ train dispatching center
4. _____ station train log
5. _____ dispatch order
6. _____ cloud computing

A. instructions issued by train dispatchers
B. an internet-based computing model
C. vital documents about history of train movements kept by station
D. overseeing and controlling train operations within stations in real-time
E. a local area network established at each railway bureau.
F. a department responsible for train operation scheduling and command in the railway system

Word Bank

New Words

approximately /əˈprɒksɪmətli/ adv. 大概；大约
punctual /ˈpʌŋktʃuəl/ adj. 准时的
commander /kəˈmændər/ n. 指挥官
integrate /ˈɪntɪɡreɪt/ v. (使)合并，成为一体
subordinate /səˈbɔːrdɪnət/ adj. 从属的，下级的

supervision /ˌsuːpərˈvɪʒn/ n. 监督，管理
adjust /əˈdʒʌst/ v. 调整，调节
accurate /ˈækjərət/ adj. 准确的，精确的
analyze /ˈænəlaɪz/ vt. 对……进行分析
stability /stəˈbɪləti/ n. 稳定(性)
jurisdiction /ˌdʒʊrɪsˈdɪkʃn/ n. 管辖区域
hazard /ˈhæzərd/ n. 危险，危害

Phrases & Expressions

departure interval　发车间隔
train dispatching command system　列车调度指挥系统
central LAN (central local area network)　中心局域网
railway bureau　铁路总公司
dedicated lines　专有线
station base level network　车站基层网

train dispatching center　调度中心
freight loading and unloading　货车装卸
train flows　车流
dispatch order　调度指令
cloud computing　云计算
station train log　车站行车日志
be composed of　由……组成
real-time information　实时信息

Task 4　Passage Study 习情境案例

Task Description: Read the article, complete the following exercises, and learn about train dispatching command systems and responsibilities of indoor equipment maintenance communication worker.

任务描述:读懂文章,完成练习,了解列车调度系统以及室内维护通信工的职责。

The "Strongest Brain": Train Dispatching Command System

The train dispatching command system, known as the "strongest brain" of railway transportation, uses advanced information technology to monitor, dispatch, and command train operations in real-time, ensuring the safe and efficient operation of trains. It **is composed of** the China Railway Corporation, the railway bureau TDCS central LAN, and the station base level network, forming a modernized railway transportation dispatching and control system covering the entire network.

The technical features of the train operation dispatching command system are mainly reflected in the following aspects:

Communication technology: The system uses computer network technology to achieve **real-time information** transmission between trains and the dispatch center, ensuring the timely and **accurate** delivery of **dispatch orders**.

Information technology: The system uses big data, cloud computing, and other information technologies to **analyze** train operation data in real-time, providing strong support for dispatch decisions.

Control technology: The system uses automatic control technology to remotely dispatch and monitor trains in real-time, ensuring the **stability** and safety of train operations.

To ensure the smooth operation of the TDCS, indoor equipment maintenance communication workers are responsible for monitoring and analyzing all railway communication equipment under their **jurisdiction**, transmitting the hazard analyzed to on-site maintenance communication workers in time, and tracking and tackling the **hazard** timely to ensure good communication quality during train operation.

Task 4.1　Read the passage. Then, choose the correct answers.

1. Which of the following is NOT a primary technical feature of the train operation dispatching command system?
   A. Utilization of advanced information technology.
   B. Manual control of train movements.
   C. Integration of communication technology.
   D. Application of automatic control technology.

2. What role does control technology play in the TDCS?

    A. Monitoring passenger behavior.

    B. Ensuring timely snack delivery.

    C. Remotely dispatching and monitoring trains in real-time.

    D. Managing ticket reservations.

3. Indoor equipment maintenance communication workers are primarily responsible for ensuring the smooth operation of which system?

    A. Air traffic control system.

    B. Train operation dispatching command system.

    C. Subway signaling system.

    D. Highway traffic management system.

Task 4.2　Read the sentence pairs. Fill in each blank with the best word or phrase.

1. communication technology/information technology

    A. _____ uses big data, cloud computing, and other tools for real-time analysis of train operation data, aiding dispatch decision-making effectively.

    B. _____ uses computer network technology for real-time information exchange between trains and the dispatch center, ensuring prompt delivery of orders.

2. on-site maintenance communication workers/indoor equipment maintenance communication workers

    A. _____ monitor and analyze railway communication equipment, ensuring timely transmission of identified hazards.

    B. _____ need to track and tackle the hazard timely to ensure good communication quality during train operation.

 # Task 5　Vocational Situation Experience 演职场情景

Task Description: Experience the situational conversation and complete the following exercises, so as to enhance English application ability related to professional positions.

任务描述：体验岗位情景会话，完成练习，提升与职业岗位相关的英语应用能力。

Task 5.1　Listen to the conversation, and fill in the blanks.

Situation description: An instructor who works as a dispatcher is introducing the new train operation dispatching command system to a foreign trainee.

    Trainee:　Hi, Zhang, I've heard you have introduced an intelligent train dispatching system.

Instructor: Yes, it's fantastic and has greatly reduced our 1. _____ .

Trainee: Can you tell me more about it?

Instructor: Sure. Previously, we had to manually adjust train schedules during bad weather. Now, the system can automatically adjust the train schedules based on 2. _____ and traffic conditions.

Trainee: That's great, it can significantly improve work efficiency.

Instructor: Yes, and it can also 3. _____ train operation status in real-time. If any abnormalities are detected, it will immediately issue a 4. _____ .

Trainee: It not only improves efficiency but also enhances safety.

Instructor: Exactly. With the advancement of technology, the train dispatching system will become even 5. _____ _____ , providing safer and more efficient services for passengers.

Trainee: I hope our country's high-speed rail can also adopt this intelligent train dispatching system.

Instructor: I'm sure it will.

Task 5.2 Listen again and mark the statements as true (T) or false (F).

____ 1. The train dispatching system has reduced the workload of train dispatchers.

____ 2. The train dispatching system can only monitor train locations but not their operational status.

____ 3. The train dispatching system does not provide any communication platform for issuing warnings.

Task 5.3 Act out the roles with a partner.

Task 6 Vocational Writing Practice 练职业写作

Task Description: Please describe the main functions and specific roles of the train dispatching command system (TDCS) to better understand its application and importance in railway transportation.

任务描述：请描述列车调度指挥系统 TDCS 的主要功能及具体作用，以便更好地理解其在铁路运输中的应用和重要性。

Functions and Roles of TDCS

Main Functions	Roles
Developing train schedules	① Understand transportation needs and actual conditions ② Develop train schedules ③ Ensure timely operations
Automatically generating station operation logs	① Automatically record station activities: train arrivals and departures ② Analyze and optimize data ③ easy to check
Automatically drawing actual train operation diagrams	① Collect real-time train operation data ② Automatically generate actual train operation diagrams ③ Provide a clear understanding of actual train operations
Automatic collecting and tracking train numbers	① Automatically identify and track train numbers ② Accurately monitor and manage the status of each train

Task 7 **Telling Stories of China Railway 讲中国铁路故事**

Task Description: Watch the story of railway role models and complete the following exercises to develop the awareness and ability to tell stories of China Railway in English.

任务描述：观看铁路榜样故事，完成练习，培养用英语讲述中国铁路故事的意识和能力。

7.1 What is Lv Yidan's main responsibility in her work, and how does she contribute to the safety of the Shanghai-Kunming high-speed rail line?

7.2 Watch the video again and search online for more information about Lv Yidan, introduce her major achievements and get to know how she was known as the hundred mile "sky eye". Also, share the inspiration and motivation you gained from her spirit. Work in small groups to tell the story of Lv Yidan.

Module 4　Railway Telecommunications　铁道电信

train operations in real-time.

译文:被称为铁路运输"最强大脑"的列车调度指挥系统使用先进信息技术实时监控、调度和指挥列车运行。

7. The system uses computer network technology to achieve real-time information transmission between trains and the dispatch center, ensuring the timely and accurate delivery of dispatch orders.

译文:列车调度指挥系统通过计算机网络技术,实现列车与车站之间地实时信息传输,确保调度命令的及时准确传达。

8. The system uses automatic control technology to remotely dispatch and monitor trains in real-time, ensuring the stability and safety of train operations.

译文:列车调度指挥系统通过计算技术,实现对列车的远程调度指挥和实时监控,确保列车运行的稳定性和安全性。

9. Control Technology: The system uses automatic control technology to remotely dispatch and monitor trains in real-time.

译文:控制技术:列车调度指挥系统通过手动控制技术,实现对列车的远程调度指挥和实时监控。

10. Indoor equipment maintenance communication worker are responsible for monitoring and analyzing all railway communication equipment under their jurisdiction.

译文:室内设备维修通信工负责监控分析辖区所有的铁路信号设备。

Task 9　Self-assessment 评学习效果

Task Description：Tick the items and self-assess learning outcomes.
任务描述：勾选选项，自我评估学习效果。

教学目标	评分项目
自主学习完善	☐Have a good habit of independent learning 有良好的自主学习习惯 ☐Be clear about learning objectives 明确学习目标 ☐know about learning content 了解学习内容 ☐Complete learning tasks effectively 有效完成学习任务 ☐Finish the section test consciously 自主进行知识检测
语言思维提升	Master the pronunciation, spelling, definition, and simple usage of the following vocabulary: 掌握下列词汇的发音、拼写、释义及简单应用： ☐dispatch ☐command ☐supervision ☐integrate ☐adjust ☐subordinate ☐analyze ☐stability ☐jurisdiction ☐hazard ☐Train dispatching center ☐Cloud computing ☐Train operation dispatching command system ☐Station train log ☐be composed of Be able to read and understand articles related to this topic and talk about them in English: 能读懂本主题相关文章并用英语简单介绍： ☐The advanced technologies of TDCS 　列车运行调度指挥系统的先进技术 ☐Functions and roles of TDCS 　TDCS 的主要功能和具体作用 ☐The job responsibilities and work attitude of onboard signalman 　室内设备维修通信工岗位的工作职责与工作态度
职场涉外沟通	☐Be able to understand workplace situational conversations related to this topic 　能听懂本主题相关的职场情景对话 ☐Be able to simulate workplace situational conversations related to this topic with a partner 　能与搭档一起模拟本主题相关的职场情景对话 ☐Be able to introduce the given theme in written form 　能用英语完成主题相关的书面表达
多元文化交流	☐Be able to work in groups to tell the story of China railway role models in English 　能小组合作用英语讲述本主题相关的中国铁路榜样故事

参 考 文 献

一、图书

[1] 中国国家铁路集团有限公司运输部.铁道概论[M].北京:中国铁道出版社有限公司,2022.

[2] 佟立本,王伶俐,孙琦.铁道概论[M].北京:中国铁道出版社有限公司,2019.

[3] 刘慧,林春香.行知行业英语[M].北京:高等教育出版社,2019.

[4] 洪从鲁,员珍珍.铁道机车车辆专业英语[M].成都:西南交通大学出版社,2016.

[5] 罗荣凤,刘德辉.桥隧施工及养护[M].北京:中国铁道出版社有限公司,2023.

[6] 杨维国,许红叶.铁路桥梁与隧道工程[M].长沙:中南大学出版社,2016.

[7] 李建平.铁路轨道与修理(第三版)[M].北京:中国铁道出版社有限公司,2019.

[8] 李朝阳,刘思源,孙莉.高速铁路概论[M].成都:西南交通大学出版社,2023.

[9] 吴冰.铁道机车英语[M].北京:外语教学与研究出版社,2020.

[10] 宫艳芳.铁路机车车辆[M].北京:中国铁道出版社,2017.

[11] 刘涛,李纯.铁道概论[M].北京:北京交通大学出版社,2021.

[12] 王海星.铁道概论[M].北京:中国铁道出版社有限公司,2020.

[13] 纪书景,张进奎.铁路客运组织[M].上海:上海交通大学出版社,2023.

[14] 赵立冬.铁路线路养护与维修[M].北京:中国铁道出版社有限公司,2019.

[15] 中国国家铁路集团有限公司货运部.铁路货物运输[M].北京:中国铁道出版社有限公司,2023.

[16] 毛鹤,王萌萌.铁路普通货物运输(第2版)[M].北京:人民交通出版社,2021.

[17] 王邠,李永芳.铁路通信技术(第2版)[M].北京:中国铁道出版社,2016.

二、网站

[1] https://zhuanlan.zhihu.com/p/675770617？utm_campaign = shareopn&utm_medium = social&utm_psn = 1780631220134215680&utm_source = wechat_session&utm_id = 0.

[2] https://zhuanlan.zhihu.com/p/655954397？utm_campaign = shareopn&utm_medium = social&utm_psn = 1780636963805720577&utm_source = wechat_session&utm_id = 0.

[3] https://www.zhihu.com/zvideo/1698640244189048833？utm_psn = 1780635133486964736&utm_id = 0.

[4] https://www.bilibili.com/video/BV1Ft421u7ai/？spm_id_from = 333.337.search-card.all.click&vd_source = 00646e8e10904efc3a7c5f8a727ef0a8.

[5] https://www.sohu.com/a/709143748_121123834.

[6] https://article.xuexi.cn/articles/video/index.html？art_id = 15370079451239232115&study_style_id = video_default&source = share&share_to = wx_single.

[7] https://zhuanlan.zhihu.com/p/669524719?utm_campaign=shareopn&utm_medium=social&utm_psn=1780633374161793024&utm_source=wechat_session.

[8] https://zhuanlan.zhihu.com/p/591673695?utm_campaign=shareopn&utm_medium=social&utm_psn=1780645289990795264&utm_source=wechat_session&s_r=0&wechatShare=1.

[9] https://article.xuexi.cn/articles/video/index.html?art_id=10453384191138659036&read_id=31701e96-201d-4121-8ad6-db666f88d6af&ref_read_id=&reco_id=&mod_id=&cid=&source=share&study_style_id=video_default.

[10] https://www.163.com/dy/article/IGSCJIMN0514RDBQ.html.

[11] https://max.book118.com/html/2019/0314/6224045205002014.shtm.

[12] https://m.thepaper.cn/baijiahao_18318727.

[13] https://m.thepaper.cn/baijiahao_18657196.

[14] https://m.thepaper.cn/baijiahao_17666359.

[15] https://www.xiaohongshu.com/explore/6512804b000000002202b7ae?app_platform=android&ignoreEngage=true&app_version=8.38.0&share_from_user_hidden=true&type=normal&author_share=1&xhsshare=WeixinSession&shareRedId=N0o0MDs1NkI2NzUyOTgwNjczOTpGSzk6&apptime=1717171627&share_id=f0ab71e4f0cf48e5b4c2c46f8f7bde0b&wechatWid=085cd904ad1e1a4bda9959ab90db07cf&wechatOrigin=menu.

[16] https://www.xiaohongshu.com/explore/6512804b000000002202b7ae?app_platform=android&ignoreEngage=true&app_version=8.38.0&share_from_user_hidden=true&type=normal&author_share=1&xhsshare=WeixinSession&shareRedId=N0o0MDs1NkI2NzUyOTgwNjczOTpGSzk6&apptime=1717171627&share_id=f0ab71e4f0cf48e5b4c2c46f8f7bde0b&wechatWid=085cd904ad1e1a4bda99 59ab90db 07cf&wechatOrigin=menu.

[17] https://wenku.so.com/d/7ca2e5050ae7523378d85e451d689034.

[18] https://baike.so.com/doc/7327281-7556932.html.

[19] https://baike.baidu.com/item/%E5%88%97%E8%BD%A6%E8%B0%83%E5%BA%A6%E6%8C%87%E6%8C%A5%E7%B3%BB%E7%BB%9F/20868587?fr=ge_ala.

[20] https://mbd.baidu.com/newspage/data/videoshare?nid=sv_2709437986011074993&source=search&tpl=search&sid_for_share=&ruk=gQE0VRfyxCCNpDdzTQ25Fw.

[21] https://mbd.baidu.com/ug_share/mbox/4a83aa9e65/share?domain=mbd.baidu.com&product=smartapp&rs=2889815830&ruk=gQE0VRfyxCCNpDdzTQ25Fw&share_url=https%3A%2F%2Fvhsagj.smartapps.baidu.com%2Fpages%2Flemma%2Flemma%3FlemmaTitle%3D%25E5%2588%2597%25E8%25BD%25A6%25E8%25B0%2583%25E5%25BA%25A6%25E6%258C%2587%25E6%258C%25A5%25E7%25B3%25BB%25E7%25BB%259F%26lemmaId%3D20868587%26from%3DbottomBarShare%26_swebfr%3D1%26_swebFromHost%3Dbaiduboxapp&tk=cfc182985c213abf8594233231acaec2.

[22] https://m.baidu.com/video/page?pd=video_page&nid=6514236120004756441&sign=&word=CTCS-3%E7%BA%A7%E5%88%97%E8%BD%A6%E8%BF%90%E8%A1%8C%E6%8E%A7%E7%B3%BB%E7%BB%9F&oword=CTCS-3%E7%BA%A7%E5%88%97%E8%BD%A6%E8%BF%90%E8%A1%8C%E6%8E%A7%E7%B3%BB%E7%BB%9F&atn=index&ext=%7B%22jsy%22%3A1%7D&top=%7B%22sfhs%22%3A1%2C%22_hold%22%3A2%7D&_t=1726834534587.

三、公众号

[1] https://mp.weixin.qq.com/s?__biz=MjM5MDA3MDM5OA==&mid=2652948700&idx=1&sn=f8e7c2832e75dba0a3c04f60f2ad15e2&chksm=bc8cccf18d60d11764122369616b7a00038fbc3bb6171fe3c34394c0b13b61718273d3fc14ca&mpshare=1&scene=23&srcid=0606tox9SE2OLjKrzbPYCKpH&sharer_shareinfo=0050073c1693247fa466799b2a3c7917&sharer_shareinfo_first=a0dfcc616335b20df04c1bafbcd398c2#rd.

[2] https://mp.weixin.qq.com/s/JNMWRqqTCgsG-yUxiGme0w.

[3] https://mp.weixin.qq.com/s/3zmexTfnE2yIXw7-g5UtBw.

[4] https://mp.weixin.qq.com/s?__biz=MzA4OTM2OTMzMw==&mid=2651697720&idx=1&sn=64004fac050f898f83320fe6fcfb4754&chksm=8be2eda2bc9564b434bed2d27651c7977a38eb8023bac75e7445fbf2f665d47eb4b387870f3e&scene=27.

[5] https://mp.weixin.qq.com/s/cG2Wlux04q_tmcXub08feQ.

[6] https://mp.weixin.qq.com/s/n0oMdZDuID6TK7Yo8vUrzA.

[7] https://mp.weixin.qq.com/s/2hxovMeSiDch-RKbc-B04Q.

[8] https://mp.weixin.qq.com/s/aaAVhGkrxvnm8hP3Zs6k0Q.

[9] https://mp.weixin.qq.com/s/UwbNRU56WXTEZmIGHRKbCQ.

[10] https://mp.weixin.qq.com/s/Bt5zj5n-1KScFy6HP2MwAg.

[11] https://mp.weixin.qq.com/s/GpcHI9IUp9vq3E7wn1iTog.

[12] https://mp.weixin.qq.com/s/buec8V-G8ojl926UKnvlFg.

[13] https://mp.weixin.qq.com/s/ct5V9kIAnXVdqD1XDagdqA.

[14] https://mp.weixin.qq.com/s/VIvUR7i5ZQUqpjJC_4_xUQ.

[15] https://mp.weixin.qq.com/s/reUbext_6nErakpIlBJhsw.

[16] https://mp.weixin.qq.com/s/_z9oqasyaiKgGPkTYuT6FQ.

[17] https://mp.weixin.qq.com/s/ZhI4gGtrvmBoTwmJXavhMQ.

[18] https://mp.weixin.qq.com/s/NzvM3SAtOwtHye-7eDXN4g.

[19] https://mp.weixin.qq.com/s/rzed100he3HkxtPxOcWcqA.

[20] https://www.zhihu.com/pin/1558014140668616704?native=1&scene=share&utm_campaign=shareopn&utm_medium=social&utm_psn=1780647003652505600&utm_source=wechat_session.

[21] https://www.zhihu.com/pin/1558014140668616704?native=1&scene=share&utm_campaign=shareopn&utm_medium=social&utm_psn=1780647003652505600&utm_source=wechat_session.

[22] https://mp.weixin.qq.com/s/_VDC45MMh-4fUAcyFuxmGw.

[23] https://www.xiaohongshu.com/explore/6512804b000000002202b7ae?app_platform=android&ignoreEngage=true&app_version=8.38.0&share_from_user_hidden=true&type=normal&author_share=1&xhsshare=WeixinSession&shareRedId=N0oOMDs1NkI2NzUyOTgwNjczOTRpGSzk6&apptime=1717171627&share_id=f0ab71e4f0cf48e5b4c2c46f8f7bde0b&wechatWid=085cd904ad1e1a4bda9959ab90db07cf&wechatOrigin=menu.